GARBO and GILBERT in Love

Hollywood's First Great Celebrity Couple

COLIN SHINDLER

ORION

Copyright © Colin Shindler 2005

The right of Colin Shindler to be identified as the author of
this work has been asserted by him in accordance with
the Copyright, Designs and Patents Act 1988.

First published in hardback in Great Britain in 2005 by
Orion Books
an imprint of the Orion Publishing Group Ltd
Orion House, 5 Upper St Martin's Lane,
London WC2H 9EA

1 3 5 7 9 10 8 6 4 2

A CIP catalogue record for this book is available
from the British Library.

ISBN: 0 75287 174 9

Typeset by Deltatype Ltd, Birkenhead, Merseyside
Printed in Great Britain by Clays Ltd, St Ives plc

Every effort has been made to fulfil requirements with regard
to reproducing copyright material. The author and publisher will be glad
to rectify any ommissions at the earliest opportunity.

www.orionbooks.co.uk

This book is dedicated to the memory of
Lynn Shindler,
my loving and beautiful wife who died too young
during the writing of this book.
We met as the only two people in a cinema watching an MGM film
of the 1930s.
The story of Garbo and Gilbert and their MGM lives feels like a
fitting tribute to her and the love she inspired.

Acknowledgements

This book is not meant to be a formal biography of either Greta Garbo or John Gilbert. It is a non-fiction novel based on real events. It contains imagined conversations, but they have been written only after extensive research into the characters of Garbo and Gilbert.

My first debt, therefore, is to my esteemed editor Ian Marshall, who has unstintingly supported this journey from Maine Road to Hollywood, Lorraine Baxter and their supporting team at Orion Books. Stephen Brown did an excellent job of copy editing, and I am grateful for his many helpful suggestions. My literary agent, Luigi Bonomi, offered advice that sustained me during the writing in what developed into the worst year of my life.

I would like to thank Professor Tony Badger, Mellon Professor of American History at Cambridge, whose championing of the use of film in the study of history has enabled me to utilise the vast resources of the Cambridge University library where much of the book was completed and Neil McKendrick, Master of Gonville and Caius College, whose tireless support of my research application many years ago started the process and changed my life.

I was very pleased to have made the acquaintance of Jack Gilbert's daughter, Leatrice Fountain, who was the major source for details of her father's life. A certain amount of doubt in recent years has been cast on the double wedding and the final meeting between Gilbert and Garbo, and I was highly delighted to find that Leatrice shares my belief that both events happened much as described hereafter. Lee Stribling was my indefatigable and highly valued researcher into the history of women's fashions in the 1920s and 1930s, an area in which I am shamefully ignorant, but then it never came up during my previous books on football in Manchester. No book on the silent cinema of Hollywood can ever be written it seems to me without the help of, or in some measure reference to, the uniquely gifted Kevin Brownlow and his Photoplay Productions. Kevin is the film historian all other toilers in this vineyard aspire to match.

Some of the research was also compiled after BBC Radio Four commissioned a play on the subject, and I was fortunate enough to have Peter Leslie Wild as my sensitive and sensible director and Henry Goodman who was exactly the Gilbert I was hearing in my head.

I should really thank almost everyone I know for keeping me going through a year in which I lost my wife, my father and my best friend in a matter of weeks. But the two people in particular who shared those terrible times with me are my children, David and Amy. To them goes all the love I had previously shared with their wonderful mother.

London, April 2005

Chapter One

~~~~~

Garbo was deep in thought as she walked briskly towards the MGM commissary and didn't register the identity of the attractive man who accosted her.

'Hi, Greta,' Jack Gilbert called out cheerily with that American informality she still found so disconcerting.

'It's Miss Garbo,' she replied instinctively and continued on her way without a second glance.

'Do you know who that was?' queried the struggling young actor who had been hired by the studio to interpret for his fellow Swede, as he hurried to keep step with Garbo's long, rapid stride.

'No,' came Garbo's familiar monosyllabic reply.

'It was Jack Gilbert!'

Garbo stopped, sickened by the realisation of what she had just done. 'Should I go back and apologise?'

In the twelve months she had spent in America Garbo had learned that careers could be broken by the wrong word to the wrong person at the wrong time.

'The damage is done now. Best not draw attention to it.'

Garbo strode into the MGM commissary, shrugged off the long wrap-over coat the studio had given her for her last premiere and let it fall over the back of the chair, not caring if the fur shawl collar touched the floor or not. She sat down and wondered if her brief Hollywood career was about to come to an end. She couldn't talk to anyone at the studio about it. After work she would drive over to Pacific Palisades and talk to Mauritz Stiller, the man who had directed her in the first feature film she acted in. Even after a year in Hollywood she still felt as much a foreigner as when she and Stiller had docked in New York. Stiller was her only source of comfort and advice, even though he had been fired by MGM and was now

1

working for another studio. Despite the constant presence of her interpreter, Sven-Hugo Borg, Garbo felt alone and friendless, cast adrift on the tide of false bonhomie and drama that washed around the MGM studio. She was aware that people on the MGM lot, mostly men of course, stared at her and, even if the staring was in its own way a compliment, it made her feel uncomfortable.

Greta accepted the fact that, since she was an actress, audiences looked at her. That was the unfortunate trade-off she had to make. But it was one thing to be stared at on a screen in some remote backwater when she was tucked up in her bed at the Miramar Hotel or writing letters to the family and friends she had left behind in Stockholm. It was quite another matter to be stared at in the flesh, especially by film workers who had plenty of stars to stare at if they were so inclined.

Greta weighed 127 lbs and stood five feet seven and a half inches tall, which was considerably taller than the average American woman, and in many cases almost as tall as her leading men. Occasionally, on set, she had been told to lean against a table or chair when she was being photographed alongside a hero who was self-conscious about his relative lack of height.

Greta was descended on her father's side from Swedish farmers and that ancestry was responsible for her long limbs, large feet and broad yoke of collarbone. She was oddly scrawny for the stardom that was gathering itself like a storm cloud out at sea to descend upon her. She had been philosophical about her relatively small bust for years. Now it suited the latest fashions perfectly. Costume designers struggled to fit many of the stars in their charge into the straight, almost boyish cut of their designs, but Greta, in this respect if no other, was no bother to them.

It was already apparent to the studio executives and the directors whom they assigned to her films that Greta Garbo had a magical presence on screen. Her close-ups mesmerised audiences. She had a face so perfectly shaped that it had no bad angles. Though black and white films gave no hint of their extraordinary colour, her eyes were of the deepest blue and she had the longest natural eyelashes anyone had ever seen. Her eyes had so impressed Louis B. Mayer, head of the recently formed Metro-Goldwyn-Mayer studio, when he first saw her on screen that he had quickly agreed to take her to Hollywood along with Stiller. With those eyes he knew he had the makings of a star. When she moved she did so with a feline grace and all her awkward proportions shifted into sensuous adjustment to each other. The sexual magnetism that Garbo radiated was far greater than the sum of her constituent parts. Later generations would call Garbo 'sexy'. In 1926 it was widely agreed that she had 'it'.

John Gilbert – Jack to his friends – also had 'it'. He was nearly six feet tall, with curly black hair and flashing dark eyes, which screen make-up accentuated. He was a walking definition of the 1926 woman's fantasy of the tall, dark and handsome man. Extremely photogenic and openly emotional, Jack Gilbert was as romantic off screen as the characters he portrayed were on it. He was certainly not used to being slighted by virtual unknowns in his own back yard. Jack had heard all the stories about Garbo's unique sexiness, which was why he had been so keen to meet her, but he returned to the set of *Bardelys the Magnificent*, a costume epic set during the reign of Louis XIII, distinctly unimpressed.

'I just said hello to that dumb-ass Swede,' he said to his director and close friend, King Vidor.

'Give the poor girl a chance, Jack. She's spoken for,' replied Vidor lightly. The director was deep in conversation with his cameraman over the lighting for the next shot but he knew well enough that you didn't wilfully antagonise your leading man – especially if he was the biggest male star in Hollywood and earning a rumoured $10,000 a week.

'I'm going to. Nothing would persuade me to talk to that snooty bitch again. Trouble is, the studio front office want to team me with her in *Flesh and the Devil*.'

Vidor whistled through his teeth and broke away from the conversation with the cameraman.

'I hear the stuff she's doing on *The Temptress* is sensational.'

'She's a good-looking girl but no more than that.'

'You can't have seen her on screen. Did you see *The Torrent*? Everyone's talking about her.'

'Yeah, they're saying she's a snooty bitch.'

'But a snooty bitch with a fantastic face for the camera.'

Garbo did have a good excuse for her behaviour, but it wasn't one she wanted to share with the rest of the world. In April her beloved sister, Alva, who was a year older than Greta, had died of lymphatic cancer in a nursing home in Sweden. Nobody except Stiller cared greatly that they had both felt so alienated since they had arrived in America in July the previous year. Americans didn't care for gloomy faces or depressed people. Garbo and Stiller were working in the fastest-growing, most exciting industry in the world. Hollywood was in California, the golden state, the final frontier of the pioneers who had travelled overland from the East Coast in search of their manifest destiny. They were living in the United States of America in a decade in which a working man could make his fortune on the stock market in the space of a few weeks. Scott Fitzgerald told of the time he went to visit his barber only to find the shop closed because the barber had retired, having sold the shareholding that had made him a millionaire. The newspapers called it the 'Era of Wonderful Nonsense'.

Garbo agreed that it was all nonsense but she didn't find much of it to be wonderful. Devastated by Alva's death and then by MGM's cold-blooded removal of Mauritz Stiller from her professional life, Garbo couldn't understand the mentality of her co-workers. She studied the menu in the MGM commissary and yearned for the simple pleasures of a hamburger or a knickerbocker glory but, in accordance with the studio's instructions, she was soon faced with a plate of spinach and a slice of lemon. She had lost twenty pounds since she had arrived in America, and the studio was determined not to allow her to regain the weight she had so successfully shed.

'American men don't like fat women,' Louis B. Mayer had told her bluntly.

Garbo looked about her at the frenetic bustle of the studio on a typical working day. Nobody walked anywhere. They ran. And they joked constantly. She found all this forced jollity extremely stressful.

'I've never seen anyone look unhappy here. They smile and smile all day long and sometimes I get angry. I would like to say "Shut up", but the only thing to do is smile again and pretend that's what you've been doing all your life.' Her young interpreter agreed. And smiled.

At exactly five o'clock Garbo's coloured maid, Alma, appeared on set with a glass of herbal tea. The maid lifted the lid of the make-up box, and Garbo immediately turned, took the pins out of her hair and shook it vigorously. It was another of Stiller's inflexible demands. Although Garbo was not quite twenty-one years old and still in the flush of youth, Stiller was anxious that the impact of working under the hot lights should not line her face prematurely. Accordingly he insisted that she stop work at 5 p.m. promptly. The studio was not comfortable with this unilateral decision. Normally it operated as a factory with no labour laws. It was not uncommon to work until midnight during shooting and then be in again at 6 a.m. the following morning.

In her dressing room Garbo thankfully stepped out of her loose, low-waisted chemise dress and changed rapidly into Fair Isle patterned baggy trousers with the wide legs she felt so comfortable in. The MGM costume designer had spent hours pointing out to her the delights of her dress, decorated with glass beads on fine net fabric, which sparkled and danced as she moved under the studio lights.

The memory of her poverty-stricken upbringing in Sweden was still too recent to make her feel anything but relieved to be back in her own clothes. Although she did not feel comfortable in these clothes that were setting the world of women's fashion alight, she understood that, combined with the headband which covered her forehead, they made her look quite sensational in the party scene they had just been shooting. It was all part of the job. However ridiculous she felt the sparkly dresses, the ox-blood lipstick and the cloche hats were, she knew that they were giving her a pioneering look and this look was contributing to her growing status at the studio. That was why when she left her dressing room with the rest of the cast still hard at work on the set, nobody stopped her as she strode purposefully across the parking lot to her little roadster. Mayer tried to tell her that this wasn't the custom in Hollywood, but shortly before 5.30 p.m. every day she just got into her car and left.

The studio had soon learned to shoot around her to keep her films on budget. MGM suspected from the reception of her first movie, a melodramatic potboiler called *The Torrent*, that they had stumbled on a special talent who could become a major revenue stream for them. So long as her films continued to turn in big profits, it was best to let her have her way. Once her films started to slip, it would be a different matter.

She removed the cloche hat, which suited not only the fine bone structure of her face but also her fashionably bobbed hair, and took down the top of the car before negotiating her way carefully towards the gate and freedom. As she passed the security guard she shook her hair free so she could feel the wind rushing through it and then drove at high speed the few miles from Culver City, where the MGM studio was being built around them, to Pacific Palisades, where Stiller had rented his house. He had not cared to live permanently in the Miramar Hotel up the road in Santa Monica, where Garbo had remained in a self-contained apartment since their arrival on the West Coast. She loved this time of day, when the heat started to fade and the play of the sun on the Pacific Ocean reminded her a little of summer days by Lake Sillen, south of Stockholm.

Stiller tried to calm her anxieties and talked, as he had always talked, of the dazzling future that lay before his protégée, provided she obeyed his basic set of rules.

'American directors never talk about ideas, Moje. They just tell me where to sit or stand or walk,' she complained.

Stiller could only nod in sympathy. His attempts to instil a European sensibility into American movies had failed miserably.

'Rush, rush, rush. Money, money, money,' he agreed. 'These

Americans are only interested in money and time is money so we have no time and we make bad films.'

Stiller told her it was unlikely that she had mortally offended John Gilbert, but, unless they were going to make a film together, it wouldn't damage her career if she had.

'Do you like him?'

'Who?'

'Gilbert.'

'I've seen his pictures.'

'And?'

'He overacts. He does everything you tell me not to do – the big gestures, the rolling eyes . . .'

'Americans like him for more than his acting. Do you think he is handsome?'

Garbo didn't like these questions about her sexual taste when they weren't related to the character she was playing.

'Does it matter?'

'If you were to play in a picture with him, it could help if you thought he was attractive. But of course it is more important that the character you are playing thinks he is attractive.'

'I think John Gilbert is very attractive,' stated Garbo matter-of-factly. Stiller felt an entirely unwelcome and unexpected stab of jealousy. Garbo saw it and instantly regretted her honesty. She glanced down at the set drawing spread out on the kitchen table. It was bad enough that he had been removed as the director of her current film, *The Temptress*, and sent off to work at Paramount, but it was much worse when she saw this tangible evidence of his involvement with another project and other actresses. She knew that his new film, *Hotel Imperial*, starred the exotic Polish *femme fatale* Pola Negri, whose highly publicised affair with Rudolf Valentino had abruptly terminated with his spectacular death. It was the first time since she had known him that Stiller had been devoting his attention to an actress other than herself and the recognition of it hurt her. As if to emphasise the chasm that was starting to open up between their lives, the telephone rang and it was clear that it was Negri on the line. Garbo comforted herself with the knowledge that her beloved Moje was a homosexual, and Negri would probably soon lose interest in him once she had discovered the fact for herself.

They parted sadly, aware that Mayer, who had fired Stiller from *The Temptress* for being too slow, was unlikely to team them together ever again. Indeed, they were both coming to terms with the real possibility that Stiller's contract at MGM was not going to be renewed, and where did that leave her? wondered Garbo, as she drove furiously along Sunset Boulevard, turning left along Ocean Front on her way back to the Miramar. The answer wasn't long in coming.

Louis B. Mayer sat behind his mahogany desk, a large piece of antique furniture mounted imperiously on a carpeted platform, nearly a foot above the rest of his wood-panelled office. He was small of stature but powerfully built with a notoriously short temper, which occasionally erupted into physical violence. He might have blinked owlishly through his glasses but he was at heart a street fighter. He also possessed strong business acumen and an instinct for commercial movies and showmanship that his many enemies ignored at their peril.

Behind him stood the Stars and Stripes on a small flagpole and a marble statue of the MGM lion. Next to the neatly arranged paperwork on his desk were a series of telephones, many of them white to emphasise his importance, a prayer book, rarely used, photographs of his wife and two daughters and a tintype of his mother.

'What's the matter, Greta? Come on, you can tell me,' he cajoled.

'Mr Mayer,' began Garbo hesitantly.

'Call me Chief. Everyone else does.'

Garbo knew exactly what everyone called L.B. Mayer behind his back and it was rarely 'Chief'.

'I am tired. I am sick. My sister . . .'

Her voice trailed away. She didn't much enjoy confronting Mayer or playing the games she knew were important if she were to maintain her position in the studio's hierarchy, but the death of her sister didn't require any acting. Mayer, too, knew that Alva's untimely death had been a terrible shock to his newest star.

'I've got great news for you,' Mayer started cheerily. 'We're going to team you up with the biggest male star on the lot. You're going to make your next picture with John Gilbert.'

The studios were quickly learning that one good way to make a new star was to team him or her with a more established one. If the newcomer was any good, the other's star quality somehow transmitted itself to the neophyte. Mayer was hoping for a response of tearful gratitude. He didn't get it.

'Mister Mayer, Chief, I am so tired. I have had no time to mourn my sister. I am so nervous and anxious. I am going to have some kind of a breakdown.'

Garbo's reply wrong-footed Mayer. He knew actresses only too well and understood how deeply they feared unemployment and how easily they became addicted to the fame and money that stemmed from a successful movie career. All they ever wanted from him was a better acting role. They never threatened him with refusing to work. He had been expecting Garbo to demand a pay rise, which he was determined to refuse, but now he was afraid that if he didn't get this young woman into another film quickly the bloom might desert the rose and the chance to make some serious money out of her would be lost.

'I'll tell you what I'll do, Greta,' he wheedled. 'You start your costume fittings for the Jack Gilbert picture and I'll make sure you get a good long holiday when you finish shooting. You can even go back to Sweden.'

Mayer wondered why he was pleading with this twenty-one-year-old girl. She had signed her contract. He could make her play as cast or he could place her on suspension, even threaten to cancel her contract and throw her out on her ear and whistle up a replacement.

Only he couldn't. He was smart enough to know he had stumbled on a special talent, a girl whose face was uniquely photogenic. He could see it there for himself, and her two directors so far had confirmed it. Garbo was going to be a huge star and teaming her with John Gilbert was going to create a gold mine for the studio. He needed her cooperation and something told him he was facing an opponent whose inner steel belied her youthful good looks. He spun the story of *Flesh and the Devil* to emphasise the wonderful role he was offering her, a role that would make her world famous. To his amazement, Garbo simply shook her head again.

'I don't want to play another bad womans.'

'It's a great part,' protested Mayer.

'I have played this part. A bad womans. She attracts men and then she dies.'

'Audiences love that kind of woman.'

'I am an actress.'

'Sure you are. That's why we hired you.'

'I don't want to play this part. Please find me another one.'

Mayer had a short fuse at the best of times. Greta Garbo had just lit it.

'You'll play the girl in *Flesh and the Devil* or you're suspended. That means no pay and the time you miss is added on to the end of your contract. Plus you can't work for anyone else unless I give you permission. And I won't be doing that,' he added unnecessarily.

Garbo stared at him, unfazed, then slowly clipped her handbag together and stood up.

'I tank I go home,' she announced, and walked out. It was a parting line MGM employees would become used to hearing over the next fifteen years.

Mayer was stunned and furious. Stars, especially young pretty actresses who could barely speak the language, simply did not talk to him this way. He picked up the phone and bellowed into the intercom.

'Irving, get in here!'

If his plain dealing wasn't going to have any effect on this uppity Swede, maybe it was time to unleash the diplomatic charms of his young vice president in charge of production, Irving Thalberg. He knew Thalberg and Gilbert were friends. Thalberg would find a way to get Garbo back to work before the delay started to cost the studio money.

*

While Mayer and Thalberg continued to argue with Garbo, shooting began on all the location scenes in which Garbo's character was not scheduled to appear. The director of *Flesh and the Devil*, Clarence Brown, took the unit up to Lake Arrowhead in the hills above San Bernardino, to shoot the location sequences for the Isle of Friendship – the romantic island where the young Leo and his best friend, Ulrich, swear their eternal friendship sealed by a blood oath. It was also to be the setting for the climax of the film, when the two men, now played by Gilbert and the Swedish actor Lars Hanson, decide not to proceed with their duel even as Felicitas, the character Garbo had initially resisted playing and the object of both their passions, is falling through the ice to her suitably cathartic death.

Jack Gilbert loved being out on location making movies. He was also quite happy making films on the studio lot in Culver City. Jack just liked working: he liked the company of cast and technicians, he liked the satisfaction that can be derived from creating something powerful, dramatic and magical out of the barest of scenarios, he liked the money that MGM was pouring into his bank account every week, and he adored the attention that came with being a rich, handsome and successful movie star.

He particularly enjoyed it all because he had not forgotten his impoverished background. His father had abandoned him shortly after he was born, and his mother, an unsuccessful actress, had palmed him off on to distant but stable relatives when he was twelve. From the age of fourteen he had effectively been on his own and times had been desperately hard. He was twenty-seven years old now, and true recognition had only arrived less than two years before, when *The Merry Widow* and *The Big Parade* had opened. Since then he had discovered he could do nothing wrong. It was an intoxicating sensation, the only negative being he had been a little headstrong in his relations with women other than his pretty second wife, the actress Leatrice Joy.

Yet what was he to do when women threw themselves at him? They bribed hotel doormen to be allowed to slip into his bedroom when he was on location; they pressed telephone numbers and house keys into his hand on a few minutes' acquaintance. Leatrice was rather straight-laced about this sort of thing. It came from working for that arch-hypocrite Cecil B. DeMille, Jack thought, but it was extremely unfortunate that she had come home unexpectedly to find him and two friends passed out on the living-room floor with an incriminating telegram from Broadway actress Laurette Taylor open on the kitchen table. There was also a previous incident involving two teenage girls but he had thought he had successfully talked his way out of that one. Now, after discovering what appeared to be yet another adulterous liaison, she had decided to serve divorce papers on him, even though she was only a few days away from giving birth to their first child. Each night, after shooting scenes on *Flesh and the Devil*, co-star Lars Hanson and director Clarence Brown talked to him about his new leading lady, Greta Garbo. They, like almost everyone else on the MGM lot, had heard or seen evidence of Garbo's beauty. Jack had not responded particularly well to the snub of 'It's Miss Garbo' and was unimpressed. There were dozens and dozens of pretty women in Hollywood. Why was this one so special?

'Just wait till you meet her,' smiled Lars Hanson.

'I met her already. She walks like a man.'

Jack wasn't the first to make the observation that there was something mannish about Garbo. However, the men who acknowledged the truth of the observation also found themselves attracted to her powerful sexuality. By the time the location shooting had been completed, Gilbert had become convinced by all the arguments. Garbo had now settled her differences with the studio, and he was eagerly anticipating meeting her again.

He couldn't help admiring the confrontational manner in which she had taken on MGM. She was still young, and it took enormous strength to defy the bullying tactics of L.B. Mayer. As the studio's hottest male star, Gilbert was safe from Mayer's rages, but Garbo, for all the positive word-of-mouth, didn't have three huge hits, like he did, to back up her demands. Maybe they were right. Maybe this girl had something.

Outwardly, however, he maintained a deep scepticism about Garbo so everyone on the set of *Flesh and the Devil* was waiting for some kind of explosion when the two stars began working together. Clarence Brown made the introductions, and this time Garbo was fulsome in her admiration for the actor. Gilbert nodded graciously. This was more like it. It took him about five minutes to forget the hostility that had been building up for weeks. He mentally congratulated himself on having agreed to Irving Thalberg's suggestion that he take their new European discovery as his next co-star. Five minutes after that Jack Gilbert was in love with Greta Garbo.

This was by no means an unusual event in Jack Gilbert's life. In fact five minutes was the standard amount of time Jack took to fall in love. What was surprising to everyone was that the moody, stuck-up Swede, as everyone had thought her to be, appeared to be undergoing the same emotional transformation and in the same amount of time.

Their first scene together was the first time the characters met in the film. The set was a railway station, and amid the bustle of arrivals and departures and family reunions it was necessary to convey to the audience that Leo was instantly smitten by the beauty of Felicitas. He doesn't know at this time that she is married to an elderly man. He knows only that he has just seen the love of his life. Felicitas has also registered Leo's existence but being a woman she is not permitted to convey the fact that she finds him attractive too.

The next day came the scene of the party in the great house. Leo refuses to be distracted by the bouncing enthusiasm of Ulrich's kid sister and he searches each room looking for the beautiful woman he glimpsed earlier. Eventually he finds her and leads her out onto the balcony and then into the garden where the two lovers are confronted with the overwhelming nature of their passion for each other.

Everyone on the set could see the two actors were instantly entranced with each other. From the moment they first looked into each other's eyes the rest of the world slowly dissolved and Garbo and Gilbert seemed to disappear into a world of their own creation in front of the rest of the cast and the crew on the MGM studio floor. Clarence Brown, to his amazement, watched his two stars falling in love not just in the story but also in front of his eyes. William Daniels, the lighting cameraman, took his director to one side.

'Clarence, have you seen what's happening here?'

'Yes, Bill. I've never seen anything like it.'

'It's fantastic. We've got to do something about it.'

'You mean stop it?'

'Christ, no. I mean let it rip.'

'How?'

'In this garden scene do they light cigarettes?'

'They can.'

'I'm going to give Jack a small lamp he can cup in his hands. When he lights her cigarette it'll illuminate her face. It'll be something special.'

It was. Daniels's imaginative lighting work created a magical effect. Everyone seemed to be caught up in the atmosphere of breathless romance. They knew that they were privileged to be present at the start of a grand passion. Show-business folk frequently gossiped about the possibility of two actors falling in love while pretending to be lovers, but it was usually an affair of convenience between two bored actors hanging around on location waiting for the weather to change. What was happening on the set of *Flesh and the Devil* was very different. When Garbo and Gilbert kissed, the whole world, through the magic eye of the camera lens, could see that they were truly besotted with each other.

At the end of the scene Brown saw that his two stars couldn't take their eyes off each other. The director's assistant and the camera operator looked at him, waiting for the command 'Cut!' that would end the scene, but Brown just signalled silently to stop the cranking. On a silent-movie set the director would cheerfully shout out his instructions but in this instance he felt it would be almost sacrilegious to puncture the atmosphere that had descended on them all. The crew tip-toed away leaving the two lovers still locked in an embrace, still staring into each other's eyes. Nobody wanted to break the mood, nobody wanted to make a joke or talk loudly. They were in the presence of a great romance and they knew it had to be allowed to run its course without the rude jokes or the cutting comments that would usually accompany a romance on the set.

The passion that appeared to overwhelm the two of them aroused in Garbo a predatory feeling as she instinctively tried to take the initiative in the days that followed the filming of that first fateful meeting at the railway station. In the next scheduled love scenes when they kissed she would hold Gilbert's face between her hands, controlling the pace and the intensity of the embrace. Clarence Brown and the technicians watched fascinated as Garbo, contrary to long-established practice in films, opened her mouth to receive her lover's kisses as if she were about to devour him. After one such take Brown talked very privately to the lovers.

'How far do you want to take this?'

'Clarence!' exclaimed Jack leaping to the most extreme of conclusions.

'What do you mean, Mr Brown?' asked Garbo.

'These love scenes are wonderful because they are so truthful.'

'It is acting, Mr Brown,' said Garbo carefully.

'Not entirely, Greta,' added Jack, grinning.

'I want you to continue doing whatever feels most comfortable.'

'Like what?'

'Like lying down, horizontal with each other.'

'Can we do that?' asked Jack in surprise. 'Won't someone object?'

'Maybe,' admitted the director. 'It depends what you two come up with.'

While Bill Daniels re-set the lighting for the next scene the three of them went off into Jack's dressing room to rehearse. When they emerged Clarence Brown was still not entirely sure what would happen when the camera turned. He gave instructions to the cast and crew to prepare for shooting. It was the scene on the chaise longue when the lovers are eventually discovered by the man who reveals himself to Leo's great dismay as the husband of Felicitas.

When the embraces became even more intense than anything they had seen previously, the first assistant looked questioningly at the director. Surely he wasn't going to let this display of naked passion continue? Brown motioned for him to leave them alone. Garbo, as he suspected, was not content to lie on her back, passively accepting her lover's kisses. She soon wriggled out from under him and started to straddle him. For the first time in his career Jack Gilbert was playing the part of the seduced not the seducer. It was clear that the Great Lover liked this new sensation.

The sensual pleasures of kissing never failed to arouse Jack. Usually it was just a physiological response, and many actresses regarded it as an insult if the man they were kissing did not feel that spark of passion. Greta wasn't one of them. In her previous films with Ricardo Cortez and Antonio Moreno she had been offended by the protuberant flesh that stuck uncomfortably into her thigh. Now it was different. Much to her own surprise she found Jack's eagerness a sign that something special was happening on the set and for almost the first time in her life she was starting to revel in the power of her sexuality. The actor playing Felicitas's cuckolded husband waited a long time for his cue to burst in upon the lovers.

The following day they shot the scene in the church where the two still-secret adulterous lovers are taking communion. Clarence Brown, as was his wont, painstakingly explained the narrative background to the pantomime they were about to perform. He could tell that his actors were benefiting from his decision not to talk to them as the camera was turning. The acting was so good, the passion so intense, Clarence Brown felt sure that the audience would be completely entranced by the movie.

'OK, Greta, this is the scene where the audience knows there's trouble brewing. You married Ulrich when you should have waited for Leo to return from exile. Now you're all taking communion together, and I need to know, I need the audience to see, that the two of you are going to carry on screwing even if it jeopardises your marriage and Leo's friendship with your husband.'

Brown retreated to talk to Bill Daniels, and Jack reached out to hold Greta's hand.

'Just lose yourself in the part, do something, anything, whatever you feel is right. You're not Greta any more, you're Felicitas and you'd do anything for love. Do you understand?'

Greta squeezed back gratefully.

The cameraman turned the cranking handle, and the priest passed down the row offering the wine and the wafer to each member of the family in turn. Greta kept her eyes fixed on Jack as he drank and handed the chalice back to the priest. The priest then carefully turned the cup round for hygienic purposes before giving it to Greta, who was still staring at her lover with a wild intensity. Greta saw what the priest did and instantly knew what she had to do. Deliberately she turned the chalice round in her hands and lifted it to her mouth so her lips could touch the exact spot on the goblet so recently vacated by her lover's own lips. It was sensuous and spine-tingling. Greta's instinct was perfect. Both Jack and his director now knew that they were in the presence of a young woman who was destined for greatness.

After filming was finally completed for the day, Clarence Brown sat in Irving Thalberg's office and related to him what had been happening, though Thalberg's spies had long since broken the news to him of the new romance that was the talk of the studio.

'Honestly, Irving, it's the damnedest thing you ever saw. It's the sort of behaviour Elinor Glynn used to write about. When they got into that first love scene . . . well, nobody else was even there. Those two were alone in a world of their own. All I could do was to turn the lights off and leave them alone to get on with it.'

'And did they? Get on with it?'

'She's not that kind of girl. She's special. She saves it all for the camera. That's why it's so amazing and why Jack's so focused. If they were doing it at night they'd leave it in the bedroom, but as it is we all get the benefit.'

Thalberg was thrilled and promised to tell the MGM publicity department immediately. Brown didn't think that was a very good idea.

'What happens if it doesn't last? Won't they look stupid?'

Thalberg sighed. Sometimes sensitive directors like Clarence Brown were just a little too sensitive.

'That's OK,' he explained patiently. 'That just means more publicity. I keep telling you – they're movie stars, they're not even actors. And you know my opinion about actors.'

It was true. Clarence Brown did know the studio executives' standard attitude to the actors they kept under contract. The conversation was over. Clarence Brown got up to leave. It was now clear to him that Garbo and Gilbert were going to be fed to the press in a cynical attempt to create the sort of hysteria that would result in a bonanza for the studio at the box office. It wasn't going to be pretty but it was going to be exciting. He was right about the excitement, but not even MGM's script department could have devised the story that was to follow.

Chapter Two

~~~~~~

They were lovers to the world but not to each other. Despite the very obvious passion they exhibited towards each other both on and off screen, Greta had not yet decided how far she wished this romance to go. Jack did his best to control himself but inside he was screaming with frustration. He wasn't used to this indecision. If women liked him personally and found him sexually attractive they simply gave themselves to him. Greta was not the sort of girl to give herself to anybody.

To all his friends Jack let it be known that Greta was dynamite in bed. When they asked for details he gave them and was instantly believed. After all, what Jack told them was exactly what they had been expecting. When Greta heard what Jack had been saying about them she was horrified.

'How can you say this?'

'If you'd let me take you to bed, I wouldn't have to make it all up.'

'I'm not ready.'

'Greta, the whole world already thinks we're lovers, what's the point in holding out?'

'I have not yet decided.'

She may not have decided, but MGM's publicity department didn't care. They suddenly found themselves with the hottest celebrity couple in the world on the payroll and they were determined to make the most of it. Greta wanted to run into her bedroom, lock the door and hide, but Jack persuaded her that the publicity would only help her career. Stiller accepted too, albeit with great reluctance, that the torrent of publicity would help to make *Flesh and the Devil* a guaranteed hit. It was just unfortunate that it would also benefit John Gilbert rather than himself but there was nothing he could do about it.

Now that Rudy Valentino was dead the fan magazines pronounced John Gilbert to be the handsomest, sexiest man in Hollywood and therefore the world. He read the articles with increasing satisfaction for they were written confirmation of what he had long believed – namely that there was scarcely a woman alive who would not leave her husband for the chance of an hour in bed with John Gilbert. Of course, it also made Greta's stubborn refusal to consummate this grand passion even more incredible to him. When he showed her the magazine covers and the publicity shots, she threw them into the corner of the room. Jack laughed. He had never seen such an aversion to publicity. Every actress he knew, certainly every actress he had dated, regarded this sort of exposure as the very oxygen of life. The studio's publicity department regularly fixed up dates between stars, or between gay actors and starlets whose very obvious and photogenic sex appeal would be sufficient to suppress any rumours of homosexuality. Most actresses on the make in Hollywood couldn't live without the attention that made them feel whole and most of them were distraught when the limelight was suddenly withdrawn. They would have prostituted themselves for the publicity that was being lavished on Greta Garbo. Some of them did.

At first Greta tried to close her eyes to what was happening. Behind the high walls of the MGM studios in Culver City, guarded by men with guns, she felt safe. The power of the mob was kept at bay, and she could concentrate on the serious business of acting and the more enjoyable sensation of being truly in love for the first time in her life.

It was what happened when they left the security of the studio that distressed her. At first she dismissed the publicity as embarrassing and, as far as she was concerned, irrelevant. But Jack was a party animal and he not only liked to go out at night, he liked to be seen going out at night. Greta loved the idea of a romantic candlelit dinner for two in some remote restaurant where they could hold hands under the table and listen to the gypsy violinist. She also loved the ocean: the unspoiled beaches of Santa Monica Bay were only a few minutes from her hotel.

Within days of their relationship being made public, however, these two outlets were effectively denied her. Crowds of eager admirers started to follow them. They were waiting outside the restaurant when she and Jack drove up. She could never work out how they knew in advance that this was where they were going to eat. She simply couldn't believe it when Jack told her that the studio's publicity department was responsible.

'How do *they* know, then?' she asked reasonably.

Jack shifted in his seat and looked a little uncomfortable.

Bathing in the Pacific Ocean in Santa Monica Bay had to be abandoned very quickly. These ghastly people with their autograph books and their glossy photos of the two actors were not just curious fans, Garbo decided. They were the baying and unruly mob that had attacked the Bastille, had cackled as the aristocrats were guillotined in the Place de la Révolution and had stormed the Winter Palace and deposed the Tsar just eight years before. They terrified Garbo.

'I'm never going there again,' she said to Jack as they drove away from Venice beach and the adoration of the imploring multitudes, who had come to watch these gods of the silver screen lying on the beach on a towel.

'We can go further north to Malibu. Or south to Palos Verdes,' he offered.

Greta shook her head and stared grimly ahead.

'The swimming pool in the new house is almost ready,' said Jack. 'Maybe it would be better if you came and swam there.'

'It's not the same as the ocean. I like to feel the current pulling against my body.'

'But it's very private.'

'Could I swim there naked?'

'You can *only* swim naked in my house. It's a very old rule.'

'But it's a very new house.'

'Yes, but I inherited the rule from the original owner of the land. He would only sell me the land if I agreed to observe that rule.'

'Liar. Why would he do this?'

'Because he has the house next door and a pair of powerful binoculars.'

Garbo slapped his forearm playfully, and Jack deliberately steered the car towards the ditch at the side of the road until she screamed and he quickly righted the steering.

Jack realised this was the perfect time to show Greta his newly built house at 1400 Tower Road, in Benedict Canyon. It was a two-storey Spanish-style hacienda which made it far from unique in Beverly Hills, although his more individual taste for Gothic interior decoration somewhat surprised her.

'Like it?' he asked, as the door opened on to a cavernous hall and a blood-red living room.

'It's so large,' wondered Greta. 'You could have a party right here in the hall.'

'I do. Let's go upstairs.'

Greta shrieked. Jack turned round.

'What?'

'Yackie, there are owls in the fireplace!'

Jack smiled, childishly pleased to have evoked such a reaction.

'What? Oh, that's just the fire irons. I had them shaped like owls.'

'Why?'

'I like owls. And their eyes are supposed to light up when the fire is lit. C'mon upstairs.'

Greta was determined to keep the upper hand in the relationship. Jack's impassioned lovemaking had all the ardour of adolescence. She continued to tease him.

'I wonder what is so important upstairs?'

'Well, you won't find out down here.'

'I tank I stay downstairs.'

'I told you, the view is unbelievable. You've got to look at it. You can see all the way to the mountains on one side and the ocean on the other. On a clear day you can see Catalina Island. It's the best view in Los Angeles.'

'I tank I know what you want me to look at. And it is not Los Angeles.'

Eventually Jack persuaded Greta to climb the stairs, although she tried to obfuscate by talking about the carved walnut furniture on their way up.

'Is it seventeenth-century Spanish?'

'Kind of.'

'It looks very expensive.'

'It is. I paid some guy in Michigan a fortune to make it look like that.'

Greta was fascinated by the lock on Jack's bedroom door.

'It's from a mediaeval Spanish castle. That's what the guy from Long Beach told me.'

Jack struggled to get it open.

'It needs oiling,' he explained, as he finally managed to unlock it. He flung the door wide open.

'This is the master bedroom. I told you there was a great view. You can see all the way downtown.'

Greta stood at the floor-to-ceiling picture window and stared fixedly out as if to make sure Jack was telling the truth.

'I can see Los Angeles,' she stated flatly, as if ticking it off on a list of promises Jack had made her.

'Sometimes,' Jack admitted proudly, 'Los Angeles can see me.'

Garbo turned to him, puzzled. It must be my limited English, she thought.

'I like to take all my clothes off and stand there, where you are,' he explained, 'naked as a jaybird, and yell at the place.'

'What do you yell?' asked Garbo, curious. Jack raced to the window and battered on the glass as he leapt in the air and began doing star jumps.

'It's all mine, you bastards! Mine! Can you hear me?' He turned back to face the surprised Garbo and moved matter-of-factly towards the bed.

'And this is really comfortable,' he added, bouncing up and down on it.

Greta swept back out onto the landing like a prospective purchaser.

'Show me the guest room you are always boasting about.'

Jack shrugged and did as he was bidden. The spare bedroom was something else. Greta gasped when she saw what was inside.

'Yackie! What have you done?'

Jack was a little hurt that Greta seemed not to recognise the décor.

'It's a replica of one of the sets from *The Merry Widow*. You remember that scene where I try to seduce Mae Murray?'

'It's a monk's cell!' she protested.

Jack grinned and nodded in agreement.

'Don't you just love the crucifix and the prie-dieu?'

'This is your spare bedroom?' asked Garbo in wonderment.

Jack decided this was the time to strike.

'I've been talking to a friend at the studio. He's a designer, and I showed the place to him and he said he could transform it into a miniature Louis Seize boudoir in blue and ivory and gold and black. It'll be spectacular.'

'Louis the Sixteenth?'

'I think. Maybe he said Louis the Fifteenth. Who cares?'

'Why would you redecorate it?'

'For you, Greta. It'll be yours.'

Jack was now becoming swept away on a tide of his own enthusiasm. He was in love and money was no object.

'And in the master bedroom I'm going to install black marble walls with a sunken black marble bathtub with gold fixtures. What do you think?'

Greta had no doubt as to what she thought. She thought he was crazy. Jack tried to reassure her.

'It's only going to cost fifteen thousand dollars.'

Greta was horrified. Jack was surprised. They clearly had different attitudes to money, or, at least, to the spending of it.

'Who cares so long as we both like it?'

Greta picked up immediately on the use of the plural. She strongly suspected it was not the royal 'we'.

'We? Who is we?' she asked suspiciously.

Jack could no longer contain the words that had been bubbling up inside him.

'I'm crazy about you, my Swedish meatball. I love you, I love you, I love you.'

Greta was not impressed. For all her familiarity with the absurd exaggeration of the language of show business, she was never comfortable with it. And of course, like most things, it was worse in America.

'Oh, you Americans, you are the crazy ones.'

She neatly ducked away from Jack's arms, which were seeking to embrace her. Her efforts were in vain. Jack caught her and held her close before kissing her, softly at first and then with increasing passion. Greta responded. She couldn't help herself. All her training had been to avoid these emotional entanglements because they only led to heartache and were invariably an obstacle to the fulfilment of Moje's dream that she would become the greatest actress in the world.

Her legs became weak and seemed incapable of supporting the weight of her body. She was being held upright only by Jack's arms. He guided her gently to the bed where he kissed her tenderly. His hand went to the bottom of her skirt and he started to lift it up her legs, but Garbo recovered her strength and he could feel her legs snap shut like the gates of the mediaeval castle he had described to her in such fulsome detail.

Well, he thought, if she didn't want sex she must want love. Most women did. There was no reason to suppose that Garbo was any different. Despite the discomfort caused by the swelling in his groin he dropped to the floor on both knees. He realised that traditionally the words he was about to speak were delivered on one knee rather than both, but she couldn't see that and, more to the point, there was no camera or audience to observe.

'Greta, I do love you. Please, *please*, will you marry me?'

Garbo struggled to sit up.

'Now you really are crazy.' Jack had his fall-back plan in place.

'Then live with me. Here. Please, Greta.'

But the surprising Swede surprised him again.

'Make love to me.'

'What?'

Greta smiled.

'I thought you wanted to.'

'Of course. It's just that you always . . .'

'Now, Yackie, now!' She pulled him onto the bed and rolled on top of him, kissing him with the all the urgency he always longed for. Her hands went to the buttons of his shirt and she undid them with a sureness that belied her inexperience.

Of course, thought Jack, she's acting. It's what she knows. With a mighty effort he pulled her down flat on the bed with him and gradually, as if they were in a genuine wrestling contest, he slowly forced his way on top of her. This time when his hand slipped beneath her skirt there was no resistance. As the gates of the citadel swung apart Jack breathed a deep sigh of relief. Thank God, he thought, for he had started to doubt his much-vaunted sexual magnetism. This was the conquest that would truly confirm his reputation as the Great Lover.

Afterwards, as they lay contentedly in each other's arms, he whispered with genuine feeling the words that came so easily to him.

'I love you, Greta Garbo. You are the most enchanting creature I have ever known.'

'I'm hungry,' replied the enchanting creature. 'Where can we eat?'

There was any number of local places to eat that Jack enjoyed patronising. Musso & Franks on Hollywood Boulevard had been established as early as 1919, and the Brown Derby, Ciro's and Romanoff's had followed soon after. Greta hated all of them. For a start, she was fussy about what she ate; more importantly she loathed having to run the gauntlet of the crowds gathered round the entrances, of the photographers who took unflattering photographs and sold them to the press and of the press agents who seemed to lurk at every table.

Even tonight when they drove downtown into the heart of Los Angeles and away from the obvious celebrity restaurants of Hollywood there was an incident. They had a secured a table in an alcove; the lights were dim and the atmosphere sedate. Greta was obviously starting to relax for she responded to Jack's attempt to insert his leg between hers by slipping off her shoe and sending her long leg into his lap where it rummaged brazenly, rubbing the length of his crotch.

Just as Jack grabbed the leg and was about to tickle the sole of her foot a drunken man in a dinner jacket sat down at their table uninvited.

'Do you mind? We're having a private dinner here.' The man stared at Jack and then at Greta.

'Hey! You're that pansy from Hollywood!'

'Can you leave us, please?' said Jack coldly as Greta's features began to freeze over. The drunken man then vomited all over the table. Jack grabbed him and hauled him to his feet as two waiters arrived to drag him outside. He refused to go quietly.

'Goddamn pansy!' he yelled. 'And you're that Swedish piece of ass! Wait till Louella Parsons hears about this!'

Louella was the syndicated gossip columnist for all the newspapers owned by the press magnate William Randolph Hearst. Jack didn't like her and wasn't very good at disguising his feelings. He knew Hearst had only given her the job because she knew where the bodies were buried – literally. A couple of years before she had been one of the guests in a private party on the Hearst yacht and a witness to the death of the producer Thomas Ince. Jack had been among the first to hear the rumour that Hearst had become insane with jealousy because he believed his mistress Marion Davies was having an affair with Ince and had shot him in a fit of jealous rage. Davies, a talented, self-effacing comedienne, was a contemporary of Jack and the two had been friends since the days of their early struggles in Hollywood. Jack told Greta the story with glee.

'And it was all untrue?'

'Only part of it.'

'What do you mean?'

'Well, Marion's a beautiful kid and W.R. is old and a pain in the ass.'

'So?'

'So she was having an affair OK but not with Ince.'

'Then who?'

Jack smiled. He was enjoying teasing out the story and glad to see that the Swedish iceberg was as hot for the gossip as any regular Hollywood actress.

'Tell me!'

'Charlie.'

'Charlie Chaplin?' Greta exclaimed.

'The same. You want to meet him?'

'Do you know him?'

'Honey, I'm Jack Gilbert. I know everyone. Just make sure you don't get too close. Charlie's well known for liking girls a lot. Still, you're twenty-one now, so you're probably too old for him.'

Charlie turned up at the next Sunday brunch Jack arranged. Greta had been in Hollywood for a little over a year but she had spent nearly all her time when not working at the studio either with Moje or writing letters home. Her self-consciousness about her poor English in addition to her naturally shy, reserved demeanour combined to keep her out of the Hollywood social scene. Jack's desire to demonstrate his love for her persuaded all his friends to turn up.

Greta wore her new little black dress, the latest creation of the hottest designer of 1926, Coco Chanel. Against her white, almost alabaster, skin the black dress positively shimmered. Ironically Greta herself preferred the healthy glow of an outdoors girl, but the assembled guests were quick to admire the contrast between the dark fabric and the light skin – the result, thought Greta unhappily, of too many hours in a dark, unhealthy studio. When she was rich and powerful she would devote herself to keeping healthy.

In addition to Charlie, Greta encountered the cream of Hollywood society that afternoon – actors like Buster Keaton, Richard Barthelmess, Colleen Moore and Bebe Daniels and writers like Donald Ogden Stewart, Carey Wilson and Adela Rogers St Johns. She thought they would overwhelm her with their clever talk but they went out of their way to be kind to her and include her in their conversations, explaining those areas of American or Hollywood life with which she was unfamiliar.

Last to arrive was Irving Thalberg, the twenty-seven-year-old *wunderkind*, Louis B. Mayer's second-in-command at MGM. He wasn't much taller than Mayer, a mere five feet six inches against Mayer's five feet four, but he was painfully thin, unlike the stocky, well-built Mayer. He constantly looked ill and he never weighed more than 120 lbs, no matter what he ate. Many of the actresses on the lot envied him this ability. He had been struck down with rheumatic fever when he was seventeen years old and everyone knew he had a weak heart. Greta had only really known him as a remote studio executive whom she placed on the same level as the hateful Louis B. Mayer because that was how Moje regarded the pair of them.

Now, around the swimming pool at 1400 Tower Drive, she saw why Jack had always talked warmly of Thalberg. He wasn't the insensitive executive she had imagined but a gentle, rather frail young man who talked of his passion for the movies and the way in which they could make people's lives better. MGM would bring to the screen the great classic works of literature – Dickens, Tolstoy, Victor Hugo. He didn't mind if they lost money, as long as the studio made a profit at the end of the year. He felt Hollywood had an obligation to bring culture to the masses. Greta was entranced. Without denigrating Mayer, Thalberg let Greta know that he would watch over her career with great care and ensure that she was only cast in the sort of roles in which she would be happy and could grow as an actress. He wondered how she felt about the possibility of playing Anna Karenina.

Greta caught Jack looking at her from the shade of the eucalyptus tree. Seeing her happy was making him happy. Seeing him happy was making her happy. This must be what it is like to be in love, she thought. And she smiled at Jack. He smiled back, holding one hand over his heart as if he were a bad actor in a bad movie. She laughed. He held both hands lasciviously over his crotch. She blushed. And Jack laughed.

After lunch it was time for tennis. Greta knew it was time for tennis because Big Bill Tilden, the best tennis player in the world, showed up in his whites. Jack introduced them proudly.

'You want to play some doubles?' asked Tilden.

Greta looked at Jack for permission as she would have looked at Moje had he been there. Jack smiled his assent.

'Thank you. Who do we play?'

'Charlie and Buster.'

'You'll be OK. I mean, they're funnier, but Bill's the better tennis player,' said Jack, as he handed Greta a tennis racket.

'Charlie's a damn fine player,' said Tilden quickly. 'Let's hope he and Buster just want to fool around, otherwise we're in for a tough game. Hey! You always hold the racket like that?'

'Like what?'

Greta was holding the tennis racket about two inches from the top of the handle, just below the throat.

'Is it wrong?'

'It's the way a kid would hold it.'

'I always do this. Since a little girl in Sweden.'

'You play how you want, my Svenska flicka,' Jack reassured her. He liked showing off his knowledge of Swedish, although in truth it didn't go much beyond the most basic vocabulary along with the words for the male and female genitals and this nickname for his new girlfriend – literally 'Swedish friend'.

Charlie Chaplin was an excellent left-handed tennis player but he had never before encountered an opponent quite like Greta Garbo. Bill Tilden covered the back of the court with enormous strides leaving Greta to volley at the net, which she did with her ludicrous grip but with enormous power. The two greatest film comedians in the world were roundly trounced to the great delight of the assembled guests, particularly Jack, who embraced Greta passionately after she smashed the final volley so hard it bounced over the wire netting at the back of the court. Buster collapsed spread-eagled on the ground. Chaplin didn't take defeat so well and, having seen it meant nothing to his partner, disappeared from the court as quickly as he could. Three minutes later his Pierce Arrow was pulling out of the driveway.

Greta celebrated her victory by leaping fully clothed into the pool and swimming briskly for ten minutes. She then clambered out, shook off the excess water like a dog, grabbed a cushion from a chair and to the incredulity of everyone except Jack – who thought the whole routine utterly charming – she proceeded to stand on her head to the sound of delighted applause as her wet tennis skirt slowly dropped over her head, revealing long, tanned legs and a pair of white cotton panties. Suddenly realising the display she was making of herself, Greta abruptly stood upright.

'Anyone want to come for a hike?'

There was a short silence.

'Aren't you just the teensiest bit tired?' asked Adela Rogers St Johns.

'I love to hike up these hills.'

'You do know they're full of rattlesnakes,' said Buster Keaton.

'There are drinks on the veranda if anyone can't keep up with Greta,' announced Jack, aware that Greta's physical exuberance could sometimes become quite exhausting for others. The guests turned gratefully away.

Then, just as suddenly, she seemed quite deflated and she retreated to the house.

'Where's Greta?' asked Irving Thalberg, an hour later. 'I want to say goodbye.'

'She's lying down. She's bushed.' It was the first in what became a line of excuses that Jack would make for what his friends would think was Greta's anti-social behaviour. It annoyed him, but he loved her so much he couldn't bring himself to challenge her.

Of course there was that time when Carey Wilson threw a dinner party and she decided at the last minute that she didn't have a suitable evening gown and that was why she couldn't go. Jack was incensed.

'You're going, Flicka, we gave our promise.'

'You go. You can explain.'

Greta was wearing a long dark-green dress with a high neck and long sleeves. Jack had an inspired idea.

'Wait here,' he said briefly and dashed into the kitchen where he rummaged in various drawers before finding the pair of scissors he was looking for. He ran back up the stairs and into the bedroom where he brandished the scissors with what he hoped was an evil smile straight out of a Victorian melodrama.

'What are you doing, Yackie?' asked Garbo a little worried as her lover started clicking the scissors manically in front of her.

'Just a few little alterations, madam.'

And with that he hacked off the sleeves and snipped a low back and a classic décolletage off the green dress. He stood back to admire his handiwork.

'You could pay five hundred bucks for a dress like that on Fifth Avenue.' Garbo looked at herself critically in front of the full-length mirror then turned to her lover with a wide smile.

'I like it. I tank we go now.'

Jack was so taken with Garbo's reaction that they arrived a good thirty-five minutes late. The time, he thought, had been well spent.

The relationship between the twenty-seven-year-old movie star and the twenty-one-year-old neophyte quickly developed beyond the sexual.

'We're so alike you and I,' he murmured softly to her one morning after they had already made love for the second time. Greta ran her fingers gently down his chest and through his dark matted chest hair.

'How can you say that?' she responded spiritedly. 'You come from a theatre family, you are in the movies from the time you are seventeen, you are an American, you are used to all this.' She waved her hand vaguely. Jack laughed, caught it and kissed her arm all the way from the wrist to the shoulder as he had so often done to women in the movies.

'I mean I had a miserable childhood too.'

'Did your father die when you were fourteen?'

'I have no idea. I don't know whether my father is dead or alive.'

'That's horrible.'

'And to tell the truth, the way he walked out, I don't much care.'

'So what do you care about?'

'I care about you.'

Jack was the first man Greta opened her soul to. It surprised her how much she revealed. She never talked like this to Moje, even though he knew about her domestic circumstances. Jack seemed to be fascinated by her life, and she found herself gradually revealing more and more to him.

For the first time Garbo started to tell Jack about her relationship with her father, a relationship that had been troubled enough to affect the way she saw the world and the way she approached any kind of intimacy with another person. Karl Gustaffson had suffered uncomplainingly from kidney problems and struggled to hold down labouring jobs. As a result more pressure fell on his wife Anna, also of peasant stock, who was not impressed by Karl's inability to look after his family as tradition dictated. He died of kidney failure when Greta was fourteen. Her father's misfortune confirmed Greta's belief that life was hard and a burden to be carried, not an experience that could uplift or enrich.

Jack nodded as he saw a little more clearly into the Nordic gloom that surrounded Garbo so much of the time.

'Don't look back,' urged Jack. 'Just keep looking forward.'

'To what?'

'To our movie. I have the feeling it's going to be a smash hit.'

Jack was right about the movie. The word of mouth on *Flesh and the Devil* was exactly what the studio and the film-makers had hoped for. First, there had been the widely publicised affair between the two stars, and the extraordinary intensity of that first love scene fuelled the always popular belief in the worldwide audience that what they were watching was not acting but reality, not actors' technique but real love.

Second, there was the impact of Garbo herself in a well-written, well-directed film. Jack knew how good she was because he felt the power emanating from her as he acted with her. But when he first saw the impact Garbo had on screen it rather frightened him. Not only was she better than any actress he had ever seen before (and he had worked with the great Lillian Gish) but she also seemed to have found a new style of acting. *Flesh and the Devil* was a *Sturm und Drang* old-fashioned melodrama set in a fantasy European kingdom. Both Jack and Lars were good as the sworn blood brothers who fall out over the beautiful Felicitas, played by Garbo. Greta herself was acting with such utter truthfulness that she had no need of the big gestures and the facial grimaces which movie-goers had grown used to over the years. Audiences were captivated.

Jack was sure the film would be a hit and he couldn't wait for the New York premiere, which took place at the Capitol Theater early in January 1927. Predictably Garbo hated premieres with a passion. Had it been up to her she would have turned and run away, but Moje knew this film could be a major breakthrough for her and he forced her to go. Greta reluctantly agreed to travel east for the big occasion, but when the studio limousine drew up at the corner of Broadway and 51st Street she turned ashen-faced at the sight of the milling throng. Jack, in contrast, was as thrilled as the studio executives they were travelling with. What is the point of a premiere after all if nobody faints with excitement and has to be revived in front of the assembled reporters and cameramen?

Jack helped Greta out of the car with a huge smile on his face. The crowd screeched its approval at the familiar dashing figure of Jack in his tuxedo, now accompanied by Greta in a stunning black backless satin dress designed by her favourite costume designer, Gilbert Adrian. It was a bitterly cold night, and Greta shivered as she pulled her silver fox wrap more tightly around her exposed shoulders and back, although the shivering was as much due to the proximity of the unruly crowd as to the low temperature.

Jack bathed in the adoration the crowd was lavishing on him. The premiere of his previous film, *Bardelys the Magnificent*, had evoked nothing like this hysteria. The difference was Garbo, or, as he rapidly told himself, the potent combination of Gilbert and Garbo and their world-famous steamy love affair. For a moment he thought it was sublime to be praised and envied and paid handsomely for the not too unpleasant task of making love to the most beautiful woman in the world. Then came the doubts: what if this romance were to die? Would his career, his popularity, his life die with it? He dismissed the thought and concentrated on the applause that accompanied their slow walk up the red carpet towards the man in the tuxedo standing by the large radio microphone.

What to Jack was a roar of applause was to Greta a fearful noise of a horde that was out of control.

'Yackie, I am frightened,' said Greta, clutching his arm.

'We're fine,' Jack comforted her. 'The cops won't let them get past the rope.'

'I feel like they will eat me alive.'

'Just keep smiling and waving, precious,' said Jack, smiling and waving as they proceeded along the red carpet. 'I'll do the talking.'

The radio station's host was almost as excited as the fans who swayed dangerously against the line of policemen.

'And now, ladies and gentlemen, the moment you have all been waiting for, the fabled lovers of the silver screen, Hollywood's greatest stars, the handsome John Gilbert and the beautiful Greta Garbo!'

Greta would have preferred death at that moment. The thought of standing there in high heels which pinched her feet, having an 'intimate' conversation with a man she had never met, in front of five thousand lunatics and God knows how many more with their ears glued to their radio sets across the nation, froze her to the spot.

'John, please say a word to our listeners. Is *Flesh and the Devil* as great a movie as we have all been hearing?'

'Greater. You did ask for a word, didn't you?'

The audience rocked with laughter at the hilarity of his witticism. Greta felt the blood draining from her face. In a moment, she was sure, her vision would blur and her legs would give way.

'Greater than *The Big Parade*? Greater than *The Merry Widow*?' The announcer was happy to play along with his new friend, the big movie star. 'How can this be?'

'Because *Flesh and the Devil* stars Greta Garbo, the greatest movie star of all time.'

That's it, thought Greta. I'm dead. Literally, dead.

The announcer was thrilled to get this kind of response from Jack. He knew his bosses were listening and wouldn't they be impressed at his easy, familiar way with the stars? He'd be in line for promotion after this. The general feeling of euphoria emboldened him to ask the one question all America, maybe the whole world, wanted to know the answer to.

'Now, John, we've all read the stories about how you two fell in love while you were making the movie. So tell us, and I promise you we won't tell anyone else . . .'

The interviewer grinned, waited for the laughter and applause to die down, then drew a large breath.

'When are you two getting married?'

There was a deathly hush. The announcer thought for a second he had gone too far, but Jack was equal to the occasion.

'Just as soon as Greta says "I do",' replied Jack evenly, without giving his interviewer a glance.

As Jack had anticipated, his answer provoked a huge cheer. The announcer grinned and turned to Garbo, confidence and adrenaline flowing through him.

'Now, Greta, we all heard the proposal. What are you going to say? Do you, Greta Garbo, take John Gilbert to have and to hold from this day forth?'

There was an excruciating pause before Greta broke away from Jack and fled into the relative security of the movie-theatre lobby. The crowds cramming the sidewalk muttered but the hundreds of thousands of people still listening to their wireless sets had no idea why their radios appeared to have gone dead. Jack leapt into the breach.

'She's very shy and doesn't speak the language very well. But if you all go and see *Flesh and the Devil* you'll soon realise the wedding is just around the corner!'

Chapter Three

Jack was right. *Flesh and the Devil* was a smash hit. Louis B. Mayer and Irving Thalberg sat in Mayer's office one night towards the end of January 1927 and pored over the reviews and the box-office receipts with evident satisfaction. Thalberg went for the reviews, Mayer for the financial returns.

'Have you seen the *Herald Tribune*?' crowed Thalberg. ' "Never before has John Gilbert been so intense in his portrayal of a man in love . . . Frankly we have never seen a seduction scene done so perfectly.' "

Mayer ignored the comment. He didn't like John Gilbert and he wasn't going to waste time pretending he did. The fact that he was Thalberg's friend simply widened the breach. Instead he gazed happily at the figures from the Capitol Theater.

'The Capitol Theater is going to hold it over for a third week,' he announced. 'First time ever.'

Thalberg knew it was going to make money. For him that was no longer the issue. He gloried in the creation of a new team that would carry all before it. Who knows what great movies they could now make? Maybe Garbo's rising star would even help him realise his dream of bringing Tolstoy's *Anna Karenina* to the screen.

'Look at this one: "The old film vamp was relentlessly cruel but Garbo shows a frail physique and a fragile, ethereal air. She is infinitely more civilised and all the more subtle for not being so deliberate." I told you there was something special about that girl.'

Mayer put down the papers he had been scanning and looked indignantly at his young lieutenant.

'What do you mean, you told me? I was the one who went to Berlin and signed her, wasn't I?'

'Sure you were, L.B. I'm just tickled it's worked out so well.'

'The Capitol's taken one hundred and thirty-two thousand, five hundred and five dollars in two weeks. That's about four hundred thousand people.' For a man with little formal education, Mayer's mental arithmetic was impressive.

'I haven't seen anything like it since *The Big Parade*,' Mayer added.

Thalberg couldn't resist teasing the older man as soon as he mentioned Gilbert's previous big triumph.

'Wasn't that also a Jack Gilbert picture?'

Mayer was not to be provoked into the slightest degree of praise for the actor whom he hated with a fine fury.

'Goddamn degenerate bum,' he grunted.

It irritated Thalberg that Mayer remained so adamantly contemptuous of the studio's biggest male star.

'What is it about Jack you hate so much, L.B.?'

'I told you, he's a degenerate bum,' he repeated.

'How? I mean, what makes him such a degenerate bum?'

'He called his mother a "whore" to my face.'

'He meant it metaphorically. His mother abandoned him when he was very young. So did his dad. He's had to make his own way in the world since he was about twelve.'

'You think my life was a bed of roses? I was picking scrap iron off tips when I was six . . .'

'I know, I know,' said Thalberg hurriedly, instantly regretting having led the discussion down that particular corridor. The subject of Louis B. Mayer's life and hard times was something he did his best to avoid, although it wasn't always possible.

'You know, Louis, everyone at the studio loves Jack. He's kind, he's a good worker, a serious actor, the public loves him . . .'

Mayer looked unimpressed.

'Then that's fine. As long as the public loves him. But God help him when the public don't love him 'cause he's still gonna be a degenerate bum.'

Thalberg couldn't stand another minute on this topic.

'How's it playing in Portland, Oregon?'

Mayer ran his forefinger down the page.

'Let's see. More than treble what *The Torrent* did there in its opening week,' he said with evident satisfaction.

Jack also knew exactly what the success of *Flesh and the Devil* meant. MGM was bound to team Gilbert and Garbo in more movies and the two of them would become the most romantic couple in the world. They would take over from Douglas Fairbanks and Mary Pickford as king and queen of Hollywood. Fairbanks and Pickford lived in Pickfair, the house made famous all over the world by the stories of the celebrities who made the obligatory visit to the film capital's royal family. Jack figured that the royal couple had probably had their day by now. They'd had a good ten years at the top and Doug, for all his trademark athleticism, which he delighted in showing off in his films, was nearly forty-five years old. Mary was sweet – at least she seemed so to the public – but she wasn't sexy.

Garbo on the other hand was sexy, unbelievably sexy, but not in an obvious way like the pouting starlets he had to fight off – sometimes unsuccessfully. He was sexy too, of course, but he rather dismissed that and concentrated on the combined impact that Greta and he would have together. It wasn't just the torrents of cash that excited him, it was the chance to be somebody other than the Great Lover. Jack was as good an actor as Greta was potentially an actress, but this new level of box-office success gave him more power to pick and choose the parts on offer at MGM. Irving would see him right. Irving was his friend and he was the one person in authority at the studio he could trust. Besides, with his newly cemented status not even Mayer would dare to challenge him.

Yes, life was good for Jack, and marriage to Greta, the next logical step, would make it even better. He was sorry his marriage to Leatrice hadn't worked out but now he saw it had all been for the best. He was being saved for Garbo. He was sure she would marry him soon. He knew how potent his brand of boyish enthusiasm was on women: she was bound to submit, sooner rather than later. Perhaps he would go round to King Vidor's house after work and discuss it all with his best friend Vidor and Vidor's fiancée, Eleanor Boardman. They had been talking about their own forthcoming marriage for weeks. It had been driving him crazy and fuelled his desperate desire for Greta to say 'yes'.

He went over to the liquor cabinet and poured himself a shot of whisky. It was good stuff, although that wasn't surprising. He was on the delivery list of the best bootlegger in Hollywood. It was important to be seen employing the right people and in the seven years since the government had introduced Prohibition, having the right gangster to deliver your illegal booze had become something of a status symbol.

Garbo didn't much care for his drinking, but Jack was quick to defend it as nothing more than a social lubricant. The fact that Leatrice had cited his drinking as one of her main reasons for suing for a divorce, well, that just showed what a silly, stuck-up, frigid bitch she was. How could Leatrice refuse to see that Cecil B. DeMille was nothing but a hypocrite? He pretended to be this great moralist – a lay preacher and a pillar of the Presbyterian Church. Christ! He kept his mistress in a house at the bottom of his garden and his foot fetish could be seen by anyone who watched his movies with a brain that was still functioning. All those bathroom scenes were just excuses to get the actresses to take their clothes off. He had genuinely loved Leatrice, and the way that DeMille had driven his wife from him made him feel as angry as if he had discovered that the two of them had been lovers, though he was sure they hadn't. He reached for the bottle again.

In her sitting room at the Hotel Miramar, Garbo was looking at Moje as he steadily worked his way through the huge pile of reviews of *Flesh and the Devil*. It was clear that he was not particularly enjoying the experience. She thought for a moment that he was just having his usual trouble with the English language. Her knowledge, though not spectacular, was far better than his. He was already fluent in Swedish, Yiddish, German and Russian, so maybe at the age of forty-three he was simply too old to learn another language. The manner in which he threw down the last of the newspaper clippings, however, told Garbo immediately that he understood the tenor of the reviews well enough.

'So now you are a star.'

'Just as you told me I would be,' she agreed.

'It hasn't worked out as I imagined.'

Garbo nodded. Through the dark days after their arrival in America, when they were being ignored by the studio, they had sustained themselves with the dream of making great films together – the beautiful, talented actress guided by the genius film-maker, the master puppeteer. Now that vision was dead. She might go on to achieve those heights, but it would be with other directors. Whatever life held in store for Mauritz Stiller, it was unlikely to be Hollywood success.

'I wanted to be the director who introduced your great talent to the world.'

'You are. If it hadn't been for you, I would have been nothing.'

It was the truth as far as Greta was concerned. He had plucked her out of obscurity as a teenager in the Stockholm drama school, he had cast her in *Gösta Berlings Saga*, her first film, negotiated for her second when she made *Die Freudlose Gasse* in Germany, worried about her as they decided whether or not to come to Hollywood. He had directed not just her career choices but also her life choices. How could a working-class girl from Sweden have achieved so much so quickly if it hadn't been for Stiller? Only a few years ago she had been lathering men's faces in a Stockholm barber shop. She owed him everything. She told him so but he demurred.

'No, you would always have been Garbo. It makes me so frustrated to see Louis B. Mayer and Irving Thalberg take the credit. They destroyed me and stole you.'

'They didn't. Nobody could steal me from you, Moje.'

'Not even Gilbert?'

'Not even Gilbert.'

It wasn't quite true, of course. The frenzy of her love affair with Jack had changed everything, but she was very conscious of Moje's unhappiness and of what she owed him.

'He doesn't know I am here with you. He cannot stop me seeing you. You are everything to me. We are closer than husband and wife. They have secrets from each other. We have none. I think I will never marry, but if there is one man I would have liked to marry it is you, Moje.' She sounded unaccountably bleak.

Stiller nodded, but his heart was broken. He knew perfectly well he had lost his protégée just as he had always feared he would, not just to American commerce, which was bad enough, but also to a virile young man, which was much worse. At least they weren't in direct competition for Greta's delectable body. Maybe if he could have satisfied her sexually, it would have bound her more tightly to him, but he knew that had never really been an option. Oddly, for a woman with whom half the world was already in love, Greta herself had never before shown much interest in young men. It was one of the things that had made her so attractive to him. Freed from the shackles of constant sexual longings, she could focus her mind entirely on what he wanted her to achieve – becoming a great actress. He had his own occasional dalliance with young men, but really, despite the fact that he spent much of his creative life communicating to audiences the manifold delights and dangers of sex, he wasn't much interested in it himself, at least not as an active participant.

'Does he think we are lovers?'

'Maybe.'

Stiller was relieved.

'You haven't discussed me ... it ... with him?'

Greta was scandalised.

'No! I would never discuss you like that. Not with anyone!'

Stiller nodded, pleased that even in the throes of passion Greta was able to exercise discretion. There was no talk like pillow talk. It was insidious and could never be stopped. That was another reason he hated the sexual hi-jinks of the business he had embraced. But if Gilbert didn't know that Stiller was homosexual, he would assume that he was heterosexual; in which case they were obviously both rivals for Greta's body. He didn't want to be caught in a pointless duel for her love like Ulrich and Leo on the Isle of Friendship.

'Then he thinks we are lovers.'

'I told you, I never ...'

'I know men, I know actors. And I know Mr Gilbert.'

*

Jack had been in love before, but never quite like this. He knew he fell in love easily. It was one of life's pleasures and women who saw how completely he was in love with them were very easy to persuade into bed. The trouble was that, however genuine the original passion, he fell out of love just as quickly. He never thought of himself as a scoundrel because most of the time the women couldn't wait to take off their clothes. Sometimes, when he knew he had fallen out of love minutes after ejaculation, while the woman was still nestled against his naked chest, he wondered if perhaps all men were like this and he couldn't really help it. But when he had fallen for Greta, he had done so in a way he had never previously experienced, not even when he first fell in love with Leatrice.

Greta enchanted him and enslaved him: he would do anything for her. She came and went from his house as she pleased. She was like no woman he had ever known. Although she was anxious to look her best for the camera, she spent little time worrying about her appearance. She wanted what pleased her and what pleased her was invariably simple. She wore her longish fair hair very simply coiffed, she preferred plain flowered dresses and no make-up. Her skin was exquisitely smooth and he adored those long but natural eyelashes.

What he did do was build what was effectively a new and secret suite on to the house especially for her so she could live in it without being seen by anyone in the main house. It was possible to wander through the main house and be entirely unaware of Garbo's separate quarters, which had been dug into the side of the hill. The main feature was a large, elaborate bedroom with closets spacious enough to walk into (though Garbo never even half-filled them). There were mirrors along one wall and (particularly enjoyed by Jack) on the ceiling. The bathroom contained a shower and an outsize tub as well as the bidet that Jack knew was integral to every European home. The entrance into the main house was through a closet on the main floor so Garbo could pretend that she was entirely on her own or she could choose to favour Jack with her company for the night.

She came and went from his house as she pleased. Jack never knew where she was or what she was doing other than when she was at the studio. It bothered him when she slipped her naked body between his sheets that he didn't know where she had been and couldn't bring himself to ask. He didn't think she'd been with another man – apart from Stiller, and she couldn't be sleeping with him: he was old enough to be her father. Besides, the way she nestled into him, the intensity of her kisses, the unblinking stare that emanated from those mesmerising eyes, all these convinced Jack that Greta was as much in love with him as he was with her. But, though she certainly slept with him – sometimes – was she even technically living with him? He didn't know. Sometimes she would stay away from his house for as long as a week. Would the occasional night of intoxicating passion convince her to marry him? He wasn't confident of the answer to that question.

She was Swedish, that much he understood, and she missed her homeland. If the situation were reversed, he would certainly miss America. Jack decided he would recreate a little of Sweden at the back of 1400 Tower Road. Accordingly he used Greta's frequent absences from the house, especially when she was filming, to engage a team of builders to construct a log cabin, plant a pine grove and create a waterfall, such as might be found in any part of the Swedish countryside. His friend King Vidor had suggested that the sight and sounds of such a landscape might help to alleviate the worst effects of Greta's homesickness. Jack soon got the taste for this kind of therapy and wondered what else he could do. Vidor suggested opening a mail-order account at a bookshop in Stockholm. Jack thought it was a brilliant idea because Greta always complained that reading books, which she loved to do, was very difficult for her in English.

When Greta returned to the house after an argument and a spell back in the Hotel Miramar, everything was ready. She barely had time to turn off the engine before Jack almost dragged her out of the car. He was as excited as a little boy with a new toy. Greta started to complain at the way he was pulling her through the trees.

'Yackie, where are we going?'

'C'mon, slowpoke.'

'Stop pulling me!'

'It's just through there. Stop a minute and listen.'

He halted, turned and held her in his arms. He kissed her ear, inhaled the delicate perfume rising from her hair and whispered softly to her.

'Can you hear it?'

Running through the trees all she could hear had been the snapping of twigs underfoot, but in the luscious silence she could now discern the sound of rushing water.

'Is it raining?' she asked, puzzled.

'You bet!' laughed Jack and he pulled her onwards through the trees until the sound of rushing water became ever louder. He held up a branch of the last tree and waited for her reaction.

'Yackie! A waterfall! Where did it come from?'

'I had it built for you. You can't have that log cabin and not hear the sound of rushing water.'

'You are crazy, crazy!'

'Isn't it just like Sweden now?' asked Jack, eager for his efforts to be validated.

Greta laughed.

'No, it is like Beverly Hills now.'

Greta's smart reply crushed Jack completely. He looked so downcast her heart changed immediately. He really was just a little boy, for all his $10,000 a week. She took his face in her hands, looked at his forlorn face, then closed her eyes and kissed him. He stood there motionless as she covered his face with quick kisses.

'You are the sweetest man.'

'I opened a mail-order account with a bookstore in Stockholm because I want you to be happy living here with me. I'll do anything for you. You only have to ask.'

'I do not deserve this.'

'Of course you do. This and a whole lot more.'

'This must have cost a fortune.'

'What's the point of having all this money if I can't spend it on the woman I love?'

'Do you love me, Yackie?'

'Yes, Greta, I love you. Now until the day I die. I will never stop loving you.'

As they lay together afterwards on the carpet of bracken that had been carefully laid by the construction company, Jack couldn't help realising that in some weird and inexplicable way the traditional male and female roles in a relationship had been completely reversed. He was content to be Garbo's lover as and when she demanded, for the sheer exultation of hearing her declare her love for him. When she did, occasionally and in her halting English, declare her feelings for him, his heart soared. She wouldn't, however, use those declarations of love he had heard so many times on stage and which he now believed were the only valid way to express true love. Garbo scorned the traditional phrases, and Jack was left only with the intensity of her lovemaking to tell him how much she loved him. It was never enough. Greta knew he wanted more but she couldn't give it to him.

For all her determination to maintain her independence Garbo still turned to Jack when she wanted support in her ongoing battles with MGM. Irving Thalberg had spent three hours coaxing her into accepting another 'bad womans' role in a film to be called *Women Love Diamonds*. He had found the process just as frustrating as Garbo did. Every actress on the lot would love to play these 'bad' women. They got fed up playing sweet, simpering heroines and longed to chew up the scenery and drive men to frenzy for love of them. Garbo's resistance was inexplicable. However, Irving, calling on all his famous powers of persuasion, felt at the end of the meeting that he had won this particular battle and told the wardrobe department to instruct Garbo to come in and look at the designs for the role. She never showed up.

Thalberg was furious. He was not used to having his legendary charm flouted so brazenly but he kept his temper and persuaded her to meet the new director off the lot. He would come to the lobby of the Hotel Miramar, where she still kept her room, and talk to her there. Greta agreed and went downstairs to meet him as requested. The director had been rehearsing his speech of persuasion for days but unfortunately when it came it made absolutely no impact on the actress.

'No,' she said firmly. 'I do not wish to do this.'

'But you don't understand,' he blustered. 'You have no choice. The studio can just make you do it.'

'No,' said Greta bluntly. '*You* do not understand. I do not wish to work for you.'

And with that she got up and went back to her room. She had not lost her temper or yelled or made any kind of a scene. She simply could not be persuaded to do something she did not wish to do. The legal letter from Louis B. Mayer, informing her she had been suspended and would therefore receive no salary, arrived by messenger within hours.

Jack was impressed by her steadfastness in the face of MGM's bitter threats and all the weapons they swore to deploy against her. They signed Pauline Stark to play the part in *Women Love Diamonds* with Lionel Barrymore and Douglas Fairbanks Jr. Greta affected not to care. They called her an ignorant thickheaded Swede, but, though she didn't like the terminology or the fact that she was no longer being paid, it just made her even less inclined to accede to the studio's demands. They threatened to deport her when her visa ran out. Greta let them know that Jack Gilbert was only too willing to provide an American passport through marriage.

Indeed, Jack found the whole episode hugely entertaining. He entirely supported Greta's stand, which displeased his friend Irving Thalberg and positively incensed Louis B. Mayer. Garbo's intransigence was going to cost MGM a fortune and it was all the fault of Jack Gilbert. With his experience, Gilbert knew precisely what the weak points of the studio's argument were and – worse – he knew the man who could exploit those weaknesses. He introduced Greta to his own business manager, Harry Edington.

Now, with Edington's help, Greta was able to state explicitly what she wanted from the new five-year contract MGM was pressing her to sign. She wanted her salary increased from $750 to $5,000 a week and, just as important, she wanted a say in what parts she was going to play for that money. The front office started to release stories in the press about greedy foreign stars. The smear campaign couldn't be too aggressive because Mayer and Thalberg still hoped she would come to heel and they would have to start promoting her again. Louella Parsons was again roped in, this time to suggest in her syndicated column in the Hearst press that Greta was – in addition to being greedy of course – wilful, spoilt, childish and temperamental.

At Jack's next Sunday brunch Irving Thalberg didn't show up. Jack was sorry to have alienated his friend, but he knew it was only temporary. He tried to explain as much to Greta.

'Trust me. It's a really good sign.'

'Why?'

'He's frightened of you.'

'Me?'

'Yes, you, my Svenska flicka. He doesn't want to see how unmoved you are by this stupid war the studio's waging against you.'

'Jack's right, Greta,' said King Vidor, who had been back home to change into his tennis whites. 'They'll have to give in eventually. The public just loves the two of you.'

'What's happened to *Women Love Diamonds*?'

'I talked to Eddie Goulding. It's going to be a disaster. Won't take a dime at the box office.'

Jack and Greta exchanged glances of deep satisfaction.

'Hey, you two, I can't stand the smug way you look at each other. Eleanor and I were going to play. Want to make it mixed doubles?'

Greta and Jack took the court against King and his fiancée, Eleanor. Greta vented her anger by playing at the net, smashing every weak volley that came her way. Sometimes it didn't matter if the ball was going anywhere near her or not.

'Get it back, Yackie!' she called, as a mis-hit cross-court forehand dropped just over her head.

'OK, mine!' shouted Jack, but Garbo was already running to the back of the left-hand court.

'No, let me!' she screamed, but her attempt sailed a good six inches out.

'That's out,' shouted King catching the errant ball.

'It was in. I saw it. It was in!' yelled Garbo in frustration.

King was unmoved by this unusual outburst of Scandinavian fire.

'It was a foot over the base line, Greta,' he said firmly. 'Sorry! That's 6–4 to us. Do you want another set?'

'No. I want the point replayed.'

Jack was anxious to calm down his agitated partner. 'Let's all have some iced tea. Eleanor, how about it?'

'That sounds like a real good idea. It's so hot.'

They walked over to where the pitcher of iced tea has been laid out by Jack's butler and started to drink thirstily. Greta was first to finish.

'Good. Now we replay the last point.'

'Why don't we just play another set?'

'I'm sorry, Yackie. I played really bad.'

'You were fine. King's service was unplayable.'

'No, it was all my fault. I should win when I am at the net.'

'It's just a silly game of tennis,' said Eleanor who didn't want the silly game of tennis to spoil what had been an idyllic afternoon.

Jack was quick to help change the subject. 'Did I tell you Greta signed with Harry Edington?'

King and Eleanor knew of Greta's ongoing battle with the studio and were generally supportive.

'He will not charge me any commission,' said Greta proudly. 'He says he will do it just for the prestige of having Garbo as a client.'

'Does Mayer know?' asked King warily.

'He does now,' grinned Jack. 'Harry told him he wanted to raise Greta's fee from seven hundred and fifty to five thousand dollars a week.'

'L.B. must have hit the roof.'

'Not just his roof. He hit every roof for five miles,' laughed Jack briefly, suddenly becoming conscious that King and Eleanor were not joining in. Maybe the conversation shouldn't always centre on Garbo, particularly when their best friends were about to get married. He spotted something on Eleanor's hand, which was glinting in the bright afternoon sunlight.

'Hey, is that the engagement ring?'

Eleanor was relieved that her supposed best friends had finally noticed what she had been waving under their faces since midday. It was an 18-carat gold band with a white diamond solitaire, pear cut, weighing some 2 carats. She could not see how Greta and Jack had avoided mentioning it for as long as they had. Men, she knew, were particularly slow on the uptake in matters of jewellery, unless they had just paid for it, but Greta must surely have noticed this gigantic rock. Was it possible that she finally possessed something of which Greta was jealous?

'Isn't it just beautiful?' gushed Eleanor deliberately. 'King won't tell me how much it cost,' she added.

'I think that keeps the mystery of the romance alive,' said King, pouring himself a third glass of iced tea.

'That's why he took the Woolworth's price tag off before he gave it to you,' smiled Jack.

King didn't find that at all funny, so he deliberately threw a hand grenade into the conversation, knowing how much it would discomfort his best friend.

'Say, why don't we make it a double wedding?'

For a few moments, no one spoke.

'What is a double wedding?' asked Greta.

'It means you marry Jack the same time as I marry Eleanor,' said King brightly.

'King! You can't embarrass Jack and Greta like that. You really put them on the spot.'

'Eleanor, nobody can embarrass Jack Gilbert. This is the guy who proposed to Greta live on national radio.'

'Anyway, it's not something we can arrange ourselves,' argued Eleanor. 'It's not our house. We're getting married at Marion Davies's hacienda. We can't just impose another hundred guests on her.'

'Nonsense, think of the scoop the Hearst press would have.'

Jack saw the logic immediately and all the wonderful publicity that would ensue. It would be the perfect coronation. Of course he'd have to share the day with his best friends, but with all due respect to Eleanor, who was a fine actress, and King, who was one of the best directors in Hollywood, there would no doubt which newly married couple would dominate the headlines.

'I think a double wedding's a great idea. Mr and Mrs King Vidor, Mr and Mrs John Gilbert. Doesn't that sound wonderful?'

Eleanor saw exactly what Jack saw and didn't like it one little bit. It was her wedding day. She had no intention of playing the part of a bridesmaid while wearing the white wedding dress on which she had already lavished a month's salary.

'Oh, this isn't romantic at all,' Eleanor complained. She turned to Garbo: 'You just ignore them, honey.'

'You want romance? I'll give you romance. You wanna direct me, King?'

The boys were enjoying the play-acting.

'Sure. OK, Jack, on your knee . . .'

Jack, intentionally misunderstanding, dropped onto both knees, his eyes staring straight at Greta's crotch.

'Just one knee, you asshole. You look like a kid. OK, now take her hand and kiss it. No! Bend your face. Don't pull it to your lips. That's better. Now tell her you love her.'

Jack cleared his throat and in a very silly high-pitched squeak said the words that gave him such pleasure.

'Greta Garbo, I love you.'

It was such a silly voice that everybody laughed.

'It's a bit too rich and fruity, that voice,' King commented. 'Could you go up another octave and say it again?'

Jack's voice dropped an octave instead and, in a good imitation of the stage star John Barrymore, rolled the words around his mouth like a vintage port.

'Greta Garbo, you are the sun to my moon, the great North star to all the little stars, the cream in my coffee . . .'

Eleanor still didn't like the conversation.

'Jack, stop it. You're embarrassing poor Greta.'

But Jack was acting for all he was worth.

'Will you accept my proposal of marriage and make me the happiest man on earth?'

Eleanor looked at Greta and saw that she wasn't finding it funny either. To her horror it appeared to Eleanor that Greta was taking it very seriously.

'Yes, Yackie, I will. Why not?'

There was a general gasp of astonishment.

'Did you just say "yes"?' asked King, amazed.

Jack was beside himself with excitement.

'She did, she did. She said yes. You both heard her, didn't you?'

Chapter Four

The very next week MGM announced they were going ahead with their adaptation of Tolstoy's novel *Anna Karenina*, and that, since Garbo was still on suspension, Jeanne Eagels, who was currently starring as the notorious Sadie Thompson in the hit Broadway play *Rain*, would play the title role. Now Greta was really upset. Jack tried to calm her, aware that the slightest problem might damage the prospect of their forthcoming marriage.

'Don't panic, don't react. That's what they want.'

'Mayer said he'd let Joan Crawford play the part before he gave it to me.'

'He's bluffing.'

'How do you know?'

'Because Mayer's a nasty evil sonofabitch but he's not stupid. It would take a stupid sonofabitch to cast Joan Crawford as Anna Karenina. The public still loves you.'

'But if I don't make another movie soon, the public might forget all about me.'

'Not when you get married to the top movie star in Hollywood.'

'But Douglas Fairbanks is already married.'

'Svenska beetch!'

She laughed and dodged the playful cuff that was coming her way. She raced out of the house and through the pine trees. He allowed her to get to the log cabin first so she could open the door but he was too close behind her to allow her to close it. He stuck his foot in the door and gradually his superior force pushed the door open. He pretended to twirl his small moustache as if he were playing a particularly evil Victorian villain in a melodrama. Greta shrieked and fell obligingly on her back onto the couch. Jack threw himself on top of her and started to kiss her. His fingers sought the buttons of the fly on her trousers.

'I wish you'd wear skirts like other women.'

'I'm not like other women,' Greta whispered into his ear.

'It makes me feel like I'm going to have sex with a man, trying to take your trousers down.'

'Would you like to have sex with a man?' asked Greta, genuinely curious.

'Me? God, no!' said Jack with evident disgust. Then he realised that, as with most of Greta's more outrageous pronouncements, there was more to the question than he had originally thought.

'Why do you ask?'

'No reason.'

'Do you want to do it with another woman?'

'Maybe.'

'Who?'

'Who would you like me to do it with?'

Jack's mind was whirling. For all his reputation as the Great Lover, this was an area he had never ventured into. He didn't know what to think. Images seared into his brain. Greta and Eleanor, Greta and Leatrice (DeMille would like that one), Greta and Clara Bow . . . Greta could feel how excited he was, and they made love with as much passion as they had managed in the weeks since MGM's war of attrition had started to intensify.

Next day Greta was told that she was to play a chorus girl in *Her Brother From Brazil*, a romantic comedy, starring Aileen Pringle and Lew Cody. She picked up the phone to talk to Harry Edington.

'It's a ploy. Best thing is to go along with it.'

'Harry, I can't play a chorus girl, a tiny supporting part.'

'They don't want you to. It would defeat their strategy of capitalising on your star status.'

'They want me to have costume fittings.'

'Do it. Mayer wouldn't dare risk destroying the studio's investment in you. They're telling everyone you won't cooperate. So, cooperate!'

When Aileen Pringle discovered that the studio had cast the most controversial young actress in Hollywood in her film she was horrified and marched straight into Louis B. Mayer's office.

'You can't do this to me, L.B.'

'I can't do what? You got the lead. The Swedish bitch is a supporting act.'

'You think anyone's going to look at me when she comes on the screen?'

'You want me to suspend you too?'

Aileen Pringle knew she was taking a risk. You didn't cross L.B. Mayer lightly.

'L.B., you know how much I love working for you. Can't you see if you cast Garbo in this picture it's MGM that's going to look stupid?'

Pringle's question became more compelling a few days later when the executives in New York decided that keeping Garbo on suspension was pointless. On suspension she was not making money for MGM and there was a real danger that the studio might end up tarnishing its own golden girl. The parent company's powerful attorney J. Robert Rubin travelled to the West Coast to supervise Garbo's new contract. Soon Harry Edington was able to tell his client that her new five-year deal would pay her $3,000 a week rising to $5,000 over the length of the contract. To all intents and purposes Garbo had won.

Jack took the news as a reason to celebrate. He immediately opened bottles of champagne, and a spontaneous party started in the house. Jack loved drinking, he loved beating the studio, he loved Greta and, indeed, by nine o'clock that night, he loved the whole world. He took the needle off the spinning record on the gramophone and called loudly for silence. It gave him great pleasure, he told the equally merry guests, to announce not only the successful conclusion of Greta Garbo's contract talks, which would enable her to start production shortly as Anna Karenina, but also her marriage to himself at a ceremony to be performed in Marion Davies's Beverly Hills house at the same time as their closest friends King Vidor and Eleanor Boardman were also plighting their troth.

He told them also that this was a big, big secret and they were to tell absolutely nobody about it.

The announcement was greeted with cheers of approval. Bottle in his left hand, Jack held out his right hand for Greta to join him in a public demonstration of their world-famous love. As the noise gradually died away to an embarrassed silence it became clear that Greta Garbo was no longer in the room. Indeed she was no longer in the house. Jack shrugged and opened another bottle.

At the time Jack was making his speech, Greta was driving west along Santa Monica Boulevard towards the little house where an increasingly sick Mauritz Stiller was still living.

'He drinks, Moje,' Greta said to her old friend once she was installed on his sofa. 'He drinks all the time.'

'Most people in Hollywood drink. It's expected of you.'

'He drinks in the morning. Not just at parties.'

'Swedish people drink. Especially in the winter.'

'Not like Yackie drinks.'

'Are you still going to marry him?'

'I don't think I am cut out for marriage.'

Stiller smiled. Garbo's words restored his spirits.

'No. You are to be a great actress. The greatest the world has ever seen.'

Greta basked in the certainty of Moje's belief. He had been saying this to her almost every day for three years and he was a great director. Everyone in Europe knew that. Only the fools in Hollywood couldn't see it. He took her hands in his and raised them to his lips, touching them softly. His eyes filled with tears. Greta brought his hands to her lips and smothered them with her kisses. She wondered, not for the first time, why Nature had to be so cruel. She knew Moje loved her in a way Jack could never challenge. It was just that he needed the bodies of young men for his own release. As for her, she loved Moje with all her heart, but still there was something missing from the relationship, apart from the fact that Nature had made such a pursuit entirely pointless. They didn't need to speak words to each other, they just looked each other in the eyes and they knew how hopeless it was. Maybe she should go through with the marriage to Jack after all.

Jack was furious at the way Greta had just slipped away from the party without saying anything to anyone. And he knew where she'd gone. She'd been seeing that old goat Stiller. How could she let him touch her? He was old, he looked decrepit, he was just this failure of a director who couldn't speak English.

Jack drove through the gates of the Culver City studio the next day in a foul temper. He was making a picture called *Twelve Miles Out*, a highly topical action melodrama about bootleggers and their ongoing battles with the coastguards and federal agents who faced the impossible job of enforcing Prohibition. The leading lady was Joan Crawford. He didn't much care for this kid from San Antonio, Texas. She was exactly the same age as Greta but she had no class, not the way Greta did. She looked like what she was – an ex-waitress and shop girl who had been invited to Hollywood because she had won a Charleston contest in Kansas City.

Rumour had it that she had also starred in movies that were never going to get released in movie theatres or reviewed in the newspapers. The way she looked at him with those big black staring eyes, the way she rubbed up against him at the slightest opportunity, the way she made it quite clear she would do anything to get ahead in the business left Jack in no doubt that the rumours were true. He was pretty sure Louis B. Mayer had 'auditioned' her, and there had to be a reason that the producer Harry Rapf was advancing her cause. He couldn't conceive of Greta doing anything like that. In fact Greta's sexuality was still a puzzle to him but at least it wasn't obviously available to a man who could advance her career.

Joan knew about Jack's affair with Greta but she figured she would see just how strong this so-called attachment to the enigmatic Swede really was. As they sank onto the couch in a clinch and the camera remained on their faces, she let her hand travel swiftly up Jack's inner thigh. Jack pushed her roughly away and stormed off the set. He marched into his dressing room and picked up the phone. Carlos told him Greta had gone back to the Miramar. She had a private number at the hotel but when he dialled it all he got was the long, wailing tone of a disconnected number. He rang reception at the Miramar and asked someone to go and check whether there was any problem in Greta's room.

The reply incensed him. Apparently her room was empty and she had taken the phone out of the wall. When the chambermaid reinserted it Jack rang it again and again only to receive the same dull tone in his ear. On further enquiry he discovered that Greta had changed the number.

Jack was frustrated that Greta would only agree to marry him in conditions of the strictest secrecy, and she had not been amused by his drunken announcement at the party for which he had to apologise very humbly. If they were to get married at the same time as King and Eleanor they couldn't invite their own guests. Greta still demanded that so far as it was now possible it should be a surprise to everyone except the other bride and bridegroom and their host and hostess – and presumably whoever was going to marry them. Jack thought it a crazy idea. 'We're the most famous lovers in the world. What's the point of keeping it a secret?'

'I don't like the press, the reporters, the cameras . . .'

'We can't do it anyway. As soon as we apply for the licence and take the blood tests the press will be all over us.'

'We have to apply in our real names, don't we?'

'I guess so.'

'They say, "Aren't you Greta Garbo?" I say, "No, I am Greta Gustaffson." Anyway, what is your name?'

'John Cecil Pringle.'

Garbo burst into laughter.

'Really?'

'Really.' Jack was disgruntled.

'No one will mistake you for John Gilbert,' she trilled. 'Not with that name.'

The irritated Jack was determined to force home his original point.

'Are you really trying to tell me you're going to buy a wedding dress, stand there in the store and try it on and then pretend it's for someone else?'

Jack's point was valid. Ten days before the scheduled event Greta called Eleanor to bemoan the fact that she had no wedding dress and didn't know where to turn for help. Eleanor offered to take her shopping for a dress she could get married in but which wasn't a traditional wedding dress. Greta agreed willingly, which relieved Eleanor, who now felt she stood a chance of not being completely overshadowed on her own wedding day. Eleanor and her chauffeur drove all the way out to Santa Monica to collect Greta who took nearly thirty minutes to come downstairs while Eleanor waited in the back of the car before it became too hot and she went into the Hotel Miramar's bar to cool down. The stores in Beverly Hills didn't contain anything Greta wanted so Eleanor agreed they should drive on into downtown Los Angeles.

Greta then decided she wasn't going to buy a dress at all but she needed shoes. In the fourth store, having tried on what appeared to the now fretful Eleanor well over a thousand pairs of shoes, Greta finally found a pair she liked. In fact she liked them so much she kept them on her feet when she walked out of the store with her old ones in a bag. Instead of making for the safety of the back of the car Greta decided she would go for a walk to test out the shoes.

They crossed the street and started to walk briskly along the sidewalk when Greta suddenly hobbled to a stop. She slipped off one of the new shoes and examined the inside carefully.

'Stone in your shoe?' asked Eleanor, hoping that it hurt.

'No. No stone. My foot is sore.'

'They're new. Your feet have to mould the leather.'

'I can't wear shoes that hurt me.'

'We all do it, Greta. They're very stylish. That's the price we pay to look chic.'

'We must take them back.'

'You've worn them, Greta. And you've scuffed them. Look.'

'Don't be silly. I am Greta Garbo. We take them back.'

Greta was quite right of course. With evident reluctance the store clerk took the shoes back and refunded the money. Greta slipped on her old shoes, and they walked back to Eleanor's car.

'Oh, these old shoes are wonderful,' cried Greta in relief.

'So why did you buy that pair?'

'I have no idea. I really like these shoes.'

Eleanor had always known that Greta was somewhat self-obsessed but she had found her idiosyncrasies endearing. You couldn't help but feel sorry for Greta and her social awkwardness when she was clearly so shy and was finding the English language so difficult. However, Eleanor was always surprised that when she and King and Jack went swimming in the pool at Jack's house Greta showed no shyness at all in stripping off completely and jumping in stark naked.

'This is how people swim in Sweden,' she used to explain in a matter-of-fact tone. Eleanor would watch King unwaveringly as they frolicked in the pool. Her basilisk stare was enough to prevent any untoward physical response from King to the sight of the bare breasts of the Divine Garbo floating on the surface of the water.

Eleanor and Greta hardly exchanged a word on the way home. By the time they had driven all the way from downtown Los Angeles to the edge of the ocean at Santa Monica, dropped off Greta at her hotel and driven back to her house in Tower Road, Beverly Hills, Eleanor was exhausted and Garbo had bought nothing that could be used at the wedding.

'How come you're so tired?' asked King when he got back from the studio to find Eleanor asleep on the couch at 7.30 p.m.

'I've been not shopping with Greta.'

'How did you get on?' asked King, splashing soda into his whisky.

'We spent the whole day together. I drove her all the way from Santa Monica to downtown and back, and you know what? She never even had the grace to say "thank you". She got out of the car and went straight up to her room. She's a bitch.'

'But a very photogenic bitch.'

On the day before the wedding Jack was woken by the sound of a car starting in the driveway outside. He turned over idly in bed and reached out to touch his fiancée's naked skin, but though the sheets were still warm there was nobody in the bed but himself. He clambered out, dragging the sheet awkwardly with him, pulled back the drapes and was just in time to see Greta driving her little Ford coupé out of the gates and turning down Tower Road towards the Beverly Hills Hotel.

Grabbing a pair of shorts, he raced downstairs to find Carlos, the Filipino servant, setting the breakfast table.

'Miss Garbo, did she say where she was going?'

Carlos bowed deeply. In certain circumstances this display of formal servility rather pleased Jack but now it just made him impatient.

'Carlos! Where is she?'

Carlos bowed again. Jack ran to the door, opened it, realised he was only wearing shorts and raced back inside again to get dressed more conventionally.

She wasn't at Stiller's place, although at first he hadn't believed the old man. With great reluctance Stiller had let Jack into his house and sworn at him in Swedish or Russian or Yiddish or some combination of foreign languages. Jack had no time for Stiller and had been happy to let the director (who to be honest looked really sick and miserable) know that.

He knew Garbo had got cold feet about the wedding, which was appropriate because she did literally have cold feet. He complained when she tucked ten icy toes under his bare bottom to warm them up, but his complaints rather dwindled when she started to move her feet into other areas of his body. Literal cold feet he could cope with. He just didn't want the metaphorical cold feet to destroy the wedding of the century.

At the Hotel Miramar they told him that Garbo sometimes, very early in the morning, went out to the beach so he drove mournfully along Ocean Front, past the beach houses of W.R. Hearst and Louis B. Mayer. It was a status symbol to own a house right on the beach at Santa Monica. He wondered if he was just going to make a laughing stock of himself. He passed the start of Sunset Boulevard, which was commonly regarded as the last outpost of civilisation by the sophisticated citizens of Hollywood. He had nearly reached Malibu when he saw her – a lone figure standing on the beach gazing at the rolling waves of the Pacific Ocean. He found her car and waited by it for fifteen minutes. How long could a person just stand on the beach and look at the ocean? he wondered. The answer, as far as Greta was concerned, was clearly longer than fifteen minutes.

He examined her back. Even from behind she appeared to be calmer than he had known her for weeks. Somehow she needs this bonding with the ocean, or at least with Nature, he thought. He was no longer angry with her for what seemed to him to be her running out on him but full of love and tenderness. He thought he was indeed a fortunate man to have found for a life partner not just a sexy young woman and a talented actress who was on her way to becoming the biggest movie star in the world but a person of such depth and soul.

Eventually he realised he could be waiting for her for hours so he walked out across the flat sand and stood next to her for a moment. He didn't dare to speak and break the perfect silence that enveloped them. Her body started briefly when she realised there was somebody who was approaching her, but she didn't utter a word and the atmosphere surrounding her remained undisturbed. Jack was childishly thrilled when Greta slowly stretched out her hand to reach for his, and when their fingers interlocked she squeezed his hand with such feeling that it seemed to be the most eloquent declaration of love he had ever known. It was all he could do to stop himself from bursting into tears or dropping to his knees and burying his face in the crotch of her trousers. He restrained himself from doing anything to let her know how needy he felt. At least he had the comfort of that hand squeeze. She did love him after all. He was sure of it.

That was why when he lay in bed and heard her car starting early the next morning he didn't panic. She was obviously just going to her usual haunt to commune with Nature again. The double wedding wasn't scheduled to start in Beverly Hills until four o'clock.

Indeed most of the guests would put in nearly a full day's work at the studio first, so there was plenty of time for her to drive up to Malibu and back before the main event. When King rang to make sure everything was all right, Jack told him that Greta, quite enchantingly, had decided she would not see him until the moment of their meeting in front of the judge. It was a charming old-fashioned gesture, and he was entirely in favour of it.

Midday came and went and Jack suddenly didn't feel so confident any more. He roared out to Santa Monica and then up the coast, stopping whenever he saw a lone figure, but there was no sign of the bride-to-be. He called home but she hadn't returned. With great reluctance he dialled King's house.

'Hi. It's Jack. Is Greta there?'

'Here? What the hell would she be doing here?'

'I . . . I can't find her.'

'I thought you said . . .'

'I know what I said.'

'So what makes you think she isn't going to show up at four o'clock at Marion's?'

'I . . . I don't know. I just thought she might have wanted to talk to Eleanor.'

'Well, Eleanor doesn't want to talk to her. Do you know what Greta did the other day?'

'Another time, King, please!'

'You'd better get dressed and get over there. I'll warn Marion.'

'No, don't do that! Marion's a gossip. You're probably right. She'll show up at four as planned.'

King put the phone down and told Eleanor the news. The bride-to-be was not happy. 'I don't know why you agreed to this stupid idea in the first place.'

'Everyone liked it. That's why.'

'I didn't. I never did. I told you this was supposed to be our wedding day and the Swedish Ice Queen and your drinking buddy would steal it.'

'So now we've got our wedding day back. If Greta doesn't show, you'll be the only bride there.'

He moved towards her to kiss her, but she shrugged him aside impatiently. King wondered if this was going to be the tenor of the marriage. He had already been through one expensive divorce: he really didn't want another. Damn Garbo and damn Gilbert too. They deserved each other.

It was the Wednesday after the Labor Day weekend that traditionally marked the end of the long summer vacation and Hollywood's royalty duly arrived for the novelty value of the double celebrity wedding. King was at heart a company man and he made sure Louis B. Mayer and his family were invited despite Jack and Greta's feelings about the way his studio had behaved. Irving Thalberg was there to pour oil on troubled waters if it was needed, but Marion Davies and W.R. Hearst clearly expected nothing but a wedding party otherwise they would not have invited Sam Goldwyn, whose feelings about Mayer as a person and MGM as a studio coincided entirely with Greta's and Jack's after he had been ejected from the original Goldwyn Company by a hostile takeover.

Marion was the first to spot Jack's inebriated state when he arrived. Marion herself was partial to a drop of bootleg liquor but W.R. didn't approve and she had had to resort to the practices of the confirmed alcoholic, constantly seeking new places to hide the bottles. One look at Jack and she knew he had been drinking steadily all day. She also knew there was trouble in store, although she tried to calm the agitated bridegroom as best she could.

'She'll be here. You know Greta.'

'I do know Greta. That's why I'm worried.'

'She hates publicity, she hates parties, she hates small talk.'

'Perfect for a bride, don't you think?'

'She'll come at the last minute, you just see.'

' 'Course she will,' said Jack who had as little faith in Marion's prediction as the hostess herself had.

The noisy chatter from the assembled guests grew louder and louder as the 4 p.m. deadline passed, and there was no sign that the wedding might be about to start. There was also no sign of one of the brides. After half an hour the other one took her intended groom aside and laid into him.

'This is my wedding day. I am not going to have it spoiled.'

'It'll destroy Jack if we go ahead without him.'

'She's not coming. It's not our fault.'

'Another ten minutes.'

'It's after four thirty. They all know she's not coming. Let's just do it now.'

'I'll talk to Jack.'

The small orchestra had exhausted its repertoire of Gilbert and Sullivan and Viennese operetta music and was looking for arrangements of marching tunes by Sousa as King climbed the stairs to look for Jack. He found him sitting on the bed in one of the guest bedrooms with his head in his hands.

'I don't understand, Jack. I thought you said she was deliberately hiding herself until four.'

'I lied. She drove away at eight o'clock this morning without a word.'

'Did you try the hotel?'

'Of course I tried the hotel, you idiot!'

'Easy, Jack, easy.'

'And I tried Stiller's place. He's an asshole. I really wanted to punch him in the kisser. Then I drove up the coast to Malibu. Sometimes she goes up there to look at the ocean.'

'Look at it or swim in it?'

'Look at it. She loves me, King.'

'Maybe, but she doesn't want to marry you.'

'Another half-hour, please,' pleaded Jack desperately.

'We're already late. Marion and Hearst are getting restless.'

'What's another half an hour when it's so important?'

King was starting to feel a little of what Eleanor had been experiencing ever since Garbo had accepted Jack's proposal, when an angry bride stuck her head round the door. She saw Jack slumped on the bed, King standing awkwardly at his side.

'Did you tell him?'

Jack looked up.

'Tell me what?'

'Jack, this is our wedding too. It's not just about you and Garbo.'

'I know she'll come.'

Eleanor snorted. 'Be sensible, Jack. No woman runs away on her wedding day if she really wants to get married.'

'OK, you two start. I'll wait for Garbo. We'll do it after you instead of at the same time.'

'Jack, you need to get it into your thick head. She's not coming!'

'All right, Eleanor, that's enough now,' said Vidor.

'Tell the orchestra to start, King. I'm just going to freshen my make-up.'

Eleanor left. King hurried after her.

Jack got slowly to his feet and walked out onto the landing in search of another drink. The door to the guest bathroom opened to reveal the grinning face of Louis B. Mayer, blinking owlishly through his thick spectacles. He must have had reports of good box-office returns, thought Jack, as Mayer smiled and clapped him on the back with a hearty thump and a broad smile.

'Hey, Gilbert, where's your blushing bride?'

'God knows.'

'Don't tell me she's stood you up again. Well, well. The screen's Great Lover gets left at the altar.'

Oddly enough the jibe was spoken in a tone of voice that suggested good fellowship and male bonding rather than the usual malevolence that made Jack want to hit Mayer every time he saw him.

'She'll be here,' said Jack grimly.

On later reflection Jack thought that possibly Mayer had meant what he next said as a piece of helpful advice. After all, it pretty much echoed the philosophy by which Mayer lived his own life.

'Don't get too depressed,' sympathised the head of the MGM production studio. 'After all, Garbo's just an actress. What do you have to marry her for anyway? Why don't you just fuck her till you're through with her?'

Unfortunately Jack was unable to take the advice in the spirit in which it might have been intended. He loved Garbo; he adored her. It was ironic that after their last bitter argument, in which Jack had besmirched the good name of all women, or at least all mothers, whom Mayer had dedicated his life to protect and exalt, the positions should have been so completely reversed. To Mayer actresses were there to earn the studio money and provide sexual diversion for important executives. Garbo was no exception. To Jack Garbo was all women in one – his mother, his sister, his lover, his wife, his partner through the vicissitudes of life – and Mayer was an asshole.

Jack turned on Mayer and pushed him backwards through the open bathroom door.

Mayer banged his head on the wall and cried out in alarm as he sank to the floor.

'Because I love her, you stupid asshole,' he screamed at the crumpled figure. Common sense would have dictated that Jack should pick up his boss, dust him down and hope that the damage could be repaired. Instead he threw himself on his hated boss and began to pummel him, swearing and cursing all the while. It was only a matter of half a minute before King arrived with Eddie Mannix, Mayer's thuggish right-hand man, and together they pulled Jack off, but in that time Jack had landed some hefty blows on the pudgy body of his employer.

As King lifted Jack away Mayer lashed out with his foot catching Jack a painful blow. Jack made as if to respond in kind.

'For God's sake, Jack, what d'you think you're doing?' cried Vidor. 'Are you OK, Mr Mayer?'

'My glasses are broken,' said the studio chief, examining the cracked lens and the broken frame, which was badly out of alignment.

'Jack, are you out of your mind?' King asked. Jack was beginning to calm down. Mayer was just winding himself up.

'You're finished in this business, Gilbert,' he spat savagely. 'As God is my witness, if it costs me a million dollars, I'll destroy you.'

King hurried Jack away before Mayer could start to list the manifold indignities he would have no hesitation in inflicting upon Jack. Downstairs, Eleanor was in frantic discussion with Marion Davies. As Jack and King, the two bridegrooms and each other's best men, started coming down the stairs together the orchestra, with considerable relief, struck up the refrain of 'Here Comes the Bride'. Eleanor and Marion looked around. Had Garbo arrived?

Chapter Five

Jack was returning to his hotel in New York City after a riotous night on the town with Dorothy Parker and some of the other members of the famous Algonquin Round Table when a fan magazine, prominently displayed on a newsstand, caught his eye. On the front cover was a clearly faked photograph of Jack in a tuxedo and Greta in a flowing bridal dress. The news vendor was happy enough to take the dollar and watch the incensed purchaser march off without waiting for the change.

In his suite Jack stared at the poem that would be read by the laughing world.

> Off again, on again
> Greta and John again
> How they have stirred up the news for a while
> Making their critics first sigh with them, die with them
> Making the cynical smile.

He threw the magazine into the fireplace and stormed out of the hotel into the nearest speakeasy. He had travelled 3,000 miles in a blaze of anger at Greta's selfishness, vainly hoping to avoid precisely this humiliation. He felt as if everyone in the speakeasy, everyone in the hotel, everyone he passed on the streets of Manhattan knew what had happened on that fateful wedding day in Beverly Hills – and that they were all laughing at him. He signalled to the barman to leave the bottle of Jack Daniels and cradled the cold glass lovingly with one hand while he tossed back another shot that burned his throat. He would never forgive her behaviour. Never.

Garbo, understandably, had not dared show her face in Tower Road but had retreated to her hotel room in Santa Monica – and probably, thought Jack bitterly, the comforting arms or at least the comforting words of Mauritz Stiller. Rather than hang around in Hollywood waiting for his next MGM assignment and the inevitable backlash from Louis B. Mayer, Jack took off for the welcoming anonymity of the East Coast.

Meanwhile Garbo's failure to marry their top male star didn't seem to have caused her any problems at the studio as MGM continued preparations for Greta to bring to the screen her long-awaited portrayal of Anna Karenina. The task of adapting Tolstoy's epic novel of love and betrayal was given to the very experienced Frances Marion, but when Greta saw the scenario she was horrified at the huge cuts made to the narrative. She complained bitterly to the only man she thought would care.

'Moje, the young lovers Kitty and Levin have disappeared completely. It's stupid.'

'Then who is left?'

'Just Anna, Karenin, Vronsky and the boy.'

'How old is the boy?'

'Eleven.'

Stiller smiled. 'So you had a baby when you were ten. Good work!'

Greta didn't respond to the humour but she did when Stiller pointed out that it was at last the sort of role she had longed to play. He also added that the fact that her campaign to win the role had been successful (despite the fact that MGM had originally developed the scenario for Lillian Gish) told the rest of Hollywood that Greta's star was in the ascendant and that of the heroine of *The Birth of a Nation* and *Way Down East* was on the wane. Stiller knew only too well how quickly the jackals seized on bad news.

Greta was not thrilled that Ricardo Cortez, the shallow, if handsome, young man who had co-starred with her in her first MGM movie, *The Torrent*, was going to play Vronsky, the man for whose love Anna sacrifices everything. Neither she nor Stiller was particularly delighted with the choice of director either. Dmitri Buchowetzki had the merit of being a Russian émigré, but it appeared to be his sole virtue. Once shooting got under way, Greta was pleased to see that the studio had hired former members of the Russian aristocracy to add some much-needed authenticity, but still the disparate elements of the movie failed to merge into a work of art and that was invariably the fault of poor direction.

Nobody much liked what was happening on the screen, and the production threatened to turn into a disaster. Greta found it harder and harder to get up in the morning for her regular six o'clock make-up and costume call so she would be ready on the set by quarter to nine. She was listless and her performance was lacking in energy. Mayer and Thalberg both worried over the rapid decline in their prize asset. Two weeks into production she was sent home sick as the studio tried to reschedule and shoot round her, but despite the optimistic press releases the studio put out about her health and her imminent return to work, her condition continued to deteriorate.

As soon as Jack heard about it he raced to her side, forgetting entirely the pain of his recent humiliation and his nightly dreams of revenge. She was in trouble and she needed him. It was the siren call for the lover down the ages. King Vidor picked him up from the train station in Pasadena. Most of the stars got off there as there was always the possibility that they would be mobbed by their fans if they arrived at the busier Union Station in downtown Los Angeles. Unfortunately for Jack there were still half a dozen teenage girls who were not satisfied just with an autograph, and he and King had to outrun them to King's car. They drove off in a cloud of dust, flying gravel, burning rubber and evident self-satisfaction.

'You realise you could have had all six of them in the back of the car.'

'You mean you wanted three of them?'

'We're friends, aren't we?'

'You're just married, aren't you?'

'Eleanor knows what I'm like. She also knows what you're like.'

'I'm not like that any more, King. I'm in love with Flicka.'

'You hate Greta. How many times have you told me that in the past few weeks?'

'Hate, love, what's the difference? It's all passion. The real opposite of love is indifference, and I'm not indifferent to Flicka that's for sure.' Jack tried to explain to King the reality of mature love.

'I don't want to chase girls for the rest of my life.'

'Just girls like Garbo.'

'Can't you tell I am really, I mean really, in love with this extraordinary woman?'

'You know what, Jack? I think you're in love with Garbo, the movie actress.'

'Sure I am. What's wrong with that?'

'The woman you marry will be Greta the stuck-up Swede not Garbo the movie star.'

But Jack wasn't listening. Instead he fantasised that once Greta saw how selfless and dedicated to her he really was she would recover her health and they would marry, not like before with all the Hollywood bigwigs. This would be a quiet wedding, maybe in the log cabin in the pine trees at the back of his house. King rolled his eyes. Jack was so obsessed with marrying this girl he should start writing a column for a bridal magazine. He explained to the hyperactive star that Garbo's doctors had recommended complete rest for at least six weeks and that the production of *Anna Karenina* had been shut down. Jack was strangely comforted by the fact. The studio, more particularly Louis B. Mayer, was in trouble and needed him. Garbo was sick and clearly needed him. Maybe what had happened at Marion Davies's hacienda in Beverly Hills had happened for the best.

Garbo was pleased to see him all right but not as pleased as he hoped she might be. The fact that he had leaped onto the first available train to be by her side didn't seem to register with her.

'Flicka, I've been so worried about you.'

'Thank you for coming, Yackie.'

'Room for two in there?' he asked, smiling at her. She gave a wan smile back and shook her head. She looked pale and sickly but to the besotted Jack she also looked ethereally beautiful.

'I love you, Flicka. I've missed you so much.' The ethereally beautiful Garbo wanted to groan. Not more declarations of love. Yes, she was pleased to see him again and, well, maybe it was a certain light-headedness brought on by the illness, but she couldn't help thinking he looked extremely handsome in a plain white shirt open at the neck and a pair of becoming flannel trousers. However, she wasn't up to the strain of these protestations of undying affection even when she was feeling well and at the moment she was feeling miserable.

She switched the conversation to the problems on the adaptation of *Anna Karenina*.

'I tank I upset the studio.'

'Good. Anything that upsets that sonofabitch Mayer is a good move in my book.'

'I tank they lose a lot of money because I am so sick.'

'I sure hope so. Hope they lose money, not hope you're sick,' he added quickly.

Jack would have been greatly comforted had he known the extent of the troubles that were besetting the studio. MGM looked long and hard at the $200,000 they had spent so far on a few thousand feet of unusable film. They had to do something to recoup their costs, and Irving Thalberg knew exactly what was needed. He knew it because Greta had already whispered it to him when he first saw her in hospital after the production was shut down. He knew Mayer would not respond positively and was prepared for the explosion.

'Gilbert?' expostulated Mayer.

'It's the obvious choice. We can put Cortez into the Lon Chaney movie *Mockery* and we can get rid of the Russian and bring in Goulding to direct. I already talked to him.'

'Oh? And what did he say?'

'He said he'd love to do it. If he can have Gilbert as Vronsky.'

'It's a conspiracy.'

'It's common sense, L.B. They're still a great team, whatever you think of Jack.'

'I think he's a degenerate bum.'

'I know that, but he's box office, and as of today we're two hundred thousand dollars in the hole.'

Mayer still looked undecided, so Thalberg played his ace.

'And I think we should change the title from *Anna Karenina*.'

'To what?'

'To *Love*.'

'*Love*! What the hell kind of a title's that?'

'A brilliant one.'

'Why?'

'Think of the poster, think of the marquee!'

Instantly Mayer saw it.

'Gilbert and Garbo in *Love*!'

Mayer's smile was more of a grimace but in his ears he heard the sound of ringing cash registers.

'That,' he said admiringly, 'is a great title. You know, Boy Wonder, you're a pain in the ass most of the time but just occasionally you're a goddamn genius.'

Greta was thrilled that her tactics had worked. The fastidious English director Edmund Goulding was much more to her taste than the uncommunicative Russian who had started the picture. If she couldn't have Moje – and she couldn't, Thalberg made that quite clear – then Goulding was the best she could have hoped for, given that Clarence Brown was otherwise engaged. More to the point she had her Vronsky, her Yackie, and she knew that together their love scenes would ignite the screen just as surely as they had during *Flesh and the Devil*.

When Jack heard that Greta had been campaigning for him to be cast as Vronsky, it was as if that traumatic day at Marion Davies's hacienda had never happened. He wasn't an obvious casting choice as the dashing Russian cavalry officer, but he was in love with Greta and she was in love with him and frankly nothing else mattered.

Goulding was smart enough to see that the picture succeeded or failed not by the power of the Tolstoy story, which had been reduced to an almost conventional melodrama, but by the performances he could get from Gilbert and more especially Garbo. Vronsky was not sympathetically written. The pressure he exerts on Anna to leave her son is selfish and unfair, but Jack had no problems with appearing in such an unflattering light. Goulding was hugely relieved for he knew how rare it was for such a big star as Jack Gilbert to risk alienating the affections of his adoring audience.

It was when the love scenes approached that he really saw how unselfish Jack could be, as he still sought to display Garbo to her best advantage. She was fortunate in that, unlike most actresses, she didn't have a 'bad' side. She could be photographed from almost any angle, but inevitably in any two shot (a shot showing two actors together) there tends to be an angle that favours one or other of them. Most actors scrap furiously to ensure that they gain the advantage. Jack had done it many times himself, particularly in *The Merry Widow*, when relations with his co-star Mae Murray and their director, Erich von Stroheim, never dropped below boiling point. Now with Greta he was quick to offer help to Goulding and Greta's favourite lighting cameraman, Bill Daniels.

'It's fine, Bill. Just make it a dirty two. Then you can get the baby spot close enough to pick out her eyes.'

'Thanks, Jack. I wish we could use colour film. The world's never seen the kind of blue in Garbo's eyes.'

Goulding watched the exchange with interest. As Daniels instructed his electricians on where to rig the lights, he took Jack to one side.

'Jack, I think you should direct this scene.'

'You're the director, Eddie.'

'I just think you've got a better chance of getting inside the Swede.'

Jack smiled.

'You've been drilling holes in my dressing-room wall again!'

Goulding flushed with English embarrassment.

'Sorry, I phrased that rather badly.'

'I'll say. But it's true.'

'Exactly. So what do you say?'

'I say it's mighty generous of you, Edmund, my old fruitcake,' declared Jack, in what he thought passed for an English accent. Goulding failed to rise to the bait.

'Just talk to her. If she's unhappy I'll come back in. I'm going to take it from the moment when she lies down on the chaise longue. I'm lighting it so the camera can track past your shoulder and settle on her face in big close-up. I want you to talk to her about character and feelings.'

'That'll be no problem,' Jack assured him. Jack knew what Greta wanted so desperately and had never articulated, despite her other demands. She wanted a closed set, something that had never been granted to anyone in Hollywood. Most actors didn't want the privacy anyway; their very well-being was dependent on their being the centre of attention. Movie producers enjoyed the perk of being able to take important guests down to the set to watch their actors at work and since the action was invariably accompanied by the sound of mood music from a string quartet just out of range of the camera and the sound of hammering and sawing from the scene builders on an adjacent set, it usually didn't matter if visitors watched how the movies were made. Greta, however, was different, and it was Jack's belief that if he could secure a closed set for her, the love scenes would blossom accordingly. He was quite right. Greta opened up like a flower.

Greta was delighted to see that Goulding trusted both of them sufficiently to allow Jack to direct the scene and was thrilled when the black draped flats went up to shield her from the unwelcome gaze of the curious. She revelled in Jack's comforting words and presence. Playing a love scene on camera is not easy for most actors. It is a strange mixture of the technical ('Next time get your nose out of the way quicker!') and the profound. It is difficult for any actress, no matter how gifted, to convey to an audience of millions that she would die for this man, who she soon discovers to her consternation has bad breath, body odour and an attitude to women that requires extensive psychotherapy.

It obviously helps if the actress is genuinely in love with the actor and in *Love*, as in *Flesh and the Devil*, the two stars gazed at each other with such erotic intensity that audiences, like the camera crew in Hollywood, enjoyed the illicit pleasure of voyeurism. Despite his festering hatred of Jack Gilbert, when Louis B. Mayer saw the daily rushes of *Love*, he was thrilled. At the moment Gilbert was worth more to him as an MGM star than as a faded has-been. Revenge, after all, is a dish best served cold.

Jack knew L.B. didn't like him but really had no sense that it might mean big trouble down the line for him. Indeed, in the middle of 1927 there was no reason to suppose that his stardom and his earning power couldn't last for many years yet. He talked with Greta about it.

'Here's what I figure, my Svenska flicka. We make say a dozen more pictures together for MGM, see out our contracts then go independent, like Mary, Doug, Charlie and D.W. Griffith did when they started United Artists. We'll have enough money by then to set up our own studio or we could join United Artists if Doug and Mary don't think it's too much competition. Or we could just retire, buy our own island in the Pacific and make love till we die.'

'I tank we finish this movie first,' said the practical Swede.

Next day they shot the scene where Vronsky picks up Anna's negligee and fondles it with such lust in his eyes that it is impossible to determine where Vronsky ends and Jack begins or where Anna ends and Greta begins as she returns his looks of unbridled sexual passion. Greta had rarely been happier on a film set, and Jack encouraged her to convey her unique sensuality not just in her scenes with him but also in those with her ten-year-old son, played by Philippe de Lacy.

After Karenin has banished Anna from the house as punishment for the scandalous affair with Vronsky, the errant wife steals home and caresses her son as he is sleeping. In his director's chair Jack watched entranced as the mother embraced the waking child with a love that seemed to surpass conventional maternal love as her love for him (on screen and off) seemed to surpass that of conventional lovers. Jack's certain directorial touch, the love he showed Greta in his willingness to demand and secure a closed set, paid off as she again demonstrated her sure instinct for the dramatic and the tender. Slowly and carefully she removed her hat and took hold of the boy's face between her hands in the way Jack recognised as her trademark from *Flesh and the Devil*.

Jack discussed the next scene, in which Greta was due to give her son a bath, with the nominal director. Goulding was concerned that the scene struck the wrong note.

'Aren't you slightly anxious that at ten the boy is too old to be bathed by his mother?'

'No. Greta would say if she was worried.'

'I'm thinking of the audience.'

'Greta's instinct is perfect.'

'I think we should cut it.'

'Why?'

'All those moralists out there. I mean he's not sitting in the bath in his underpants, is he?'

'Of course he is.'

'You know what I mean. The audience thinks he's naked and she's a sex goddess and he's just too old to be bathed by his mother. There are a lot of weird people out there.'

'You can always cut it later if you don't like it, but Bill Daniels has got some great ideas on the way to shoot it. Remember what he did with Flicka and me in the garden in *Flesh and the Devil*, how he gave me a light to hold in my hands as I lit her cigarette?'

'Of course I remember. Nobody who saw that scene will ever forget it.'

'I think Bill's got something similar for this scene.'

That was enough. Goulding backed off and the scene went ahead.

Next day in the preview theatre they looked at the magical effects of Daniels's lighting. There was a gasp as Anna slowly pulled the nightshirt off over her son's head. Serezha looks up at his mother and holds his lip back showing his mother his bad tooth. The boy was a natural, they all agreed. Unscripted he starts to flex his muscles. Garbo laughs in delighted response, and though the screen was silent everyone in the small screening room seemed to hear the peals of Swedish laughter. The mother leans down and embraces her son, kissing him repeatedly on the lips. The luminous photography made of it a tableau from a pre-Raphaelite painting. When the various takes had finished, Thalberg turned to Goulding to offer his congratulations.

'You know, Eddie, I thought there might be problems with that scene. I could never see how you could make it beautiful and intimate and original and not get the Daughters of the American Revolution picketing MGM movie theatres.'

'Well, it wasn't really me,' began Goulding in confessional mode, but Jack leapt in quickly.

'You're damn right, Eddie. I could have directed that scene. When the Swede's in a mood like that she doesn't need directing. She's a genius.'

Thalberg agreed and then was called away before he could enquire any further.

'Why didn't you let me tell him?'

'Irving may be the Boy Wonder but he's also a studio head and they don't like actors to get above themselves.'

Goulding smiled in recognition of one of the eternal verities of the still-nascent film business.

'Jack, I know you're a pretty decent guy, but what you're doing for Garbo goes a little beyond simple professional courtesy.'

'I love her, Eddie, and I don't care who knows it. I've never been in love like this before. I kinda feel I'd never been in love at all till I met Flicka.'

Chapter Six

~~~~~~~

When they found out what MGM intended to do with the end of the film both Jack and Greta were furious. Apparently Tolstoy wasn't good enough for Mayer and Thalberg and they instructed the screen writer Frances Marion to come up with a better ending, a happier one of course. They shot the original ending in which Anna, having said goodbye to Vronsky, decides that life is not worth living without her lover and her son and throws herself under the wheels of a train. Some weeks later the principal actors were recalled to shoot another ending, more in tune with the optimism of life in America in the 1920s. This time Karenin has conveniently died so Anna's reunion with Vronsky violates no commandment, neither Biblical nor American conservative, the delightful child is restored to the care of his devoted mother and the lovers can fade out with a kiss.

Unfortunately, because it had been some weeks since the production had finished shooting, the wardrobe department couldn't find Jack's costume so they grabbed the first one to hand and the make-up department complained because Jack had already had his hair cut for another film. Jack's complaint that his appearance was completely out of continuity with previous scenes received the automatic response of lazy producers down the ages.

'Nobody will notice,' he was told.

'I will,' grumbled Jack.

Unfortunately the bad guys were right.

Swathes of the Deep South and the Midwest didn't give a hoot about such niceties and agreed with Mayer's dismissive response. As Mayer had suspected, the new 'improved' Frances Marion version was the ending they wanted. Offered the choice by an eager-to-please studio a few distributors and exhibitors on the East and West

Coasts stuck with Tolstoy, but the vast majority preferred the ending Tolstoy would certainly have written had he only had the perspicacity to have been born a hundred years later and been earning $2,000 a week writing for MGM. Mayer and Thalberg were very democratic about it all; they didn't mind which version was shown. As soon as they saw the box-office returns they knew they had another Garbo and Gilbert winner on their hands and profits soared over the half a million dollars mark.

'You realise, L.B., we're talking about Garbo and Gilbert now, not Gilbert and Garbo.'

Mayer smiled. Of course he realised.

'The exhibitors are doing the same thing – and most importantly so are the public,' Mayer added.

'You can't break the team up now. They're the biggest stars we have.'

'Hey, we run the studio, not the actors, and we can do any damn thing we want. She says she wants to work with Lars Hanson again and have Victor Seastrom direct them. If we start shooting by the end of the month we can get *The Divine Woman* into the theatres just after New Year's.'

It was true that Greta did want to work with the friendly, well-respected fellow Swede Victor Seastrom, who had adapted to the demands of directing in America as well as Stiller had failed. However, when *Love* finally wrapped shooting, Greta didn't care if she ever made another movie again. She was happy and in love, two sensations she had barely experienced in a life of more than twenty-two years. Jack had never been short of women and even during his two brief marriages he had been unable to resist the attractions of illicit liaisons but Greta seemed to consume him completely.

He knew well enough that her instincts were profoundly anti-social, at least by Hollywood standards. She was a dedicated actress and perfectly happy to be in bed by nine in the evening even when she didn't have to be up at 5.30 the following morning for her make-up and wardrobe call. She didn't really see the point of parties when she could go to bed with a good Swedish book but now she was with Jack, and Jack had a very different attitude to the social whirl.

Of course, with Greta, her reaction to any social occasion could never be predicted accurately in advance. In a fit of enthusiasm Jack had bought an eighty-foot schooner, which he named *The Temptress* in honour of Greta's second American film. It was a fine boat, luxuriously appointed, and Jack was quick to ensure that all his friends were aware of his new status as master of the ship. They trooped on deck on Friday afternoon and set sail for Catalina Island the following day at noon. Greta stayed below and refused point-blank to mingle. At the house she could disappear for a couple of hours during the Sunday brunches without attracting too much attention, but in the limited environment of a sailing boat this was much more difficult.

'Where's Greta?' they all asked as they admired Jack's new toy.

'Resting,' he would answer tersely.

When she didn't appear for dinner everyone diplomatically steered off the subject, but it was noted that Jack was even more lavish than usual in his distribution of illicit alcohol. Very shortly nobody cared whether Greta was on the boat or not.

She did leave her cabin the following day, shortly after the party had disembarked for a tour of the island. By chance they met up with another party from Hollywood and collected on board their boat for an afternoon of fun and laughter. In the distance they could make out something stirring on the deck of *The Temptress*.

'Christ, Jack, she's taken her bathing suit off!'

That brought the party chatter to an immediate halt as everyone raced to the side of the boat to stare. It did appear that Greta had dropped the straps of her suit and was walking around the deck, topless at the very least.

'Anyone got a telescope here?'

'A telescope? What d'you think this is? A pirate picture?'

'Not a telescope, what are they called? – field glasses, binoculars.'

There was a rush for the bridge and a desperate scramble before someone emerged triumphantly with the binoculars and they all raced back to the side of the boat. Mack Sennett would have been delighted with the comic effect.

'Shit! Where is she?'

'She's lying down,' came the voice of a bored female who resented the fact that the mere prospect of viewing Greta Garbo's naked breasts had caused every man on board to act like a priapic fourteen-year-old schoolboy.

By the time the afternoon party was over Jack had some difficulty in rowing back to *The Temptress*. Greta watched his fumbling attempts to climb from the rowing boat onto the ladder with evident disapproval.

'What the hell do you think you were doing?' he asked the now modestly dressed Greta when he finally managed to scramble on board.

'What was *I* doing? I was watching you make a fool of yourself.'

'Not now. Before.'

'Before what?'

'Prancing about in the altogether.'

'Altogether what?'

'In the nude. Taking your bathing suit off and showing yourself to the whole world. I mean, you won't let anyone look at you on the set, you won't come out and say hello to your guests . . .'

'. . . *Your* guests.'

'Whatever. But you have no problem in taking your clothes off and letting the whole world see you naked.'

'Oh, you Americans! I don't understand. You are like little boys staring at a girl for the first time.'

'Flicka, you are the most beautiful, the most famous woman in the world. You can't flash your breasts at men and expect them not to react.'

'Nobody reacts in Sweden. Everyone knows our bodies are private.'

'Of course they are. That's why they started designing clothes in the Garden of Eden.'

'So what you want is for me never to take my clothes off again?'

'Well, not exactly.'

By this time lust was surging through Jack's body and turning his brain to porridge. What lay beneath Greta's swimsuit was the object of his desire and she enjoyed the power her body gave her. It was still something of a pleasant surprise to her. At school she had been a plain-looking girl. By the time she had started drama school at seventeen, she had grown so tall that she was embarrassed by her height and deliberately cowered in the corner when confronted by a camera. Every producer she had ever met had told her that she was too heavy and that she had better lose weight or she could forget about a career. That now she was the imagined sex object of millions of men all over the world gave her the creeps rather than any great satisfaction, but with Jack, as ever, it was different.

Jack was the man she had always wanted – a dark, handsome, dashing, reckless cavalier of a man, a man for nights of love and romance when she was in the mood. Now suddenly, surprisingly, she was in the mood. She dropped one strap coyly down her shoulder and her breast appeared. She smiled as she saw Jack's eyes fixate, a smile such as La Giaconda would have recognised. She took him by the hand and led him below deck.

Even as they made love to the rhythm of the gentle rocking of the boat at anchor, Jack knew that he could never possess this woman. Although her body was pinioned beneath his, Greta remained apart from him, her spirit floating somewhere above their corporeal selves, smiling that irritatingly superior smile, laughing inwardly at the ridiculous pumping and heaving of his buttocks. No matter how many times he tore her clothes off, no matter how many times she allowed him access to her body, he knew she retained the upper hand in the relationship. And it drove him crazy. Two weeks later he sold *The Temptress*. There seemed no point in it any longer. And then, after a memorable weekend at San Simeon, she fooled him again.

San Simeon was the West Coast fairytale 'country' home of W.R. Hearst and Marion Davies. Jack and Greta were invited along with Ronald Colman, Sam Goldwyn, Buster Keaton, Frances Marion, Gloria Swanson and their respective partners to a weekend of gracious living in the great castle on what Hearst always called 'the enchanted hill'.

They drove up the coastal route after lunch one Friday afternoon in early April, through countryside still green from the rains of February when southern California is usually allowed a bare minimum of rainfall. Greta gazed in fascination at the profusion of wild flowers. Jack smiled.

'You ain't seen nothing yet,' he promised. Greta smiled back. She was going to enjoy herself this weekend, she was sure of it. Jack felt her certainty and relaxed. If she was happy, he was happy.

North of San Luis Obispo, Jack swung the car off the coastal route and headed into the hills towards La Casa Grande, the great mountain-top house whose imposing façade was modelled on the twin towers of a cathedral in Ronda in southern Spain which had taken Hearst's fancy. Greta exclaimed in surprise as the car passed bison, ostriches and water buffalo.

'It's like a zoo!'

'It *is* a zoo. It's Popsy's private zoo. Look!' He pointed to a sign reading 'Animals Have Right of Way' as he got out of the car to open a heavy wooden gate.

'Yackie!' shouted Greta in alarm as a zebra came racing up for a closer inspection of the sexiest, most famous couple in the world. Jack leapt back into the car and drove off before the zebra could confirm to its friends and relations that Greta and John were back together again.

Greta had been in California for nearly three years by this time and much of its glitz and glamour had worn thin. She wasn't the sort of girl who was generally impressed by the displays of conspicuous consumption that were regularly laid before her but, as Jack knew perfectly well, she had never been to Hearst's 'ranch' before. They were escorted to their guest 'cottage' through manicured gardens that would have done credit to Versailles. The bedroom contained a huge carved bed, which was reputed to have once belonged to Cardinal Richelieu. It was the epic scale on which the place had been designed that left Greta speechless. When she stepped out of the shower she found Jack sliding cases of bootleg liquor under the seventeenth-century bed.

'Yackie!'

'Sorry, Flicka, this is one of the rules.'

'What rule?'

'Popsy doesn't like anyone drinking too much.'

'So?'

'Particularly he doesn't like Marion drinking too much, so all her friends bring her up a week's supply when they are invited for the weekend.'

'That's a week's supply?'

'Marion's got a difficult life. She gets very lonely.'

'That won't help.'

'You want to swap lives?'

They walked into the cavernous reception hall and marvelled at its sheer size – it must have measured a hundred feet deep and sixty feet across, with a ceiling as high as that in the Ronda cathedral. The fireplace was framed by a mantelpiece of gargantuan proportions, almost certainly imported with enormous effort and at a ridiculous cost from Europe. In it the huge logs were making a blazing fire as they tried their best to heat the reception area. They moved into the more intimate surroundings of the dining room and were seated at the longest refectory table in the world, removed from a now defunct European monastery. On long poles over the heads of the guests were several dozen beautifully embroidered banners, which had once belonged to the leading families of Florence and Siena. At intervals of a few feet down the length of the table stood ornate silver candlesticks up to three feet in height between which nestled incongruously bottles of tomato ketchup and a pile of paper napkins. Greta sat down in the chair and immediately sprang up in alarm.

'It's OK, Flicka,' smiled Jack. 'They were designed for the bottom of a monk wearing a thick robe. Your bottom needs something more worthy of its beauty.'

He squeezed the cheeks as he made the pretence of helping her to sit down in comfort. Luxury was all around yet comfort was in short supply as 'Popsy' Hearst sat in the centre of the long table watching over Marion. Extravagant as his hospitality was, there was something intimidating about Hearst that put a damper on the evening. Everyone knew he disapproved of alcohol, whether it was consumed by Marion or by anyone else, but in deference to social custom he could be seen mixing a thimbleful of gin into the silver bowl filled with fruit punch. He hated bad language and off-colour jokes and above all, he frowned on sexual intercourse if the couple concerned was unmarried – somewhat ironic under the circumstances everyone agreed.

'Yackie, why do they give us one bed?'

'Because Marion told him we were married.'

'But I have no ring.'

'Do you want a ring?' asked Jack, his mind instantly turning to the possibility of racing Greta off down the hill to buy the first engagement ring he could lay his hands on.

'He can see we are not married.'

'Popsy sees what he wants to see.'

Jack knew from previous experience that Popsy's guests were always an odd combination of sober-suited executives from the Hearst organisation and their companions from the world of show business. They could never quite settle on a topic that appealed to both parties so the two groups tended to huddle together for protection until dinner was finished and everyone was guided into the private cinema to be shown the latest productions before they were released to the general public. Studios were quite happy to oblige Hearst in this manner, knowing that a favourable response would result in acres of free publicity throughout the Hearst press.

It was after midnight before the film finished, whereupon Marion and Hearst bade goodnight to their guests and vanished from sight inside the tiny elevator, which bore them both to the huge Gothic library situated above the preview theatre. The Hearst executives too vanished – and suddenly the night began. The actors immediately started to behave like college students after their first experience of alcohol. Buster Keaton and Ronald Colman created an apple-pie bed for Gloria Swanson even as she was performing her party piece – a brilliant impression of Charlie Chaplin. As the couples drifted back to their rooms there were panty raids and water bombs and all sorts of sophomoric behaviour. At breakfast in the morning nothing was said by the magisterial figure who presided over it all, provided no priceless *objet d'art* had been damaged or broken in the general mayhem.

Jack was in his element during this outbreak of pleasurable chaos, but Greta had other things in mind. She had seen the giant marble outdoor swimming pool. It might have been 1.50 a.m., but Garbo was ready for her swim – the fact that she had brought no swimsuit with her was no handicap. Jack, as ever, was somewhat disconcerted as Greta shrugged off her clothes and ran naked out of their 'cottage' and up the steps to the colonnaded pool. Buster Keaton took one look at the flash of her nude body and fell to the ground in what seemed to be a dead faint. It looked extremely painful to Jack, but he had seen Buster's physical antics many times before and knew the man appeared to be made of rubber, so often had he rebounded unhurt from seemingly excruciating falls.

Greta plunged into the dark, unwelcoming water in a graceful arc and began swimming strongly. Jack leapt in after her and cried out as his warm body registered the shock of the cold water. For Greta this skinny-dipping at moonlight was a reversion to her childhood days in Sweden. She thoroughly enjoyed the brisk exercise and threw herself into it with the same enthusiasm she displayed when playing tennis or hiking in the hills above the Tower Road house. It was either the exercise or the nostalgia or possibly some combination of both that overwhelmed Jack and Greta that night. They returned to the cottage to grab towels, went back out to the poolside and sat together for an hour, holding hands, saying nothing, just staring out into the vast black empty space that stretched in front of them.

In due course Greta fell gently asleep, her head resting contentedly on Jack's shoulder. He held her close. It was one of the few moments in their relationship when he felt that it had returned to the conventional pattern. He was the big star earning the big salary, the most handsome man in the world, the love object of millions of women and this was his chosen woman, a soft, sweet, tender, submissive, frightened actress from another country who needed him. She woke as he carried her back to the cottage but she was a good actress and she 'felt' the role they both now expected her to play. He laid her tenderly on Cardinal Richelieu's bed and gently removed the towels as if he were unwrapping a present of the finest Dresden china. When he entered her he felt no resistance, only a low murmur of pleasure indicating her acceptance.

Afterwards he remained on top, and she felt his slow withdrawal, crying out as he retreated from her completely. He collapsed onto his left side and gently stroked her body from her face to her legs.

'Flicka . . . ?'

'Hmm?'

'I love you.'

She said nothing but she slipped her arms round his back and pulled him towards her, burying her face in his chest and inhaling his scent.

'I want to marry you, Flicka. I want to look after you for the rest of your life. I don't want you to have to worry about anything.' She looked up at him and smiled.

'You are in love with me?' she asked.

'You don't have to ask,' he replied gallantly.

'You would do anything for me?'

'Anything.'

'Then let me sleep. I am tired.'

He could have killed her. How could she have so wilfully broken the beautiful mood they had created together? She didn't deserve him. They rolled away towards their respective corners of the bed.

They were only a few hours' drive away from the spectacular section of central California between Santa Cruz and Monterrey known as Big Sur. They left San Simeon in the middle of the afternoon the next day and drove north until they arrived in Big Sur on one of those sublime Californian evenings when the sky darkens to a midnight blue and is then suffused with a sheen of pink. To the left as they looked out of the car they saw the Los Padres National Forest and the giant redwoods and pines silhouetted against the sky. To their right the waves of the Pacific Ocean dashed themselves relentlessly, unavailingly, against the rocks, hundreds of feet below them. Jack and Greta both felt themselves in the grip of another power, not a sexual one this time but something more spiritual. For Greta the feelings were of homecoming. If she didn't know they had left San Simeon a few hours before she could have been in Sweden. For all the chill of the evening air she felt a warm glow spread through her body. Maybe this strange feeling she had at times for Yackie was what they all called love.

She wasn't sure she knew what love was, yet she was commonly called a Screen Love Goddess. It was a ridiculous name. She loved her father and her sister, that was true enough, but that wasn't the love between a man and a woman. She loved Moje too, completely, unquestioningly, but that, maybe, wasn't love either because Moje liked to go to bed with young men and not with her. Most of the time she had been grateful that her relationship with Moje had not been sullied by carnal thoughts but occasionally she thought she did not love him because they had denied themselves that ultimate consummation.

Yackie was different. She thought he was very attractive. Even when she didn't like him much she still thought he was very attractive. She knew he was utterly devoted to her, but his ease in expressing his love to her made her fearful. In her dogged peasant way, as she termed it, she felt that a love that was so openly and permanently on display could not last, could not be real. If Yackie told her that he loved her less frequently she might believe him more. Yet his feelings for her now seemed as deep and sincere as they had been on the set of that first scene they played together in *Flesh and the Devil*. She knew he would look after her, protect her against the studio, fight for her new contract, assert her right to be cast in the best parts. What more could she demand of a husband? She wasn't sure she could answer her own question. It was just that there was something, some unreasoning, nameless fear that stopped her from submitting to him completely the way he so desperately wanted.

Jack was a sensitive man and he knew well that the sights of forest and ocean, sky and mountain moved Greta. Through this shared experience, he was closer to her now than he had ever been. His hand reached for hers. She gripped his hand in confirmation that they were both feeling something that would last the rest of their lives. Jack was desperate to speak. But could he afford to break the spell? If the words came out wrong this time, after Greta's clumsy efforts last night, he would never forgive himself. But now was the time, he was sure of it. He tried again. His voice when it came was soft and mellow.

'Greta, I love you. I want nothing more than to make you happy for the rest of your life. Please will you marry me?'

It was simple, it was unaffected, it was undoubtedly true. She didn't answer for what seemed the longest time. Jack's heart sank. The only possible reason was that it was a no – or she was so transported by the wonders of Nature that she hadn't heard him. He was about to repeat the question and risk making an even bigger fool of himself when she spoke.

'All right, Yackie.'

He couldn't believe it.

'You will? You will marry me?'

She turned and smiled at him. It was a sad smile. For a moment, for a triumphant moment, he thought it was the smile of a woman who was surrendering. He had laid siege to her castle for months and months and had failed to starve or browbeat the occupants into surrender. This final artless cannon shot had finally breached the walls and the defences were down.

'Now?'

'Don't we need a minister or something?'

'I mean, tonight?'

'It's dark. I'd like to see your face when we marry.'

'We've got electric light in this country.'

She smiled. The old smile. She put her forefinger on his lips.

'Before we get back to Hollywood though? We're still registered to marry from last time.'

Greta nodded. Jack seized her in his arms and now they both acted as if they were at work. He bent her back and she let him hold her at an angle of almost forty-five degrees as he kissed her ravenously.

'So that is what it is like to be kissed by the Great Lover?'

She was sending him up.

'Women seem to like it.'

'I know. Renée Adorée, Laurette Taylor, Anna May Wong, they all love it.' She had named three actresses Jack had had affairs with. He bit his tongue.

Jack was determined to do things properly this time. They checked into the recently opened Biltmore Hotel a couple of miles south of Santa Barbara just after midnight. It was a good time to check into hotels if you were the most famous celebrity couple in the world. The night staff were themselves tired and scarcely noticed the guests to whom they handed hotel keys. Mr and Mrs Cecil Pringle certainly attracted no attention from the night clerk at the Biltmore and they reached their room with only a smirk of recognition on the face of the bellboy whom Jack deliberately over-tipped.

'Cecil Pringle?'

'Yes, Miss Gustaffson?'

'That's a very silly name.'

'I know. What the hell were my folks thinking of?'

'No wonder you don't like them.'

'In fairness that's because they are cynical, cheating, self-obsessed liars rather than just because of the name they saddled me with.'

'I like Yackie better.'

'Me too. Now, shall we destroy the sanctity of the wedding night?'

He pinned Greta against the wall, put her hands above her head and kept them pressed to the wall as he kissed her with long, slow open-mouthed kisses. Greta responded. No jokes about the Great Lover now, no mention of his former life as Cecil Pringle. His kisses made her toes curl.

'Do you know about the *ius primae noctis*?' asked Greta innocently, as Jack unbuttoned his fly and grabbed hold of her hand. He stopped.

'What?'

'It's Latin. It means the law of the first night.'

'Fascinating but I'm in the middle of something right now. Can we leave the Latin alone for the moment?' He slipped her moist hand into his shorts. She squeezed, hard. He squealed and recoiled.

'Jesus Christ!'

'I was reading a play by Beaumarchais about the marriage of a servant to a countess's lady's maid in the eighteenth century. It seems the count had the right to sleep with every bride on her first night of marriage.' Jack had slumped onto the bed and was massaging his tender genitals.

'And did the bridegroom join in?'

'No! It was the law. The law of feudalism.'

'Flicka, what are you doing?'

'I am trying to have a grown-up conversation.'

'Afterwards. After sex, then we have a grown-up conversation. Then we talk about anything you want. Gene Tunney, Jack Dempsey, Bobby Jones, Einstein, Schoenberg, Theodore Dreiser, you name it but not now. Now just kiss it better. Please.'

Greta smiled but she lowered her head as she was bidden and kissed it better.

When they woke late on their wedding day the sun was already shining out of a bright, cloudless Santa Barbara sky. Jack had heard tell of the early morning mists that rolled into town off the ocean but he had never been awake early enough to see them for himself. The sun had always burned the grey cloud away and the temperature was always seventy-two degrees. Jack pulled back the curtains in the bedroom and looked out on to the picture-book Pacific Ocean rolling gently on to the white sandy beach. He strode through to the back of the sitting room and looked out of the large window at the dramatic backdrop of the hills and the busy landscape in front of them. A major earthquake had struck Santa Barbara just a few weeks before Garbo and Stiller had docked in New York, levelling most of the downtown area. Now the town was being almost completely reconstructed in the classic Spanish style.

Greta was clearly in no mood to get up and explore so Jack kissed her briefly, grabbed his clothes and wandered outside to look at the fantasia of towers and arches and exotic gardens by the sea that constituted the hotel's exterior. Two honeymooners told him of the delights of their first week as a married couple. They had travelled all the way from Salt Lake City to enjoy the hedonistic delights of southern California because they had been told that this new Biltmore Hotel was where all the movie stars spent the weekend. It was the one blemish on their fairy-tale romance.

'We've seen no movie stars at all,' complained the very pretty bride.

'I asked the hotel manager and he said there'd be no movie stars checking in till just before Christmas,' added her husband. Jack commiserated.

'I was thinking of getting married myself,' said Jack casually, wondering why these fools didn't recognise him.

'Oh, that's swell,' said the girl from Utah. 'Is your fiancée here?'

'Greta's still asleep in bed.'

'Greta? Greta *Garbo*?' The new bride's eyes widened. Jack smiled serenely and waited for the explosion.

'Say,' said the bridegroom eagerly, 'have you seen the new courthouse they're building on Anacapa Street? I'll bet you could get married there.'

'Thanks,' said Jack staring at the woman.

'Would you like us to act as witnesses? If you haven't got your families here?' But an irritated Jack had already turned on his heel and was marching away.

He jumped into the car and roared off down the drive and back on to the main road along the shoreline and into Santa Barbara itself. He turned right on Anapamu Street and stopped just before the junction with Anacapa where the magnificent new Spanish-Moorish courthouse stood gleaming, just as the honeymooners had promised him. He admired the spacious lawns and the swaying palm trees and was greatly taken by the sunken garden. He pushed open the huge carved wooden door and found himself confronted by an ornate interior structure decorated with intricate mosaic tiles and a spiral staircase above which workmen were hanging a wrought-iron chandelier.

'Can I get married here, do you know?' he called up to the workmen.

'Sure you can,' came a helpful voice.

'When? I mean, when do you open?'

'Sometime next year I think,' came the same helpful voice.

Still, his journey into town accomplished something. Walking down busy State Street his eye was caught by the most exquisite 24-carat gold ring, which sat in a shop window calling to him. Greta was going to adore it and the price tag of $4,000 seemed cheap for such a beauty. The salesman couldn't sell it to him fast enough. Never in his entire life had he sold a wedding ring of such expense to anyone with so few words and in such little time.

Jack was suddenly conscious that he should have insisted that Greta came with him. Leaving her alone on the morning of their marriage had not been a very good idea in the past. He sprinted back to the car and drove at a furious speed back to the Biltmore. He raced up the stairs because the elevator seemed to be permanently stuck on the third floor. He fumbled with the key in the lock but managed to control his anxiety with the thought that she couldn't get out of the room at this point without his seeing her – unless, of course, at that very moment Greta Garbo was climbing down the outside of the hotel building in an insane parody of Harold Lloyd in *Safety Last*.

'Sorry, Flicka, I think we're going to have to drive to Ventura if we're going to get married today . . . Flicka?'

He started to panic. She wasn't in the sitting room, she wasn't in the bedroom, she wasn't in the bathroom. Jack cursed her, then he cursed the Santa Barbara courthouse, then he cursed himself for being so stupid as to leave her alone for as long as he had. He threw himself lengthways on the couch and started to beat himself about the head.

'Stupid, stupid, stupid idiot,' he moaned out loud.

'Who is?' asked Greta, genuinely curious.

'Flicka!' yelled Jack, running to her and flinging his arms around her. 'Where the hell have you been?'

'Downstairs to borrow a hair dryer.'

'They bring them up to the room, you know. Just call housekeeping on the telephone.'

'I didn't like to bother anyone,' replied the woman who had spent an entire weekend below deck rather than talk to friends who had come to party with her on board *The Temptress*.

Jack refused to let Greta out of his sight from now on. He even followed her into the bathroom, to her evident confusion.

'I want to be alone,' she complained.

'Not tonight, Josephine,' said Jack grimly.

'Who is this Josephine?' asked Greta disingenuously, as she called his bluff by sitting on the toilet.

'Napoleon's wife.'

'Now there's a part I'd like to play,' said Greta pulling off a strip of toilet paper.

'Josephine?' asked Jack, his head suddenly filled with thoughts of himself as the French emperor, the two of them starring in the epic love story that conquered Europe. Even L.B. Mayer would go for something like that.

'No, Napoleon,' said Greta flushing the toilet and washing her hands. 'If Sarah Bernhardt can play Hamlet, why can't I play Napoleon?'

They drove slowly southwards down the coast in the direction of Los Angeles. In Ventura they stopped at a traffic light and asked directions to the courthouse by the simple expedient of calling out to a pedestrian. Jack had no intention of leaping out of the car and running into a shop to ask. Garbo would grab the steering wheel and roar away, leaving him stranded.

'Getting nervous?' he asked smiling. Greta said nothing. She just stared grimly ahead. Though she was still sitting in the seat next to him, looking at the same travelling landscape, it was clear to Jack that Greta was having not just second thoughts but third or fourth thoughts.

'You do want to get married this time, don't you?'

Greta grunted. It wasn't much of a reply but Jack decided that it was Swedish for 'yes'.

'Look around, Flicka. No press, no photographers, no studio publicity guys. You're free.'

'Free?' echoed Greta tonelessly. It was a response that would have done credit to Kierkegaard or Sartre.

The Ventura courthouse was nothing like the architectural fantasy that Jack had seen in Santa Barbara earlier that day.

'I can't get married like this,' said Greta desperately. 'Look what I'm wearing.'

Jack's stomach lurched again. He looked at what she was wearing. She was dressed in a smartly tailored checked suit, a crisp white blouse and a very stylish cloche hat.

'It's great! What the hell's wrong with it?'

'I should have a trousseau.'

'A trousseau! Are you kidding? Now?'

'Every girl should have a trousseau.'

'You always said marriage was just about a piece of paper.'

'It is.'

Jack wanted to hit something, anything; for preference he wanted to hit Greta. He stopped the car, grinding his teeth.

'Are you calling it off?' he asked quietly but with enormous tension.

'No,' she replied in a tone of voice that screamed 'yes'.

As they walked up to the steps to the courthouse, Greta excused herself.

'I'm going to the ladies' powder room.' Jack was about to raise an objection, but Greta quickly squashed it. 'And no, you can't come with me, Yackie.'

Jack slumped onto a bench in the lobby. The rest of the world passed by, not casting a second glance in his direction. He felt as if he had been covered in a magic solution that had made him invisible. He was the Great Lover of the Silver Screen. He had a drawer in his dressing room filled with the undergarments of women who had sent them to him as a token of their appreciation for the way in which his handsome beauty had made a difference to their humdrum lives. Now here he was on his wedding day, he was marrying the most famous and beautiful movie star in the world and

. . . he glanced down at his watch. Greta had been in the ladies' room for over fifteen minutes.

He walked over to the door and hesitated. A middle-aged woman opened the door and came out.

'Excuse me, madam,' he accosted her very politely. 'My name's John Gilbert. Did you happen to see Greta Garbo in there?' The woman looked at him with large round eyes.

'Failing that, did you see a window left open, large enough for a Swedish woman to climb out of?' The woman opened her mouth wide and screamed.

'It's John Gilbert! It's John Gilbert!' And suddenly the world was very interested in John Gilbert again. Men and women and children seemed to descend on him from all directions. By the time one young guard on his first day of courthouse duty had controlled the madness and twenty-five women had raced into the ladies' room but failed to find Greta Garbo, a further ten minutes had passed.

A dishevelled, unhappy Jack Gilbert climbed into his car and drove slowly back towards Los Angeles, turned left on Sunset Boulevard and arrived back at the house on Tower Road in Beverly Hills in time for cocktail hour. This was his fourth wedding day and so far he had managed to be married only twice.

Chapter Seven

~~~~~

It wasn't the music so much as the dialogue that did it. They'd been used to hearing music with their so-called silent films, which were never silent. The early movie theatres were full of sounds – first-generation American kids translating the inter-titles for their immigrant parents, audiences commenting on the action as it unfolded in front of them, people calling out to friends in the next row, and of course the music – from a sixty-piece orchestra in the expensive first-run metropolitan theatres all the way down to a honky-tonk piano in the rural cinemas. The actors heard mood music as they emoted on the set and the audiences heard music as they watched the finished film. What they had never heard before was spoken dialogue and in particular the sort of dialogue Al Jolson was famous for ad-libbing.

Jolson wasn't the first choice for the lead in *The Jazz Singer*, in itself a fairly creaky old melodrama about the son of a Jewish cantor who betrayed his family history by singing on the stage instead of in the synagogue. On the eve of Yom Kippur, the holiest night of the Jewish year, he has to choose between opening on Broadway in the biggest break of his career or singing the Kol Nidre service in the synagogue in place of his dying father. George Jessel had played the role in the New York theatre but he wanted too much money to reprise it in Hollywood so the perennially impoverished Warner Brothers, who were gambling their very future on the sound on disc system, offered the part to Jolson instead.

The moment that changed the movies forever arrived when Jolson sits at the piano, as his adoring immigrant grey-haired old mother watches her American-born son with the rapidly receding hairline, hammering out the Irving Berlin hit song 'Blue Skies'. After the last note he turns to her and says the first words that come into his head.

'Momma, darling, if I'm a success in this show we're gonna move from here. We gonna move up to the Bronx. Lot of nice green grass up there and a whole lot of people you know. There are the Ginsbergs, the Guttenbergs, some Goldbergs . . . Oh, I don't know, a whole lotta Bergs. I don't know 'em all.'

The formally attired first-night audience, many of whom had been Ginsbergs, Guttenbergs and Goldbergs before they changed their names, roared their approval at this unexpected departure from convention.

The Jazz Singer was only partially a talking picture. It had been designed originally as a silent film with synchronised musical interludes but when Jakie Rabinowitz, now known as Jack Robin, ascended the bimah in his father's place and sang the traditional Eve of the Day of Atonement service, the age of the silent picture had been served its formal notice to quit.

Jack was in Washington D.C. shooting the exteriors for his latest film *Man, Woman and Sin* when *The Jazz Singer* opened. He was still suffering the torments of the damned whenever he thought about Greta so he did what he usually did when he was unhappy. He threw himself into his role, displaying genuine suffering as the poor boy made good who is sentenced to hang for a murder deliberately set up by the beautiful society editor of the newspaper for which they both work. The other thing Jack invariably did on the rare occasions when he was thwarted in love was to sleep with other women. His co-star was the turbulent Broadway stage actress Jeanne Eagels and Jack pursued and captured her with the minimum of fuss, mostly because the voracious actress had already decided she wanted the relationship. Jeanne Eagels was probably the only major actress whose drinking capacity matched that of Jack. Indeed, he was so impressed by her habit of drinking warm gin – she claimed it deadened the pain of her neuralgia – that he referred to her as 'Gin' Eagels.

His affair with Eagels was a temporary palliative for his obsession with Greta, but it left him slightly puzzled. In the past he had laughed at the thought of the millions of women who fantasised about him as they made love to their fat husbands. Now he was seeing Greta's face in front of his eyes as he made love to Jeanne Eagels. When he exposed and gently cupped Jeanne's breasts he was surprised that they weren't shaped like Greta's, and when he kissed her he was surprised that Jeanne's mouth moved so differently from Greta's. Instead of being delighted by this variation in sexual technique as he had been so often in the past, he was saddened by it.

'You're still in love with the Swedish broad,' said Jeanne as she injected herself with the heroin that would shortly kill her.

'I am not. I'm in love with you,' Jack declared stoutly. Jeanne looked at him as if he were mad.

'We are actors. We are screwing because there's nothing else to do in this place at night. We're not in love.'

Jack was forced to acknowledge the truth of her statement. He *was* worried about Greta; that was his problem. What he was not worried about was the possibility of talking pictures taking over from silent movies. And even if they did, he'd be all right. It was the foreign actors whose careers would be over in Hollywood if sound turned out to be something more than a gimmick.

They returned to MGM to shoot the interiors, and Jack was surprised to discover that talking pictures were not scaring the hell out of everyone in Hollywood as he had heard on the grapevine. King Vidor picked him up from the train station in Pasadena and, as soon as they had outrun the pursuing autograph fiends and jumped in the car, King told him how the success of *The Jazz Singer* had elicited differing reactions from the studio executives.

'What're Thalberg and Mayer gonna do about it?' asked Jack, quietly hopeful that Louis B. Mayer would have something else to think about besides how much he hated Jack.

'They think it's a fad, a flash in the pan. The public will soon tire of hearing actors talk.'

'I agree. I mean, who the hell wants to hear actors talk?'

'Well, at least your voice is OK.'

'You sure?' asked Jack doubtfully. 'Someone said it was a bit light.'

'Nah,' said Vidor dismissively. 'It's a pleasant light tenor. Nothing wrong with that. And the public still loves you. You can't lose whatever happens.'

'Did you tell L.B. that?'

'Mayer says MGM won't spend the money to convert the studios into sound stages because the movie theatres won't spend the money to wire themselves for sound. There's no point making sound movies for one theatre in Los Angeles and another one in New York.'

'The foreign actors will be relieved,' said Jack, thinking of course of one particular foreign actress.

'Not just the foreigners. Did you ever hear Clara Bow speak?'

'Where's she from? The Bronx?' asked Jack, trying to remember.

'Brooklyn,' King Vidor corrected him. 'They can't understand her in Manhattan.'

Jack's thoughts returned immediately to Greta. 'If sound does catch on there's one madam who won't make it. Who's gonna want to listen to that Swedish accent? "Oh, Yackie, Yackie, pliss tell me vot to do, this is not my country . . ." '

King smiled. He knew how badly his friend was still hurting.

'So where's Flicka living now?' asked Jack.

'Hey, we're here,' said Vidor with relief, as he turned the car into the driveway of 1400 Tower Road. 'We sure made quick time.'

'Thanks for the ride. I'll see you for drinks later.'

'Before you go inside the house . . .' King hesitated, thinking he had better tell Jack the bad news, despite the volcanic reaction his words might provoke.

'Yes?'

'I think she's still around. I don't think she moved out.'

'Flicka?'

'Yep.'

'She's still *here*?'

'That's what I hear,' said King uncomfortably.

'She must think I'm a fool. Where is she? I'm going to throw her and her Swedish meatballs into the road.' Jack stormed over to the house and almost wrenched the door handle off as he threw the front door open.

It didn't take him long to find Greta. She had seen his arrival from an upstairs window and came running down the stairs, almost throwing herself into his arms.

'Yackie, I am so glad you're back. I've missed you so much.' She kissed him passionately, covering his face with kisses. Jack put up almost no resistance at all.

'I thought you'd be gone when I got back,' he said, recovering his breath.

'Gone?' echoed Greta, puzzled. 'Why should I go anywhere? Besides, I need your advice about how to handle Mr Mayer.'

And that was it. Off again, on again, Greta and John again.

When they made love, three and a half minutes after King Vidor had turned out of the driveway, it was, as ever, wonderful, magical, tender, sensational, and yet, and yet, Jack couldn't work out what was missing. Something was. She still attracted him, he could get hard if she so much as smiled at him, he found her as passionate as ever as they rolled in ecstasy on top of the king-sized bed, but there was something a little too familiar about Greta. He did this, so she did that. It was very nice of course but it ever so slightly disappointed him. He felt cross with her for failing to be the girl of his dreams and cross with himself that he couldn't find happiness on any kind of permanent footing with the woman he had been living with – off and on admittedly – for over a year.

Greta had her own anxieties. In particular she was worried about Moje. He knew now that his longed-for career in America would never happen. He didn't like America and he didn't like Americans. In particular he didn't like the way they worked. They had constructed this extraordinary studio system, which made films like other factories made canned goods. In Hollywood the producer was king and the producer's only real interest was in the box-office returns. A good picture was one that made money, a very good picture was one that made a lot of money, and a bad picture was one that lost money. They didn't need to see the picture itself. They simply had to look at the box-office figures to know if the work was good or bad. If a director made, by their standards, a bad film then he was a bad director and who would want to hire a bad director?

In Europe they knew that Mauritz Stiller was a great director. He would go back to Europe.

Greta pleaded with him but to no avail. She knew he needed to return to Sweden for his own sanity, she understood how Hollywood had gradually destroyed her beloved Moje's very soul in the years they had been there but she didn't like it.

'I shall be alone,' she complained.

'You have Gilbert,' said Stiller somewhat spitefully.

'Yackie is a boy.'

'You were going to marry him.'

'But I didn't because he is a boy.'

'Do you know that the studio spread a rumour that you were my mistress, that I had made you pregnant and then forced you to have an abortion?' exclaimed Moje.

'I did not know that.'

'If I leave, that will make you free, free to be a great actress, just as I have always told you.'

'I worry about you, Moje.'

'I know. And I love you for it. But when I am back in Sweden and making films again you will have no need to worry about me. Then I will make you proud of me again.'

'I have always been proud of you,' she said and she flung her arms around him as if by her gesture she could protect him against the misfortunes that were blighting his life.

Stiller's impending departure cast a pall over Greta's very existence. She was distant again with Jack and spent much more time in her apartment at the Miramar than at the house on Tower Road. She couldn't discuss intimate thoughts with Jack at the best of times, and this wasn't the best of times. Jack begged her to come to the house on Sundays at least so the rest of Hollywood could see they were still a couple and still in love. It was important to Jack, so Greta obliged, albeit somewhat reluctantly. Entertaining was never her strong point, even now that her grasp of the English language was improving. It had certainly improved faster than Moje's. That was one reason things hadn't worked out for him.

She shuddered as she recalled the first few days on *The*

Temptress, the movie that Moje had begun to direct her in. He and her co-star Antonio Moreno had hated each other at first sight. He had insisted that Moreno shave off his moustache. Moreno had refused and the studio had supported that refusal. Greta wore size 7AA shoes and Stiller had insisted that Moreno wear shoes that were larger than his co-star's. Again he had refused and again the studio supported the actor not the director. He had been unable to direct any of the actors particularly well because his command of English was so poor. It broke Greta's heart when she heard the crew laughing at Moje as he struggled with the unfamiliar words. He couldn't talk to his cameraman, he couldn't talk to his first assistant without some miscommunication which of course slowed everything down. He frequently shouted 'Stop!' when he was supposed to shout 'Action!' and 'Go!' when he should have called 'Cut!'

The studio's decision to fire Moje after ten days was, Greta knew in her heart, inevitable, but it didn't take away any of the pain she felt as she saw him leave the studio, utterly defeated and humiliated, and it didn't assuage the guilt she felt now as he told her of his decision to return to Sweden. Why should she, the novice, have found fame and fortune when the man who had created her, just as surely as God had created Eve from Adam's rib, had moulded her, shaped her, polished her as if she were some fine piece of sculpture, why should he be the one to go home?

She went back to Jack's house that Sunday with a heavy heart. The weather seemed to be reflecting the mood for it was most unlike the typical California day. It had started raining soon after dawn and though it stopped after breakfast the grey clouds hung menacingly overhead. As she turned into Tower Road Greta heard the rumble of distant thunder. In Sweden such weather would have signalled nothing out of the ordinary – a little rain, some thunder and lightning, maybe a hailstorm, just, well, the weather. Here in Beverly Hills such a combination of meteorological events seemed to presage some sort of personal catastrophe. Greta was full of foreboding as her car came to a halt in Jack's driveway.

Jack sensed her mood immediately and knew the day was going to be a disaster. He was still in love with her and yet he knew that they were on a railway track to some kind of tragedy and there was nothing he could do to prevent it. Jack was looking for a fight and he found it immediately. He claimed he didn't like the white jumper and dark-blue sailor trousers she was wearing.

'Why do you dress like a man?'

'Before, you say you like the way I dress.'

'Before. Sure, before. Before you left me at the altar for the second time.'

Greta grimaced. She knew it wasn't going to take long before the conversation went down that road.

'You gonna spend the whole day with that Swedish scowl on your face?'

'Yackie, I am tired. Do not start with me . . .'

'I'm gonna cancel everyone. You'll disappear on me anyway . . .'

'I go now if you want.'

'Sure. Take off. Why not? It's what you're good at.'

'OK. I go home now.'

And she started to walk quickly and thankfully towards her car. Jack called after her.

'Don't think I don't know where you're going! He's old, Flicka. Can he still get it up?'

Greta broke into a run and jumped into the coupé before the insults could get any worse. When Jack was in this kind of a mood the best thing to do was to clear out and leave him to his own devices.

Jack watched Greta speeding off down Tower Road back into Beverly Hills and cursed her. Then he cursed all women. Then he got his own car out and drove, somewhat erratically, round the corner to see his friend, the playwright Donald Ogden Stewart, who was renting a flat at the bottom of the hill. The Ohio-born, eastern college-educated writer and the itinerant actor who never finished high school made an unlikely partnership. However, Don Stewart admired Jack's easy social graces and his consummate acting technique as well as his way with women. Always conscious of his lack of formal education, Jack was grateful that Don would give him lessons in cultural history without the slightest condescension.

Seeing that Jack was already in a state of mental anguish Don decided to treat his friend to a discourse on the paintings of Pieter Bruegel, a lecture that was accompanied by the worst bootleg brandy Stewart had ever been suckered into buying.

'Christ, Don, who d'ya get this stuff from?'

'Same guy you get your stuff from.'

'This is just rotgut,' said Jack holding out his glass for a refill. Don obliged with a smile.

'I want to show you these paintings by Bruegel.'

'Never heard of him.'

'Pieter Bruegel lived and worked in Antwerp and Brussels in the mid 1500s,' said Don, opening a large art book and setting it in front of his friend.

'So he was a peasant, right?'

'Well, he painted lots of pictures of peasants but he wasn't a peasant himself. I mean, if he'd been a peasant himself he would have spent all day tilling the fields not painting. What?'

Jack had turned the page and was looking with fixed eyes at one of Bruegel's masterpieces. His hand reached out for the brandy bottle.

'A wedding?'

'Sure. It's called *The Peasant Wedding*. It's only a small-scale reproduction so you have to look really close because all the details are much harder to absorb but there's so much going on here. Look at this . . .' But Jack was in no mood to look at anything. He got to his feet and stood for a moment, swaying gently like laundry on a clothesline in the breeze of an autumn morning.

'Look at the fat cow of a bride.'

'She's sitting quietly with folded hands.'

'It's Flicka. She's even got that same stupid peasant grin on her face.'

'Greta's beautiful. You can't compare . . .'

'Know where she is? Know where she is right now?'

'I . . .'

Don Stewart had no idea where Greta was and not much interest. He was aware that Jack was drunk and dangerously so.

'Jack, I think you should probably go home now and take a nap.'

'You think I drink too much too? Flicka says I drink too much. Can you believe it? I'm going over to her place to tell her what I think of her.'

'Jack, I really think . . .'

And with a final swig of the most disgusting brandy either of them had ever tasted, Gilbert was gone before Don Stewart could finish the lecture on sixteenth-century Flemish painting or persuade him to head back up the hill to Tower Road. Instead, in his white shirt open at the neck he roared out along Wilshire Boulevard to Santa Monica and to the Miramar Hotel where he suspected Garbo was lying in bed with a man, probably not just one man, maybe even the entire University of Southern California football team, which was the rumour everyone had heard about Clara Bow. He had never slept with Clara Bow, but then she was under contract to Paramount. MGM didn't like it if their stars slept with Paramount stars. It gave Paramount free publicity and Mayer hated Jesse Lasky and Adolph Zukor, who had started the Paramount studio.

Why did all those Jews who owned the studios hate each other? he wondered. Was it because they were all Jewish? Were they all related? He would have to find out. Meanwhile it looked like a good plan to him if he were to seduce Clara Bow, knowing it would annoy Louis B. Mayer. But first he wanted to screw someone else. Greta Garbo. That was the girl. That Swedish bitch needed a good pounding. Might make her see sense at last. Also he thought she might be interested in learning a little more about Pieter Bruegel.

Jack didn't so much park his car as leave it at a crazy angle, twenty yards from the front entrance of the Miramar. The hotel staff were happy to see him, as usual, and wished him a pleasant day. He responded in kind. There was a fresh-faced kid, looking no more than sixteen years old, who always carried a room key round his neck.

'Hey, kid, you seen Miss Garbo?'

'Yes, Mr Gilbert. I saw her going into her apartment about twenty minutes ago.'

'Thanks.' He flicked a dollar bill at the kid. The kid looked suitably thrilled at receiving such largesse. Jack whistled 'Come to Me, My Melancholy Baby' and ran up the stairs two at a time. He rapped imperiously on the door.

'Hey, Flicka! Open up, it's me!' There was no response. 'C'mon, Flicka, I got something to tell you.' He thought she might misinterpret what he had just said so he attempted to clarify. 'I just been to Don Stewart's. He told me all about Peter Bagel. Great painter. You'd like Bagel.'

Bagel? he thought to himself. That didn't sound quite right. He thought it was Bagel. Kind of a stupid name for a painter, though. When the invitation to discuss sixteenth-century Flemish painting was not taken up Jack started to lose his temper.

'Hey, Flicka, I know you're in there. The kid saw you. Open up!' Jack suddenly realised why she was not opening the door. 'You got a guy in there? Flicka!' Now the rapping on the door had turned into a frantic hammering. In the pause that followed, when he took his fist away from the door and examined the bruised knuckles and torn skin, Greta put her face to the inside of the door and talked softly through it.

'Yackie, go home. I am tired.'

'Open the goddamn door!'

'Have you been drinking again?'

'I haven't had a drink for nearly . . .' He stared at his watch, wondering why he had no idea what the time was even though his watch was working. 'For nearly an hour. I think.'

'Yackie, be a good boy and go home.'

'I want to see you. I love you.'

'Yackie. Tomorrow. Go home now and sleep it off.'

'Bitch! Open this door!'

He beat violently on the door. Two embarrassed hotel bellhops tried to guide him away. He resisted and a fracas ensued at the end of which Jack found himself sprawling face down in the car park. He rose slowly to his feet, looked up at the building and realised that Garbo's third-floor apartment had a balcony. Running up the wall alongside it was a vine-covered drainpipe. He'd climbed enough balconies at the studio to be quite confident of repeating the exercise here.

He took a firm grip on the drainpipe and began his ascent. His leather-soled shoes didn't have much grip and he sank ignominiously to the ground.

Inside the apartment Greta and Stiller were talking quietly, unaware of the drunken actor weaving dangerously about on the drainpipe outside.

'I don't want you to go. You are the only man I trust.'

'I'm sorry I could not . . . fulfil you any other way.'

'Oh no, Moje. You must never apologise for that. I don't care about that and besides it is because I know I am safe with you that I can trust you.'

'Then trust me to know that I am doing the right thing.'

'Maybe I should just leave with you and go back home myself.'

'You have a contract. We must honour our contracts.'

'MGM didn't honour its contract with you.'

'That's no reason for me to behave badly. I shall be appreciated in Sweden. Already I am receiving scripts from producers in Sweden. I think I might do the Swedish adaptation of that play about Broadway. The script is good.'

'Is there a part for me in it?' asked Greta, the balance of their relationship tilting back towards the status of their early days together. Stiller smiled.

'You are not free. You have films to make here in Hollywood.'

Garbo cried out in alarm. Stiller was at first inclined to offer another of his comforting speeches until he realised that her scream was not related to the conversation but to something happening outside the window. He turned to see a disembodied hand clutching the railing. Stiller rushed outside to discover its origin just as Jack was hauling himself from the drainpipe onto the ledge of the balcony.

'You!' exclaimed Stiller.

'I knew you were having an affair with him. You lied to me, you liar!' shouted Jack, still struggling to get a secure foothold on the balcony.

'Yackie, this is none of your business.'

'Of course it's my business. We are supposed to be lovers and here you are fucking this old man!'

'Yackie, you don't understand about Moje . . .'

Stiller was incensed by the charge levelled against him and he lashed out at Jack, who fought as much to control his balance as to hurt his opponent. His posture was so awkward, his mind and body were both so clouded by alcohol and his grip on the balcony was so insecure that it was easy for Stiller to loosen Jack's hold on the railings.

'She doesn't want to see you. Go home!' he said firmly and pushed Jack down by the shoulders.

'Bastard! Just wait till I . . .' But whatever Jack's threat was going to be it would have to wait some time to be carried out because at that moment he lost his footing and slid ignominiously and painfully all the way down to the sidewalk like a fireman on his first day at the fire station, burning his hands and calves as he did so.

'Sonofabitch tried to kill me!' he called out to nobody in particular as he lay on the ground. He got painfully to his feet. 'Sonofabitch tried to kill me!' he repeated. He brushed himself off and examined the bruises. He wasn't going to stand for that sort of treatment. He didn't care how great a director the old fool had been in Sweden. He was Jack Gilbert fer Chrissakes and nobody treated the Great Lover like a cuckold. He'd settle who was boss. He'd go back to the house, grab the gun and stick it in the Swede's bony belly.

And that's what Jack did. He was quite fond of the Luger service pistol. He'd bought it for $200 off some guy who had stolen it from a German prisoner in 1918. He'd had a row with Leatrice his last wife over something. He couldn't remember why for the moment, oh yes, that meaningless affair with Laurette Taylor, and he'd got it out of the drawer and waved it at her, admittedly a bit melodramatically, but it had really made her shut up for a while, which was no mean triumph in itself. She did move out of the house and serve divorce papers on him shortly afterwards but that was going to happen anyway once Cecil B. DeMille had poisoned her mind against him. Yes, he would get the gun and stick it in the belly of the Swede and then he'd go over to DeMille's place in Los Feliz on the east side of Hollywood and see how brave the big bully was when he had a loaded revolver pointing at that big stupid sanctimonious hypocritical bald head.

He was driving back towards the ocean again, along Sunset Boulevard heading west past Camden, when he suddenly realised he didn't need to do all this. Stiller was the aggressor; he was the victim. He was the biggest movie star in the world so all he needed to do was to report Stiller's actions to the cops and watch the big Swede fry in the big house. Did a charge of attempted murder lead to the electric chair? he wondered. He tried to think which movies he had seen recently in which the answer to this question could be found but his brain was too full of the new foolproof plan. Jack executed a huge U-turn. Fortunately there was no other traffic in sight on this particularly deserted stretch of Sunset Boulevard. He made a quick right turn down Rexford Drive and headed for the Beverly Hills police station. This would teach the randy old Swedish goat not to mess with Jack Gilbert.

He wondered what Garbo and the old man got up to in bed and then decided this was not a profitable line of inquiry. The old guy was probably impotent. God, he shuddered at the prospect that one day he might not be able to get it up. It was an unimaginable prospect. But then Stiller was forty-four while Jack was still in his twenties, if only by a few months. It would be another fifteen years before he reached that age of advanced senility and just think what had happened to him in the previous fifteen. In 1913 his bitch of a mother had died and he had still been in school at the Hitchcock Military Academy in San Rafael in northern California. It was fifteen years ago that his stepfather had taken Jack to the railway station in Salt Lake City, told him he would no longer look after him and given him ten dollars, his mother's make-up case and a folder of her clippings, the total legacy of her years as a failing actress. He was fourteen years old and on his own. Well, he'd made a pretty good fist of what was by any account a rotten, loveless childhood. He had every reason to be proud of what he had achieved. Having survived all that and the endemic treacheries of Hollywood, he was damned if he was going to let himself be literally pushed around by an ageing Swedish director.

Jack drew up outside the police station and rejoiced in the fact that he was a well-known and well-liked movie star. It was in situations like this that his hard-won status proved its real worth. The cops were bound to take his side against Stiller. The miserable Swede could look forward to being banged up in the slammer while he took Garbo back to the house in the hills and fucked her senseless. Yes, life as a movie star had its compensations.

He strode into the police station and noticed with pleasure the instant attention he got. This was a real police station. The officers wore clean dark-blue uniforms that could have come straight from the wardrobe department at MGM. He smiled serenely at everyone as the desk sergeant welcomed him.

'Mr Gilbert, how can we help you today?' Jack was really pleased with everything now. It was all going to end happily – just like the movies. The desk sergeant had to repeat his inquiry before Jack started to focus on the answer. Then his mind went completely blank. He really couldn't remember why he had gone there. He knew there was a reason and it was good but he was damned if he could remember what it was.

'You know,' he began, 'it's the damnedest thing.' He stopped and shook his head, trying to clear the fog that had temporarily enveloped his brain.

'How's Miss Garbo? When are you two gonna tie the knot?' Jack smiled. That was all he needed. The slightest clue and he was OK again. Of course, Garbo! Garbo and Stiller. But what was it about Garbo and Stiller that had made him drive all the way here? Then he remembered.

'Sonofabitch tried to kill me,' he stated categorically. The policeman looked interested but certainly not captivated. 'He tried to kill me,' Jack reiterated. 'Goddamn foreigner,' he added, a foreign passport being, he suspected, the only real proof policemen ever needed. This policeman was proving to be an awkward exception.

'Just calm down, Mr Gilbert.'

'Calm down! The sonofabitch tried to kill me. Now, are you going to arrest him or do I have to do it?' The policeman smiled a tolerant smile. It would be good to go home tonight and tell his wife whose life he had sorted out in the police station that day.

'You can't go around arresting people, Mr Gilbert.'

Jack was puzzled. He was a movie star fer Chrissakes. He could do what the hell he liked.

'Goddamn foreigner tried to kill me. So I went back home and got a gun.'

'A gun?' The policeman was now totally captivated. Stupid movie stars, they think life is one big long movie. What the hell made them think they could carry guns? That was for policemen.

'You have the gun with you, Mr Gilbert?'

'Sure I do.' Did this little punk think he was some kind of second-rate actor? He always had his props ready – and if he didn't it was someone else's fault.

'Can I see it?'

'Sure.'

Jack went back to the car, took the Luger out of the glove compartment, walked back into the station, twirling it round his finger like Tom Mix in the cowboy pictures, and slapped it down on the counter. The sergeant tried not to react too quickly. He opened the chamber and removed the three bullets that were in there.

'Do you have a licence for this?' he asked with a calm he did not feel.

'I'm John Gilbert. Everyone knows who I am.'

'Sure they do. OK, Mr Gilbert, you're under arrest.'

'Not me, you dumb ox! Him! Stiller! He's the guy I want you to arrest. He tried to kill me!'

'You don't have a licence for this firearm, which is a felony, and I think you'll feel a whole lot better when you've slept off whatever you've had to drink.' The sergeant summoned a patrolman who took a voluble but unresisting Jack down to the cells. The sergeant picked up the phone and dialled the number of a journalist friend who covered the Hollywood crime beat.

'Hi, Ned. Say, who do you think I've got locked up downstairs and how much is it worth to your paper?'

Jack awoke to the sound of throbbing drums. It took him quite a long time to work out that the drums were inside his own head. A young policeman was standing over him with a cup of black coffee.

'Drink this, Mr Gilbert. There's a car waiting for you outside. A studio limousine to be precise.'

'I can go?' asked Jack in surprise.

'For the moment. MGM has posted the twenty-five-dollar bail so you're free till your court appearance next Monday.'

'And nobody knows about this?'

The policeman looked a little sheepish.

'I think someone must know. There's a lot of people and cars outside.'

There were indeed a lot of people and cars outside. Howard Strickling, the recently appointed head of publicity at MGM, met him in the lobby of the station house and hurried him into the studio limo through the writhing tangle of bodies and cameras. The car sped away as soon as Strickling slammed the door.

'What the hell was all that about?' asked Jack, still shaking from the sudden exposure to direct sunlight and the frenzy of the mob.

'That was about a Hollywood star who is stupid enough to get drunk and go looking for trouble.'

'How come everyone knows about it?'

'Don't complain,' said Strickling tersely. 'It takes me months to get this sort of publicity usually.'

'Yeah, but we don't want this sort of publicity, do we?' Jack took one look at Strickling's cynical expression and for the first time in his life he really understood the meaning of the show-business cliché that there is no such thing as bad publicity.

'So what happens when I get to court?'

'You get your wrists slapped. You get told to behave as a role model to the young people who are your fans, you pay twenty-five dollars and your next picture is a huge hit. You have nothing to worry about.'

Luxuriating in his sunken bathtub that night, Jack was calmed by

Strickling's absolute assurance about the way the justice system worked in Hollywood. It made complete sense and he saw no reason to question the judgement. He thought about throwing a huge 'Get Out of Jail' party after he walked out of the courtroom but then decided against it. It was probably in bad taste and no doubt certain morals groups would be expecting him to show some sort of public contrition and to be humbled by the experience. He wondered if Garbo would be in court, gently dabbing her eyes with a handkerchief as the man who had fought so bravely for her honour took his public humiliation with the grace she had always expected he would show under such circumstances.

The following Monday a smiling Jack Gilbert found himself sentenced to ten days in the county jail by a city recorder who was clearly not a movie fan and who seemed to take exception to his court being treated as the set of a movie production. Jack was shocked. Ten days in the slammer! He hadn't expected that. Where was Howard Strickling now? Where was the studio? No point expecting help from that quarter. L.B. Mayer had probably been on the phone to the city recorder asking for life or the chair. There was no Garbo either, but he posed good-naturedly for press photos when they shut the door on jail cell number 3, figuring that at least she would see his photo in the paper. He was still front-page news. Mind you, that was cold comfort when your roommate turned out to be a terrifying Negro wife-beater or wife murderer or whatever he was. When they were left alone together Jack tried to make friends but to tell the truth it wasn't entirely successful. He wondered how he was going to survive one night let alone ten. Where was Garbo? It was her fault he was in the hoosegow. Why didn't she come and bring him a cake with a file in it? The papers would like that. Jack fell asleep on the filthy bed and tried to ignore the sound and stink of his nearest neighbour going to the toilet in a bucket in the middle of the night.

When he woke he could hear the dull hum of excited chatter – it was like listening to a waiting audience in the theatre during the last five minutes before the curtain went up. What was going on out there? To his great surprise, shortly after he had been confronted by what he was told was breakfast but, because of its texture and awful taste, could have been something created by the art department, the cell door swung open.

'Get your things, Gilbert. You're going home.'

'I am?'

'You wanna stay?'

Jack took the hint and held out his hand to his erstwhile roommate.

'Good luck, Earl. Strikes me you got a bum rap. I'll see what I can do on the outside.' Jack was very pleased with his dialogue. 'Let's see Frances Marion come up with something as convincing as that,' he muttered to himself. Some guy in a smart uniform who must have had prior warning escorted him to the front door and ostentatiously shook hands with Jack while the photographers snapped and the crowds cheered.

'Try to go straight this time, Jack,' he grinned straight at the cameras.

'Go fuck yourself,' said Jack, grinning just as inanely at the press. Hey, who did this guy think he was dealing with? Picture editors on the newspapers would crop the publicity-seeking governor out anyway.

Strickling was there with the studio limo again. He was even less welcoming, if that were possible, this time than he had been after the night in the cell at the Beverly Hills police station.

'You're more trouble to the authorities inside than outside,' he observed. 'Every starlet in need of publicity is here. Mayer's mad at you. Thought you'd like to know.'

'What does he want? I said I was sorry. I said I was drunk. That's what you told me to say, wasn't it? Then the judge gave me ten days in the slammer.'

'You changed what I told you to say.'

'One sentence. I thought my dialogue was better.'

'That was the dialogue that got you the ten days in the slammer. Pleading not guilty and then asking the judge to excuse your behaviour because you were drunk wasn't the smartest defence I've ever heard.'

'Why didn't Garbo come and visit me?'

'You were only inside for a day. Who else did you expect? President Coolidge?'

Jack couldn't deny the force of the argument. He slumped into the soft interior of the car. He shuddered at the thought that he might have had to spend ten whole nights listening to that big ape sitting on the can every night. Thank God he was on his way back to Tower Road. He wondered if Garbo would be there waiting for him, if his recent sufferings would bring her running back to him as she had done so often in the past. He had to admit to himself that she hadn't look thrilled when he had glimpsed her while he was trying to climb drunkenly onto her balcony. God, he loved her. Sometimes he wished he didn't but he really did. He thought of what their life together might still be like in a conventional husband and wife relationship. He speculated on the possibility of her accepting his proposal the next time. He sat up suddenly and looked at Strickling.

'Do you think Garbo would find a man with a criminal record attractive enough to marry?' Strickling rolled his eyes to heaven.

Chapter Eight

〰〰〰〰

It was ironic that Jack should be so disconcerted by Mauritz Stiller. Not only had he failed to detect that Stiller was a homosexual and therefore not much of a rival for Garbo's body but also he hadn't realised that, far from becoming a constant, irritating fixture in Garbo's life, Stiller was already making preparations to return to Sweden. On the way down to the train station Stiller tried hard to convince his protégée that he would be all right. She didn't believe him. Despite the fact that her career was going spectacularly well and Stiller was no longer part of it, he had been a constant presence and the dominant influence in her life for the past five years and she viewed with alarm the prospect of their enforced parting.

'I am coming home soon,' she protested, as if that would lessen the impact of their imminent separation. She was only too aware even as she spoke the words that she had said exactly the same phrase to her mother in July 1925 when she had boarded the SS *Drottningholm* with Stiller. Now she was only one year into a contract that bound her to Metro-Goldwyn-Mayer for another five years. Until that contract expired when, or even if, she could go home again was a decision that rested with Thalberg and Mayer.

Stiller kissed Greta tenderly on the lips. To him she was still the little girl with big potential he had spotted at the graduation performance of the class of 1921 at the Dramatiska Teatern in Stockholm. From the time shooting had finished on *Gösta Berlings Saga* he had been obsessed with turning her into a star. That it was happening without him was extremely painful, but at least through Greta Garbo he would achieve some measure of immortality. He felt so passionately about her that, like a good parent, he insisted that she fly the nest, even though it wrenched his guts to see her do so.

At the end, on the platform, instead of making things easy for her he made them difficult.

'You are free,' he said, looking into her deep-blue eyes. 'You have always been free.'

'I have never been free,' replied Garbo, wondering how he could invert history with such facility.

'You must go on to new triumphs and never think of me again,' he declared, knowing perfectly well that his departure was bound to leave Garbo with feelings of guilt and that these words would cause her constantly to be thinking about him. She would do so whenever she got a new script, whenever she heard who had been assigned to direct her, whenever she arrived on the set for that first awkward day of shooting a new movie with a new director and a new co-star. There would be nobody there to worry about whether the co-star had bigger feet than she did.

She stood unmoving on the platform as the Super Chief drew slowly out of the station into the unblinking noonday California sun. Not for her the tearful farewell or the manic waving of arms. She did what Stiller had always told her – stand still and make the audience come to you. As the train gathered momentum she closed her eyes and imagined a camera on the platform, like the railway platform on which she had first met Yackie, dollying in, the focus tightening all the time on her face. The heat of the sun's rays felt like the key light which Stiller had been the first director to notice illuminated her face to such spectacular effect. By the time she opened her eyes the train and her mentor were long gone.

She felt dead inside, as if Moje were taking back to Sweden a small but essential part of her soul and she would never be whole again. That theft would bind them together forever. She would never really be able to enjoy her newly won status as a movie star. She would stay in Hollywood though she despised the place. It would never be home to her, but then Stockholm could no longer be home to her either. She was stateless, rootless and sick in her heart. She wondered if those lunatics who wrote to her at the studio every week demanding her autograph and her photograph would do so if they knew how she really felt. Why couldn't they see that the movies were just an illusion? Nobody who worked in the industry ever believed in the fantasy. Except possibly Yackie. Why was it so powerful for so many millions of people all over the world?

She walked back to her car and to her dull, empty life as one half of the most famous celebrity couple in the world. Well, that might not last much longer anyway. She was tired of his childish ways and this latest stupidity was proof that a marriage to Jack Gilbert would be unmitigated folly. Admittedly he was exciting in a way, and she truly believed that he loved her, though she was never sure if what she felt for him was also love. Most days she thought herself incapable of loving anyone. What was the point? They left her anyway. Her father died, her beloved sister, now Moje. Jack would find someone else to play marriage games with. He wouldn't need her.

Besides, she wouldn't necessarily be around. Despite her long-term contract, she knew perfectly well that the arrival of talking pictures threatened her livelihood as it threatened that of all the foreign actors in Hollywood. She still spoke English quite badly and although it was slowly improving, she could never hope to pass as an American woman. She would have to continue playing foreign vamps and how long could that go on for? Sooner or later her time in Hollywood would come to an end. She couldn't see Yackie living with her in Stockholm, learning Swedish and auditioning for a part in a Strindberg play. Meanwhile she had a film to make. It would be called, eventually, *The Mysterious Lady*, because MGM was learning how to tease Garbo's adoring and growing public with films whose plots or titles seemed to suggest something of the 'real' life of the star. Garbo herself took the title to heart.

Her fascinated co-workers felt similarly. Marion Davies and her co-star, the young Swedish actor Nils Asther, in a Hearst production, *The Cardboard Lover*, were shooting on the same stage where Garbo was making *The Mysterious Lady*. One morning, to the delight of them both, Greta stood behind the camera and watched Marion and Nils at work before returning to her own set. Believing she was returning a compliment, Marion walked onto Garbo's set in the middle of a scene.

'Cut!' called Greta, much to the surprise of the director Fred Niblo and his lighting cameraman, Bill Daniels.

'What's the matter?' asked Niblo with a hint of irritation. It all seemed to have been going so well. Garbo said nothing, but inclined her head slightly towards the smiling Marion. Now Niblo had a real problem. He knew Greta well enough to understand that unless Marion Davies left, Greta would not be working that day, at a cost of time and money that would upset L.B. Mayer, which wouldn't be good for his own career. On the other hand if he told Marion Davies to clear off and she told Hearst or Louella Parsons they would find some way of paying him back either with a bad review for the picture in the Hearst press or with malicious and untrue gossip in Louella's column. To his great relief, Marion soon realised what was going on and disappeared back to her set, still smiling.

When Garbo left to take her traditionally frugal lunch in her dressing room, Marion returned to the *The Mysterious Lady* set and hid behind one of the screens, remaining there unseen by anyone until the cast and crew reassembled for the afternoon session. Niblo rehearsed Greta and her leading man Conrad Nagel in the scene and then called on Daniels to adjust the lighting as make-up and hair made minute adjustments to Garbo's appearance. Before calling for action, Niblo, as was his usual courtesy, asked Greta if she was ready to shoot.

'No.'

'No? Are make-up and hair finished?'

'Yes.'

'When will you be ready to shoot, then?'

'Just as soon as Miss Davies leaves the set.'

A red-faced Marion crawled out from behind the set like a naughty little girl caught at the back of her mother's closet looking for Christmas presents in October. She almost ran back to the set of *The Cardboard Lover*.

Jack was looking to kill off his unwanted tag as the Great Lover and the brilliant young director Howard Hawks was just the man to help him. Hawks outlined the story of a group of young fighter pilots in the Great War. One of their number is promoted to commander of the squadron and instead of being the lone ace, he is now responsible for the lives and more realistically the deaths of his young comrades. Hawks had always seen it as a talking picture, but Jack wasn't so sure.

'Does it have to be a talker, Howard?'

'The dialogue won't be mushy. There's no love interest.'

'I like that, but everyone says I should wait before I do my first talker.'

'L.B. loves the story. He wants to see me tomorrow. Come with me and together we can make sure you play the lead.'

'L.B. hates my guts.'

'You're the biggest star on the lot. Why wouldn't he want you to do it?'

'If it's good for me, he'll hate it and you'll lose the picture.'

'He already says he loves the picture. You want to do it?'

'Goddamn it, Howard, it's going to be like *The Big Parade*.'

'It'll make them offer you something more than those lousy Great Lover parts.'

'OK. Let's do it.'

The next day Mrs Koverman ushered the two men into Mayer's office. The studio chief had barely been on the lot the last few weeks as he had become increasingly wrapped up in the campaign to elect Herbert Hoover as President of the United States. The Republican Party convention was due to be held in a fortnight in Kansas City and Mayer was planning a major speech that would tie him, the studio and indeed the entire motion-picture industry to the coat tails of the Republican Party. It seemed to many at MGM that the day-to-day mechanics of running the studio were beginning to bore him and, although he left more to Irving Thalberg, his young deputy was frail and frequently unable to take up the slack. But what worried the studio relieved Jack. If L.B. was so preoccupied it would surely mean he was not planning the revenge that he had sworn that memorable afternoon at the double wedding that never was.

True enough L.B. sat quietly and politely as he heard Howard Hawks tell the story and watched Jack act out various scenes. Both men evinced great enthusiasm for the picture and made a strong case for it to be rushed into production as Jack's first sound film. Happy with their pitch, the two men returned to their chairs and awaited L.B.'s judgement with justifiable confidence. He was nobody's fool and he knew a good story when he heard one. In fact he always heard it. He rarely read. Most of the time he utilised two women to tell him the story of the scripts the studio had commissioned. They were known familiarly around the lot as 'Scheherazade 1' and 'Scheherazade 2'.

With some formality Mayer thanked Hawks and Jack for their demonstration. He turned to Hawks and asked him quietly, 'Mr Hawks, are you sure you want Mr Gilbert to be your leading man?' Hawks confirmed that he did.

'And you, Mr Gilbert, are you sure you want Mr Hawks to direct you in your first sound film?' Jack affirmed that he did and relaxed. It sounded like they were about to get the go-ahead for the movie that would do as much for his career as *The Big Parade* had done three years ago. The memory of the affair he had had with Renée Adorée, his French co-star in *The Big Parade,* raced through his mind in a montage of memorable images. That was before he had even met Flicka. God, that seemed so long ago, half a lifetime at least. He wondered what she was doing right now, whether she thought of him as often and with such passion and such emotion as he thought of her. Reluctantly he dragged himself back to whatever it was L.B. was droning on about.

He was explaining that he would decide when Jack was going to do his first sound film and nobody else. Hawks was about to stand up and walk out. If Mayer didn't want the picture after saying the previous day that he did then he would just take it to another studio. Warner Brothers had had another success with Al Jolson's second movie *The Singing Fool* and were now serious players in the industry. They had also had good reviews for their first all-talking dramatic picture *The Lights of New York*. They would bite his arm off . . .

'. . . fucking tell me what to do!' Mayer had lit up and gone off like a firework on the fourth of July but without any of the attendant pleasure. He was red faced and screaming obscenities straight at Jack.

'Degenerate bum! You do what the studio tells you to do. We pay you ten thousand dollars a week. You do what we say. You don't come into my office, you degenerate bum, and start giving me orders!' Jack could feel the anger rising in him like that afternoon when he punched the little shit and broke his glasses. Hawks saw what was happening and quickly interposed himself between the two men, hustling Jack out of the door before he could do Mayer any serious damage. Hawks, who was a pretty tough character himself, went back into Mayer's office and told the studio chief exactly what he thought of him.

'Listen to me, you sonofabitch. I don't care what you think of Jack, but I happen to think he's a great guy and a helluvan actor. You want to carry on this stupid war, do it in your own time and don't ever involve me in it, understand?'

Mayer swung a flailing fist in Hawks' direction. He ducked away from it easily.

'Get the hell off my lot. I don't want your ugly mug in this studio again.'

'I'm going, L.B. But I tell you, *The Dawn Patrol* is gonna be a great movie and you'll just be kicking yourself you missed out on it.'

'You stay here a minute longer and you're the one that's gonna get the kicking. Asshole!' he cried, but Hawks had slammed the door.

Jack was already in Thalberg's office, but his erstwhile friend was preoccupied and not particularly sympathetic.

'I could have told you that would have happened. Why didn't you come to me first?'

'Howard said L.B. had already virtually given it the go-ahead.'

'There's some trouble going on with the owners of the studio in New York. L.B.'s in a particularly tetchy mood these days. If you'd come to me I'd have told you this wasn't the time to go to him. Besides, we've already decided we're going to put you in a picture with Garbo again.'

All thoughts of *The Dawn Patrol* immediately flew out of Jack's head.

'Picture? What picture?' Thalberg smiled, knowing how Jack would react to the explosive news he was about to give him.

'We finally got the Hays Office to approve our adaptation of Michael Arlen's novel *The Green Hat*.'

Jack was surprised. *The Green Hat* had been a scandalous publishing sensation for some years now. It concerned a fast-living contemporary young woman and her marriage to a male counterpart who is stricken with venereal disease. The Hays Office was Hollywood's own self-censorship organisation and took a dim view of anything to do with sexual deviancy and drugs. Venereal disease, in the view of the Hays Office, was not a fit subject for motion pictures. It did, however, believe in financial malpractice, so instead of infecting women with a sexually transmitted disease, it was finally agreed that Garbo's husband could leap to his death from the window of their honeymoon hotel suite when the police come inquiring about certain discrepancies in the annual accounts.

'We also have to change the names of the characters and the title.'

'What's wrong with *The Green Hat*?'

'Hays Office thinks it's dirty.'

'Then get it dry-cleaned.'

'You know what I mean. They think people will associate the title with the dirty book.'

'So what are you going to call it?'

'*A Woman of Affairs*.'

'They like that?'

Thalberg nodded. Jack was mystified.

'They like a title about a woman who has affairs but they don't like a title about a green hat?'

'Looks like that,' agreed Thalberg cheerily.

'This is one fucked-up country,' said Jack, shaking his head sorrowfully. 'Which part am I playing?'

'Are you OK with Neville?'

'The spineless ex-lover who marries the other girl?'

'Do you mind?'

'I'm nearly thirty years old, Irving. Will the audience accept that my father tells me who I can marry?'

'Audiences will accept almost anything in a Garbo picture.'

'A Garbo and Gilbert picture,' corrected Jack quickly and then realised that even he was now referring to them as Garbo and Gilbert and no longer Gilbert and Garbo. Irving looked at him oddly. He too recognised that they had passed some kind of milestone, though what it betokened for the future, neither of them was as yet quite sure.

Clarence Brown was again reunited with Jack and Greta as the director of *A Woman of Affairs*. He apologised to Jack when they met on the set on the first day of shooting.

'Neville's a pain in the ass.'

'I won't play him like that.'

'You want to strengthen the part?'

'Don't touch it. Garbo's going to be wonderful. We'll all benefit.'

'You're a remarkable man, Jack. Off hand, I can't think of a single actor in Hollywood who would say something so unselfish.'

'Don't get carried away, Clarence. I'm doing it because I love Flicka. I wouldn't be saying that if it was Joan Crawford in the lead.'

'OK. But I still think . . . You happy about the supporting cast?'

'Flicka likes Dorothy Sebastian, and I've got a lot of time for young Doug Fairbanks – more than I do for his dad or his stuck-up step-mom.'

'I know Flicka likes Dorothy. They're having lunch together in her dressing room.'

'Oh.'

Clarence Brown immediately realised that Jack was unaware of this lunch date. Invariably on the two previous films he had directed with Jack and Greta the two of them had disappeared every lunchtime to his or her dressing room. 'No doubt they're going over their scenes together,' everyone on the crew had smirked to each other – a little enviously.

Jack was not pleased by Greta's decision to share her lunch with Dorothy, even though everyone knew that the ebullient, extrovert

Sebastian and the soft-spoken, unemotional Brown were living together. There were also rumours that Sebastian was having a fling with Buster Keaton, who had just joined MGM and whose own marriage to Natalie Talmadge was known to be in trouble. Maybe Garbo was as intrigued as the rest of the studio by Sebastian's eventful off-screen existence. Still, Jack thought she should know exactly how he felt at her reckless abandonment of one of their traditions and he went back to his dressing room, sat down at the desk and wrote a strongly worded message to that effect. Emerging into the corridor, he saw young Douglas Fairbanks coming towards him and motioned him inside.

'So, I hear you're fucking Joan Crawford,' he began.

'Er, yes,' replied the startled young man, wondering if he had mistakenly wandered into a previous relationship which she had omitted to mention to him.

'That's good,' said Jack, and Fairbanks breathed a sigh of relief. Whatever he had done it didn't sound as if it were fatal. It appeared as if Jack's opening statement was just breaking the ice.

'Look, I want you to do me a favour.'

'Sure. Anything.'

'Can you take this note to Flicka?'

'Miss G.? Of course. Delighted.'

Doug almost ran out of the room in relief.

On his way to Garbo's dressing room he was overwhelmed by curiosity. What could he have written to her? Why didn't he just say what he wanted to say to her face? He longed to peek but his good breeding prevented him from looking into the unsealed envelope. He knocked on Garbo's dressing-room door.

'Message for you, Miss Garbo,' he called through the door when his knocking had elicited no response at all. What could she be doing in there? Who was she with? Where was her maid? He realised this was how Jack Gilbert must be thinking all the time.

'Slide it under the door,' came the belated reply in that familiar world-weary voice.

'It's Doug Fairbanks, Miss G. Jack wanted me to deliver it to you personally.' He didn't want to be treated like a Western Union boy.

Eventually the door opened and the captivating lanky figure of the enigmatic Swede stood before him in a towelling robe with her hair in curlers. Even in such a state of dishabille, she looked a million dollars, he thought. She held out her hand for the note. Doug gave it to her and, since she didn't immediately slam the door in his face, followed her back into the room. He stared at her as she read Gilbert's scrawl with difficulty. She was utterly beguiling. He would toss Joan Crawford into the Pacific Ocean in a second if she bothered to ask him. Instead she reached for a pen, scribbled 'WHO I LUNCH WITH IS MY BUSINESS' underneath Gilbert's note, folded it up and replaced it in the envelope.

'Would you mind taking this back to Yackie, Doug?'

She had spoken to him. She had used his first name for the first time. He would happily have licked her shoes, never mind the envelope. He stared at her feet, wondering what they might taste like. Instinctively Garbo withdrew them under the table.

'So you like to look at the famous Garbo feets too?' Doug felt himself turning bright red. What had he been thinking of?

'Of course not. I . . . I . . .'

'They are size 7AA. They are not so large, I think, but everyone tells me they are.'

'I like big feet,' said Doug brightly then blushed visibly. He had told himself over and over again not to mention Garbo's feet in conversation. Garbo smiled, amused by his adolescent awkwardness.

'And how's that nice Joan Crawford?' she asked.

'So you've heard we're fucking too,' he said, and blushed again, even more furiously this time. It was also clear from her startled expression that Garbo had not heard that they were fucking. He had now rendered any future chances with Miss G. non-existent.

'I'll take this to Jack,' he said and turned to the door, almost pulling the handle off in his haste to get away. A peal of Swedish laughter followed him down the corridor.

Jack's selflessness, born out of his love for Greta and his belief that it was better to have a small part in a great film than a big part in a poor film, counted against him in the end. Clarence Brown's offer to strengthen his part might not have made the film any better, but he soon realised, as he watched the first assembly of the cut film, that he was looking unsympathetic.

It was good for the film but bad for him personally. His fans would not understand why he was playing such a weak character. They were naïve at the best of times, stupid at the worst of times, and if they saw Jack playing a weak and not particularly likeable man they would probably assume that he himself was a weak and not very likeable man. After all, they thought he was a hero when he played heroes.

Garbo, on the other hand, was a revelation in *A Woman of Affairs*. Her acting touched people in a way that Jack could see but could not duplicate. She despised what she considered to be the grandiloquent gestures so often found in silent movies though rarely among the true artists. Her acting was like watching a miniaturist at work, full of delightful little touches, such as when she put a cigarette in her mouth and then delicately picked a small piece of tobacco off her tongue.

When he kissed her he found her lips to be those of a stranger. He recognised them as her lips, the lips he had kissed so often and so passionately, but now in a weird way they seemed to belong to Diana, the character she was playing. When he kissed her it was the two characters kissing, not Yackie and Flicka. He didn't like the change and hoped it didn't mean what he was afraid it meant – that the affair was now officially over.

He tried to find solace in the litany of facts he always told himself when he felt insecure, but he knew in his heart that this time his fears were justified. For all the 'off again, on again' nature of their relationship on the set of *A Woman of Affairs*, it seemed to be transforming itself inexorably from one of sexual lust into one of just good friends. Jack would have been happy to have continued with the passion of their first sexual experiences when they were making *Flesh and the Devil*, but that was nearly two years ago, and he recognised that, whatever it was Garbo needed from him then, she didn't need it now. He wasn't going to give up completely, but, as far as Garbo was concerned, his box of tricks for arousing sexual interest in women seemed to be empty.

Jack had met the Chinese-American actress Anna May Wong, star of *Streets of Shanghai* and *Chinatown Charlie*, some time ago at a party and, high on the potent combination of her exotic charms and some bootleg liquor, he had quickly persuaded her into a coupling that had left neither of them entirely satisfied. He had therefore decided to try again and was on his way out of his front door to accomplish this mission when Garbo arrived to take up residence in her suite in the Tower Road house, which Jack had assured her would always be hers.

Jack decided that the best way of dealing with what might be an awkward situation was to be entirely honest about it. Maybe Garbo would be very hurt and angry and beg him not to see his latest mistress but to spend the night naked with her instead, being very loving and tender.

'I'm going out,' he said brusquely. Garbo was unfazed.

'I leave the door open.' That wasn't exactly the reply he had been hoping for. He decided to edge into more controversial territory.

'I'm going out to sleep with Anna May Wong,' he declared with commendable honesty. But if he thought Garbo would fling up her hands in horror, he was to be disappointed.

'I leave the door open,' repeated Garbo.

Jack was getting into the car when he admitted to himself that, sexy as Anna May Wong undoubtedly was, the fact remained that he really didn't want to do it and he was only shouting about it to Garbo because he was still in love with her. He marched back into the house.

Garbo was running water into the sunken bathtub with the black marble and gold fixtures he had had installed especially for her. She was wearing a loose pink bathrobe and when she bent forward to test the temperature of the water, it fell open a little way, sufficient to reveal a glimpse of her delightful breasts. Jack had no resistance. He fell to his knees on the bathroom floor in front of her.

'Yackie! I thought you had gone to see Anna May Wong.'

'I don't want to see Anna May Wong. I just want to see you.'

'You are seeing me now! You are seeing everything.' She smiled as she gathered the robe around her body and re-tied the cord.

'I want to see you every day when I wake up. I want to see you every night before I go to sleep. I want to know that you're mine forever. I want to marry you. Please, Flicka, please!'

'Get up, Yackie.'

'Not till you say "yes".'

'What's the point? You know even if I say "yes" now I won't marry you.'

'Goddamn it, Flicka!' Jack was beyond hurt and pain; he was just plain angry and, giving vent to his feelings, he picked up a glass jar of multi-coloured bath salts and hurled it against the wall, where it broke into pieces. The bath salts covered the floor.

'You are a very foolish boy,' said Garbo like a disapproving mother. 'You quarrel with me for no reason.'

'What the hell are you talking about? Turning me down for the third time. That isn't a reason?'

'I must do what I must do, but that is no reason to throw my bath salts at the wall.'

'Sorry.'

'And no reason that we should part.'

'You mean I can bring Anna May Wong here and fuck her in the room next to yours and you won't mind?'

'She is a nice girl. I like her.'

'Flicka, I can't live like this. Why won't you marry me?'

'I cannot be the wife you want. I cannot be the wife you need. I am in love with no man. Why should I get married? I do not wish it.'

Jack Gilbert, the man who was a nervous ball of energy twenty-four hours a day, felt totally exhausted. He was tired of being messed around by Garbo, tired of feeling like a little boy all the time he was with her, tired of a relationship in which he had no power and she had it all.

'I'm going out to sleep with Anna May Wong,' he said in a dull tone.

'OK,' she smiled at him. 'I leave the door open.'

Chapter Nine

It happened on the set of her next picture. The movie had the working title of *Heat*, until it was realised that, just as 'Garbo and Gilbert in *Love*' were some of the best words a marquee could display, 'Greta Garbo in *Heat*' were probably some of the worst. Eventually the studio settled for *Wild Orchids*.

The movie co-starred Marion Davies's opposite number from *The Cardboard Lover*, the talented Swedish actor Nils Asther. Asther played the exotic Prince de Grace who meets an American tea merchant, played by Lewis Stone, and his sexually frustrated wife Lillie on a business trip to Java. They were rehearsing the scene in which the prince shows his new friends around his palace when a messenger boy arrived on set with a telegram for Garbo. When they had finished blocking the action, the director Sidney Franklin turned to Bill Daniels and asked how long it would take to light the set before they could start shooting the master shot in which all the action and dialogue is covered by one camera. It was a safety shot that the editor could cut back to at any time when the closer shots had perhaps confused the audience's sense of geography.

'Gimme half an hour?' asked Daniels. Franklin nodded and turned to his actors.

'Bill thinks half an hour, folks,' he said softly. Sidney Franklin was a quiet, neat director, whom Thalberg and Mayer liked because such qualities produced movies that came in on time and on budget. Thalberg had a weak heart and Mayer a short fuse, so directors like Sidney Franklin would always find work at MGM.

The actors turned to go back to their dressing rooms, knowing that someone from the production staff would knock on their door five minutes before they were ready to start filming. The young gofer shyly approached Garbo and held out the ubiquitous orange envelope.

'Telegram for you, Miss Garbo.'

'Thank you.' Garbo took it with a flash of a smile that the boy would treasure for the rest of his life. She tore open the envelope and unfolded it. Nils Asther and Lewis Stone walked on.

'If we overrun again tonight, my wife will kill me. We've got Ernst Lubitsch and his wife coming to dinner.'

'We won't overrun. Franklin is too organised and the studio doesn't like getting behind schedule. What?'

Lewis Stone looked at Nils Asther, who had stopped and was running back to Garbo's side. She had staggered against the wall and was clutching a doorframe for support. As Asther guided his compatriot into the nearest chair, Lewis Stone picked up the crumpled telegram and handed it silently to Asther, who smoothed it out. It was from Edith and Victor Seastrom, who had returned to Stockholm to see the triumphant opening of the play *Broadway*, Stiller's exciting new project. MOJE PASSED AWAY LAST NIGHT QUIETLY AND CALMLY STOP LOVE TO YOU EDITH VICTOR.

Asther knew Stiller had not been well but he had no idea he was so close to death. The actor was bisexual in his tastes and, as a beautiful youth, he had been one of Stiller's lovers ten years earlier. Nils had actually experienced the physical intimacy with Stiller that Greta had always shied away from, yet, as they both knew, her loss was by far the greater. Lewis Stone went off to get a drink of water for her as Greta and Nils Asther conversed briefly and in low tones about the life and death of Mauritz Stiller, who had been such a huge influence on both their lives.

When the actors were summoned to return to the set after Bill Daniels had completed his lighting setup, Greta was entirely composed. Both Nils Asther and Lewis Stone had individual hurried conferences with Sidney Franklin and, though everyone showed Greta every consideration, it did not appear as if she needed it. She was her usual professional self, fully prepared, invariably cooperative, the very opposite of the uncommunicative, contrary, temperamental diva in whose guise she was so frequently and erroneously portrayed.

When she left the set at one minute past five she wished everyone a pleasant good night as usual. She stepped out of her costume and gave it to Alma, her maid, to slip onto a hanger and take down to the wardrobe department where they would store it overnight. Alma knew that Garbo rarely liked to talk at the end of the working day and today she would be even less inclined to indulge in small talk so she kept her mouth firmly sealed. On the table in the centre of the room was a small but expensive bottle of perfume. Propped up against it was a handwritten card from, though probably not written by, Louis B. Mayer. 'Dear Greta, My sympathy in your sorrow. But the show must go on!' It was quite clear what he felt about Stiller's passing but then, why should he care? After all, it was L.B.'s attitude towards Moje, firing him in the bluntest, most humiliating fashion after ten days on *The Temptress*, that had effectively destroyed his life in Hollywood.

She held it all together until her car turned out of the studio gates. Moje would have been so proud of the way she had behaved during the day, she thought just before the tears started. She hadn't had a life until Mauritz Stiller had found her and given her one at the age of eighteen. Everything she had achieved, at least as an actress, she knew she owed to him. It hadn't been easy, frequently it had been so difficult it had reduced her to tears, but in the end it had worked.

Without subscribing entirely to the methods of acting pro-pounded by the Russian actor and director Konstantin Stanislavski, Stiller had shown Garbo how to strip away the artifice that doomed the work of so many silent-movie stars. The public reacted positively to her because they instinctively recognised the truthful-ness of her performances. Stiller had taught her that as surely as he had taught her which fork to use first at formal dinner parties. And now he was gone and she was alone.

She pulled the car over to the side of the road and began to cry. She didn't bother searching for a handkerchief in her handbag. There would have been no point. The stream of salt water that escaped from her eyes would have required the provision of half a dozen handkerchiefs. She couldn't remember when she had ever cried like this before. She didn't think the pain had been so great when her father had died because the rest of the family was there to share it. It wasn't as great when Alva had died because Moje had been there to protect her.

She needed Yackie now more than ever. In the abyss that seemed to have opened up in front of her she felt an overwhelming longing for the Yackie she had first fallen in love with – the strong, decisive, sensitive Yackie who had backed her in her fight with Mayer, who had patiently taught her how to use her growing star power, who had introduced her to the most interesting people in Hollywood. Maybe she had made a mistake when she had cast him aside because she no longer found his childish ways as amusing as she once had. Even if it was just for a while, she wanted to feel the strength of his arms around her. She turned the car away from Santa Monica and drove north to Sunset and then east to Beverly Hills. For as long as it took to drive to the house on Tower Road she remembered why she had twice accepted his proposal of marriage. Yackie couldn't bring Moje back but being in his arms, she felt, would make the pain go away.

At the time these loving feelings were washing over Greta, Jack was deep in conversation with Nick Schenck and Harry Edington, the influential business manager whose services he and Greta shared. Harry had been in conference with Nick all day, and the two of them had come round to Tower Road to give the good news to Gilbert.

Nicholas Schenck had taken over as head of Loews Inc., MGM's New York-based parent company, when its founder, the well-respected Marcus Loew, had died prematurely in the autumn of 1927. From Jack's point of view it was a highly fortuitous appointment because Schenck and Louis B. Mayer hated each other as fiercely as Mayer hated Jack. Naturally a friendship was easily forged out of the antipathy both men felt for the head of MGM production on the West Coast.

Now Jack got to hear the details of what it was that had so upset both Mayer and Thalberg. He whistled through his teeth when Harry summarised the position.

'William Fox wants to own both his own studio and MGM and he's even made a bid for British Gaumont as well. Nick here has sold enough MGM shares to allow Fox to complete the deal. As soon as it's signed L.B. Mayer is out on his ear.'

'And you're my ace in the hole, Jack,' added Schenck. 'How many pictures did you make last year?'

'Five,' replied Jack, but Harry knew how to press home an advantage.

'In 1924 he made ten. Ten! And they all made money for MGM but Jack didn't get so much as a bonus.'

'Before my time,' countered Schenck holding up his hands.

'Mr Schenck's offered us a three-year contract, Jack.'

'In addition, no more than two pictures a year and you get a quarter of a million dollars for each.'

'The money's the same,' complained Jack. 'Fifty weeks a year at ten grand a week, what's the difference?'

'Yeah, but you made ten pictures in 1924, you had no time to breathe and you were earning five grand a week so you got paid twenty-five thousand dollars a film. I'm offering you a ten-fold increase.'

Harry wasn't going to bite his arm off.

'Nick, United Artists want Jack and they're talking about Jack having total control over script, director and casting.'

'Well, I'm not prepared to go that far. You want to work for a *schmatte* outfit like United Artists or do you want to work for the biggest studio in the world?' The Yiddish vernacular of the rag trade – where so many of the movie moguls had taken their first steps in business – was never very far away.

'Jack wants a non-exclusive deal,' said Harry. Jack nodded. He didn't know why he wanted it, but Harry obviously thought it was important.

'OK. You make those two pictures a year for MGM and you can work for any other studio you want in between MGM engagements.'

'That's great. Jack, no one in Hollywood has a contract like that.'

'What about Mayer?'

'As soon as the deal is signed with Fox, he's out, I told you.' Jack felt like doing the Charleston but decided it was inappropriate in a room with two businessmen.

'I can't wait. Let's crack open some imported champagne and celebrate.'

It was while he was on his way back to the living room with the champagne that the front door opened and Garbo entered. Seeing her tear-stained face, Jack immediately leapt to the conclusion that she had repented of her stupidity and was returning to him to announce her willingness at last to marry him. But by the time she had draped her arms around his neck and was sobbing bitterly into his shoulder he knew he was not capable of arousing this much emotion in her. There had to be another reason.

When he discovered what it was he walked back into the living room, popped the cork and poured the champagne into two flutes he extracted from the carved walnut cabinet.

'Aren't you joining us?' asked Harry, surprised by the sombre look on the face of the man who had left the room two minutes before happy and smiling.

'Flicka's here. Stiller died in Stockholm last night. I'm going to look after her.'

'Where is she?'

'She's gone downstairs to her private suite.'

'I thought she'd moved out.'

'It's her place for as long as she wants it.'

'Tell her we're really sorry.' The two men drained their glasses and made towards the door. 'Is there anything we can do?' Jack shook his head.

'We'll go have dinner, then. Iron out the small print.'

'Thanks, Harry. I'll talk to you in the morning. Thanks for coming round, Nick. Can't wait to go to work at MGM without that bastard Mayer there.'

'February, at the latest, March,' confirmed Schenck. They shook hands in the hall and, as the two men walked through the door held open by Jack's silent Filipino butler, Jack turned on his heel and ran down the stairs to Garbo's private suite two at a time. He met Greta Garbo coming up the stairs one at a time.

'Flicka!'

'I have to go.'

'Where? Why?'

'Home. It was a mistake to come here.'

'What mistake?'

'I need to be alone.'

'No. You need to be taken care of. That's my job.'

He tried to put his arms around her and pull himself to her, but she was now standing on the stair above him and he only succeeded in pulling her bosom into his face, a perfectly pleasant sensation but inappropriate for the current situation. Garbo soon struggled free of his embrace.

'No, Yackie, let me go. I'm sorry, I shouldn't have come here.'

Jack suddenly became incensed by this latest variation of Garbo's unceasing vacillation. Whatever the provocation – and he understood, or at least he told himself he understood, Garbo's devastation at the sudden loss of Stiller – he didn't deserve to have his feelings trifled with like this. Why did she think she could just walk in and out of his life whenever it suited her? Did she not realise the impact such dramatic decisions had on him?

Yes, he thought, as he stood at the open door and watched her reverse her car badly out of the drive, he deserved better. That was the last time she would humiliate him. He was taking the decision. No more Garbo in his life. Enough was enough. He was the biggest male star in Hollywood. He was, by virtue of the contract agreed in his living room that evening, the best-paid actor in the history of the world and he could sleep with any woman he wanted. Except Garbo. And he'd had her and to tell the truth, although he wouldn't because he was a gentleman and gentlemen did not talk of such things unless extremely drunk, she was no great shakes in bed. Anyone who watched her movies and was expecting fireworks would be doomed to the disappointment he frequently felt after making love to her. He was well rid of her. He picked up his little black address book and started to thumb through the pages. This wouldn't take long. Already he felt the first stirrings below the waist.

Garbo arrived home, took off all her clothes and slipped into the bathtub, where she lay for half an hour. She had made her decision and she would no longer be deflected from it. She was going home. She would go to the cemetery where he was buried and she would honour his memory by her presence as she would honour it every day by her professional behaviour for the rest of her life.

She went to see Irving Thalberg the next day to beg for her immediate release. It was unlikely to be granted, but she had already realised from the note that had accompanied his gift that Louis B. Mayer would have no interest in releasing her from her current commitment to *Wild Orchids*. Nor, it soon transpired, did Irving Thalberg. Garbo argued her case as passionately as she could.

'You will have something dead on the screen.'

'I've seen the dailies. You look sensational.'

'That was before the telegram. Now I am dead behind the eyes.'

'I've seen yesterday's work. You're not dead behind the eyes, Greta. You have depths of sorrow such as I have never seen another actress suggest.'

'I didn't sleep last night.'

'I'm sorry. I can have the studio doctor prescribe something for you if you like.'

'Prescribe?'

'A pill. Something to keep you going.'

'No. Thank you.' She could see it was hopeless. Thalberg tried to find some comfort for her.

'Sidney Franklin says he should be finished shooting by the end of November. You'll still be able to go home to Sweden for Christmas.' It was a feeble compensation. She wanted to go home now but she knew what Moje would have demanded of her. She was a professional actress and it was her duty to act professionally. Not for the sake of Metro-Goldwyn-Mayer but for the sake of Greta Garbo – and Mauritz Stiller. As she stood up and walked out of his office, Irving Thalberg couldn't help noticing that, along with her ornate Balinese costume, designed for her by Adrian, Garbo was wearing a pair of carpet slippers.

Garbo walked back down the corridor towards the stage where *Wild Orchids* was continuing in production and realised that she was still wearing her slippers. They felt so comfortable that she was invariably irritated when she had to take them off and replace them with something that hurt her feet. She knew all about the rumours that she had enormous feet, which was why she had teased young Doug Fairbanks about them. The real problem was that they were long and thin with a very high arch and she had enormous trouble finding shoes that would not pinch her feet dreadfully.

Annoyed with MGM for its lack of sympathy for her in her grief, she decided to test the limits of her power and walked onto the set in her slippers.

'Miss Garbo, you're still wearing your slippers,' said the girl who fetched her costume.

'Miss Garbo, would you like me to get your shoes for this scene?' She said nothing and started walking through the sequence with Nils Asther.

'Greta, you're wearing your slippers, you know,' her co-star whispered to her in Swedish. She allowed him the hint of a smile. Sidney Franklin came over to ask if they were ready for him to roll the film camera.

'Sure.'

'Miss Garbo, we'll see your feet in this shot.'

'Bill, can you frame your camera to crop my feets?' she asked. Bill Daniels looked through the viewfinder.

'Sure. OK with you, Sidney?'

'Won't make it a mid-two-shot, will it?' It was a well-known rule at MGM that Garbo looked her best either in tight close-up or in long shot and her worst in a mid-two-shot. Bill Daniels looked through the viewfinder of the camera and tightened the frame sufficiently to crop Garbo's figure just above the ankle.

'No, looks fine to me.'

'OK, I keep the slippers on.' And so she did in pretty much every shot in which her feet did not appear for the rest of her career.

Just as he had promised, Sidney Franklin finished principal photography on *Wild Orchids* by the end of November, but it had not been a happy shoot. Garbo was not going to make life easy for a director whom she compared unfavourably every minute of the working day to her beloved Moje. Franklin knew perfectly well what was going on and resented it. He and his star maintained a professional relationship, but its coldness hardly helped the creation of an exotic atmosphere that was dripping with unresolved sexual tension. Franklin also tried to have himself removed from the picture, but Thalberg wouldn't hear of it.

'Why not, Irving? I know you can't replace her, but you can replace me.'

'I like what you're doing.'

'Any director could do what I'm doing.'

'Don't underestimate yourself, Sidney.'

'Any director can shoot a Garbo picture if Bill Daniels is lighting it.'

'You've got another fourteen shooting days. You'll be fine.'

Fourteen shooting days would take them to the end of principal photography, but Garbo knew perfectly well what would happen then: it was standard MGM policy. After viewing the first assembled cut of the picture, Irving Thalberg would come up with a dozen new ideas of how the film might be improved which involved days of re-takes.

Greta wasn't going to wait around until she was summoned back to the studio. She had been promising herself a trip home for three years and this time she wasn't going to let the studio stop her as they had so often done in the past. She neatly labelled all her trunks with the name 'Alice Smith', boarded the Super Chief at the railway station in Pasadena and hurried across Chicago, where she had to change trains onto the Twentieth Century, hotly pursued by the press, who had been tipped off by a studio spy. To make sure that nothing similar happened at Grand Central Station in New York she disembarked at Croton-Harmon thirty-six miles north of the city and was driven to the Commodore Hotel, where she had stayed with Moje in the summer of 1925. The following morning she embarked on the SS *Kungsholm*, the newest vessel to ply the route between Sweden and the United States.

Her journey across America had been complicated by telegrams from Mayer and Thalberg, pursuing her relentlessly across the continent. THERE IS STILL TIME FOR YOU TO RETURN TO CULVER CITY ... AND MAKE SWEDEN IN TIME FOR CHRISTMAS. RETURN OR GREAT LOSS AND DAMAGE WILL BE CAUSED US. LOUIS B. MAYER What about the loss and damage already caused to me? thought Garbo as she scrunched up the telegram and threw it into the bin where it nestled with the others. On board the *Kungsholm* more frantic radio messages from MGM repeated the same request – and met the same fate. Her Christmas present from MGM was to be placed on suspension, but she no longer cared. She was going home.

Six days before Christmas, as the *Kungsholm* passed the lighthouse that marked the opening of the harbour in Gothenburg, a small pilot boat brought the press out to meet her. Well, thought Greta, they won't be like American journalists. They will be polite and they will respect my desire for privacy. And so they did, as Greta easily fended off their questions about Hollywood. By the time the ship was ready to dock, the band had struck up the Swedish national anthem, and Greta joined with the rest of the passengers as they sang lustily, cheering at its conclusion then leaning over the rail to see the reaction of the crowds lined up on the dockside. She was home.

The feelings of elation lasted scarcely the one night she spent at the Grand Hotel in Gothenburg. She was Sweden's most famous export and an international movie star and as such she was fair game. On the six-hour train journey to Stockholm a flashbulb went off in her face every time the door to her compartment was opened, and she soon realised that life was going to be as difficult for her in Sweden as it already was in America. Her fantasy of the privacy she could expect in Sweden was exposed as exactly that – a fantasy.

On her first full day in Stockholm she discovered that the name of Moje's lawyer and executor was Hugo Lindberg. When she called him on the telephone he told her that all Moje's possessions were in a storage facility. She begged Lindberg to accompany her there to see them.

'You know he didn't leave any of them to you in his will.'

'I still want to see them.'

'They have to be sold to pay off his debts. You do understand that, don't you?'

'Please, I just want to see his things.'

'OK. But just so you know, they're all going in the New Year to be auctioned at Frey's Express.'

'I understand. Please.'

The lawyer watched as Garbo walked round the room uttering faint cries of recognition. She picked up a suitcase and looked at it reverently.

'This is the suitcase he took to America when we left here three years ago.' She stroked the rugs, which she remembered buying when they were in Turkey. It was after *Gösta Berlings Saga* had opened, when Moje still had hopes of making another film himself before the money collapsed and they had to return to Berlin where she was to make *Die Freudlose Gasse* for G.W. Pabst. She spent a long time in that room touching all the furniture and paintings, which brought back to her so vividly the man whom she missed so much. The lawyer looked on, fascinated.

'What are you doing?' he asked.

'I am remembering this room,' replied Garbo. 'In the future, in my memory, I shall live a great deal in this room.'

When she had at last finished her visit, Lindberg suggested they take a taxi back to his office but Garbo declined, preferring to walk. It was a pleasure that had long been denied her in Los Angeles. Lindberg shrugged.

'You'll be followed.'

'Not in Stockholm. So many times I have walked the streets of this city and nobody has ever stopped me before.'

'That was before you went to Hollywood and became the most famous movie star in the world.'

'Not the world. There is always Chaplin.'

'Chaplin's not in Stockholm. You are.'

Lindberg was right. As soon as they were on the street, people recognised her and began to follow them. They walked faster and faster, but the crowd simply grew bigger and bigger. Eventually they did take a taxi because the policeman who was trying to control the crowds told them it was too dangerous for her to be walking the streets in that fashion.

'People are crazy,' she said miserably. Lindberg could only agree.

'Are you going out to see his grave?' he asked. Garbo nodded. I'd better draw you a map. It's not easy to find. Unless you want me to go with you.' This time Garbo shook her head fiercely. That was one trip she knew she must make alone.

'When are you planning to go?' he inquired as he handed over the sketch map.

The traditional time to visit the graves of loved ones in Sweden is Christmas Eve, which was why a crowd of journalists and photographers waited through the bitterly cold day and night for Garbo to arrive. It was, of course, obvious to Garbo that whenever she decided to visit Moje's grave, it was not going to be Christmas Eve for precisely that reason. Besides, Moje was Jewish and was buried in a Jewish cemetery. A visit on Christmas Eve would do nothing for his dear soul, so she resolved to go when she would be assured of maximum privacy.

Hugo Lindberg told Greta that the cemetery was on the north side of Stockholm, appropriately enough within walking distance of the Filmstaden at Rasunda where Moje had directed *Gösta Berlings Saga*, the movie that had started Greta's career in 1923. Sweden had then possessed a thriving film industry, but with Stiller dead and its other significant director, Victor Seastrom, showing scant interest in returning to work, no significant figure had emerged to take their places and the industry was now in decline. It didn't help the native production business that its biggest star was working in Hollywood.

Greta walked into the Judiska Forsamling Begravningsplats and found his grave. In accordance with Jewish tradition, the stone would not be set for some months, which came as something of a surprise to Greta, as did the very look of the cemetery. It was so plain and flat; it was as if the Jews were almost embarrassed by their dead. The lilies she had bought and carried so lovingly looked out of place here and indeed another mourner soon came over to tell her why.

'You're not Jewish, are you?' said the woman sharply.

'No, I'm not,' admitted Greta.

'We don't believe in these,' she said picking up the lilies and thrusting them back into Greta's arms. Greta couldn't help thinking of the moment in *A Woman of Affairs* when she wanders out of her hospital room in a distressed state looking frantically for the flowers that the John Gilbert character has brought her every day. All the critics had seized on it as characteristic of her stellar acting, but it was proving of scant help to her now.

'I was just showing respect.'

'If you want to show respect you do this.' The woman picked up a stone from the ground and placed it on the granite slab.

'Why?'

'It indicates a visitor. You don't need to show off how rich you are.'

'I didn't mean to. I didn't know. Thank you.'

The woman's eyes began to narrow.

'Have we met before?'

'I don't think so. Thank you again.' She started to walk away as briskly as she could before the recognition dawned on her fellow mourner but she had travelled less than fifty yards when the cold air was rent by the scream she had heard so often.

'Oh my God! You're Greta Garbo!'

It's a cemetery, thought Greta. This shouldn't be happening. She broke into a highly undignified run, scattering the lilies as she went. By some lucky chance, a taxi was waiting outside the funeral gates and she escaped without further mishap.

Still, there were plenty of compensations for the loss of privacy. One morning she took a taxi to the place where she had been born and raised, a four-room, cold-water flat on the fourth floor of an anonymous five-storey block. She stood outside and remembered as much as she could, drinking in the sounds and sights that had not changed so much in the nine years since she had lived there as a fourteen-year-old, going off to lather men's beards in the barber shop while dreaming of appearing one day on the stages of Stockholm's best theatres.

Now she could take her mother and her brother Sven to lunch at the Grand Hotel. They were all thrilled to be finally dining in the rococo room with its pink-shaded lights that had always appeared to the Gustaffson family to be the height of elegance. Seated by the obsequious maître d' at the privileged corner table, they dined on caviar and champagne as the string orchestra softly played its familiar medley of music by Johann Strauss, Arthur Sullivan and Franz Lehár.

Garbo revelled in being back in her natural habitat, the city where she had grown up and the countryside beyond, with its red-painted farmhouses and thick forests of fir trees. She hadn't seen snow since she had arrived in southern California. She loved the feel and the sound of it as it crunched under her feet. She rented a car and drove slowly along the snow-packed roads, taking in the sights of the ice-yachting and skate-sailing on the frozen waters of the great Archipelago and the skiing on the hill Fiskartorpet. Like most Swedes Garbo had learned to skate at an early age and was soon luxuriating in the sensation of the cold wind beating against her face as she increased her speed on skates.

These simple familiar pleasures were supplemented by new experiences. She had friends in high society now, men and women of noble birth who threw open their homes to her where previously they would scarcely have acknowledged her existence. Above all there was the theatre. The theatre was the repository of her early dreams, it was the place where she had aspired to spend the rest of her working life, and it was where she had had her first critical break, meeting Moje, who was casting his film version of *Gösta Berlings Saga*.

She went to Oscars Teatern to see Moje's final production, the Swedish version of *Broadway*, but she couldn't enjoy the play. Memories of Moje swept over her, and the audience seemed to spend as much time looking up at her in her box as they did looking at the action on the stage. Afterwards she met up with Abraham Stiller, Moje's younger brother, who had travelled from his home in Helsinki for the specific purpose of meeting her. He was a pleasant, easy-going man, very different from his driven, tortured older brother, but Greta liked him at once and the feeling was mutual. He apologised for the fact that Greta had not been mentioned in Moje's will.

'I know he wanted to make provision for you.'

'He never told me so.'

'It's just that his debts were so heavy and the little that was left was divided between his sister, myself and my brother, as his will dictated. I'm sorry.'

'There is nothing to be sorry about. I didn't want his money. I owe him everything. He owed me nothing.'

Abraham took hold of Greta's hands and looked her clearly in the eye.

'Please, Greta, I think I know how Moje felt about you.'

'It's hard to explain.'

'I'd like it a lot if you could look on me as an uncle, a kindly uncle.'

Greta thought about the relationship for a moment.

'I think,' she said slowly, 'it would be more appropriate if you regarded me as a sister-in-law.'

Abraham Stiller looked surprised.

'But you never . . . surely . . . I mean Moje . . . he wasn't . . . you know . . .' he stammered unhappily until Garbo put him out of his misery.

'I mean only that I regarded myself as a kind of a wife,' she explained. 'I was as close to him as any wife could have been.'

'Of course.' Abraham Stiller looked relieved.

'I want to be buried next to him.'

'Oh, but you can't. You're not Jewish. The synagogue's burial board would never permit such a thing.'

'You know Moje wasn't very Jewish either.'

'I know. Listen, Greta, you are very young.'

'Not so young.'

'What are you? Twenty-five?'

'Twenty-three.'

'Twenty-three!' Abraham Stiller seemed a little shocked. 'At twenty-three you should not be thinking about where you want to be buried. You shouldn't be thinking about death at all. You should be thinking about life and love. I know you have lost your loved ones, but this is no way for a young woman of twenty-three to be thinking. It's New Year's Eve. Who are you going to spend it with?'

There was of course one man, the man she had tried to erase from her mind on the trip, which she had tried to dedicate entirely to the memory of Moje. It was true that Moje was a profound influence on her, but she didn't now have the strength to resist the dawning realisation that the man she had fallen in love with in Hollywood had wormed his way inextricably into her heart and her mind. When she returned to California she resolved to treat him better. The relationship clearly meant a great deal to him, perhaps more than she had permitted herself to reciprocate. The return to Sweden had exorcised some of the Svengali influence Moje had always had over her. It was time for Trilby to fight back.

At five minutes to midnight the telephone rang in the modest apartment at Karlsbergsvagen 52, which Garbo had leased for the duration of her stay in Stockholm. It was the international operator.

'Hello, we are ready with your call to Beverly Hills.'

'Thank you.' Greta waited but heard only silence.

'Hello? Is there anyone there?'

'You wanted "person to person", didn't you, madam?'

'Yes, that's right, person to person,' confirmed Garbo.

'I believe your party is on the line now, madam.'

'Hello,' came a familiar light tenor voice. 'Who's this?'

'Oh, Yackie,' sighed Greta Garbo, 'I miss you so.'

Chapter Ten

It was the sort of prank they both enjoyed. Jack had been the first to suggest it, and Greta seized on the idea eagerly. The whole world seemed to be in a frenzy that Garbo was returning to Hollywood and might even make a talking picture shortly. If MGM needed any convincing that they had under contract the biggest female star in the world then the manner of her departure from Sweden would have reassured them. Despite booking a number of false rail and steamship reservations to confuse the waiting journalists, they still chased her by train from Stockholm to Gothenburg and then onto the *Drottningholm*, the ship she and Moje had taken in July 1925.

It was now March 1929, and Garbo had been away from Hollywood for three months, long enough for her to realise that there was no escape from her celebrity anywhere. She was actually looking forward to returning to California, where she had at least developed a lifestyle that kept the unwanted press and public at bay for most of her waking hours. That was why Jack's suggestion had fallen onto such receptive ground.

MGM was preparing a royal welcome for the return of the studio's queen. Even as the newsreel cameramen, the newspaper reporters and the MGM top brass were lining up on the platform at Union Station in Los Angeles, Garbo and her trunks were being unloaded from the Chief at the railway station in San Bernardino some sixty miles to the east. A smiling, laughing Jack supervised their transport to Beverly Hills and he and his Flicka, carrying Jack's traditional lavish bouquet of roses, jumped into his small open-topped Ford and roared away. The thought of the anger on the face of Louis B. Mayer as soon as he discovered what had happened kept them both in good humour for twenty-five minutes – which was as long as it took for Jack to propose again.

He had sent her cable after cable from the moment he had received her telephone call. He was quite capable of dictating loving messages down the telephone to the cable operator at the same time as his latest conquest was using her mouth to demonstrate how attractive she found him. This wasn't an act of infidelity as far as Jack was concerned. He loved Garbo, this was just sex, and the girl who was supplying it knew that Greta was his one true love. The fact that she was on all fours and he had to breathe deeply to maintain his composure while talking to the international cable operator was perfectly reconcilable with his love for Greta. He doubted Greta would see it exactly the same way so he refrained from giving her the details but he knew from the world's press that she had been going to parties in Stockholm with eligible young men. He could deal with that because he was a man of the world and such well-publicised social occasions merely emphasised how important in the affairs of the world were film stars such as he and Greta.

The initial conversation had been particularly rewarding. When they kissed on the platform it was like they were back in *Flesh and the Devil*. He felt her body respond just as it had during those first amazing love scenes. When they talked – well, to be honest, he did nearly all the talking, but she was lively and animated and interested as he described his first experience of talking into a microphone.

Jack, along with the entire roster of MGM stars, had been roped into a spectacular movie designed to showcase all their talents. It was called *The Hollywood Revue of 1929* and it had been a big hit with audiences who were intrigued to see what their silent heroes and heroines sounded like and who were likely to be the new stars of this era of sound on film.

Jack Benny and Conrad Nagel were the masters of ceremony, and the film featured trick photography – Bessie Love crawling out of Jack Benny's pocket – songs – Joan Crawford singing and dancing to 'Got a Feeling for You' – and comedy – Buster Keaton pre-eminently, but also a neat turn from Marie Dressler, who was got up to look like Botticelli's Venus rising from the waves. At the end Jack described how he and Norma Shearer (who was now married to Irving Thalberg and therefore likely to get all the decent parts which didn't go to Garbo) did the balcony scene from *Romeo and Juliet* first in serious manner and secondly as a send-up, with current vernacular replacing Shakespeare's immortal words.

'How was your voice?' asked Garbo with understandable curiosity.

'It was fine. Everyone seemed to like it.'

'Even when you talked Shakespeare?'

'Well, I was nervous doing the Shakespeare,' he admitted, 'but I relaxed when we were horsing around in the modern speech afterwards.'

'Did your voice change?'

'Well, like I said I became more relaxed but I don't think you can tell the difference.' He was kidding himself, but Garbo wasn't to know.

'What did Mayer think?'

'He never said directly. That's probably a good sign. And Harry says Mayer and Irving are finally discussing my first talker.'

'Did they mention me?'

'Everyone mentions you, Flicka. And when they don't I remind them.'

Garbo laughed and ran her hand down his forearm in what he took to be a gesture of appreciation. Jack felt a prickly sensation sweep through him. It was time for him to make his move.

People loved watching movies almost as much as Jack Gilbert loved making them. He believed in the magical, restorative powers of the movies as deeply as any city housewife or any farmhand who never graduated high school. He spent almost his whole working life making love to attractive young women who always married him at the end. Hollywood's entire *raison d'être* was the happy ending and the fade-out kiss, and the moment he heard Greta Garbo's voice that New Year's Eve he knew they were destined to spend the rest of their lives together.

Jack knew the course of true love didn't necessarily run smoothly. That was what three-quarters of all movies were about, but he also knew that when the audience knew that it was right for two people to be together forever then the two lovers were bound to each other by hoops of steel. With that sort of reasoning behind him, it was obvious that he only had to keep asking Garbo to marry him and she would do so. Of course her saying 'yes' by no means guaranteed that a wedding would follow, but it was an acceptable first stage in the long negotiation. He thought he might try an original approach this time. After all, he was thirty and a man of his now mature years had to take the big issues of life seriously. He had spent a lot of time thinking about Greta as a mother of his children and though he already had a charming daughter called Leatrice by his second wife of the same name, he hadn't, if he were being honest with himself, been a very good parent.

With Garbo there was the chance to wipe the slate clean. This time round he was going to be a terrific dad – a dad who wouldn't leave everything to the nannies that Hollywood stars liked so much. He would take his kids to baseball games and things like that, play in the back yard with them, teach them to swim – physical, manly things where they would learn to adore their poppa while their beautiful mother looked on from the sidelines. Yes, Jack Gilbert and Greta Garbo would have the greatest children in the world because they were the most romantic couple in the world. This scenario had an inevitability to it that nobody could argue with. It reinforced the feeling he had always had that he and Flicka were meant for each other.

'Flicka, I've been thinking a lot about us.'

'Yes?'

'Yes, especially about our raising kids together. I know you didn't have a happy childhood and neither did I, but together with our fame and our money and our good looks we can do better, we can have a great family.'

'I do not want children.' Jack affected not to hear her demurring. He was too carried away by the force of his own eloquence.

'Flicka, I love you so much, I've been going crazy these past three months.'

'Yackie, you are crazy anyway.'

'Crazy enough to ask you to marry me for the third time?'

'No.'

'You're right. It's the fourth time, isn't it? Is that counting the time I proposed to you live on national radio at the premiere of *Flesh and the Devil*?

'No. I mean no.'

'Well, third time or fourth time, who's counting?'

'Enough, Yackie.'

'You bet it's enough. One time is usually enough for most couples.'

'I do not wish to marry any man.'

Jack froze. He couldn't believe what he was hearing.

'Are you turning me down again?'

'Yes. For the third time or the fourth time. Why won't you believe me when I tell you? I don't want to marry you because I don't want to get married.'

'Stiller's dead for Christ's sake.'

'I know that. I still don't want to marry you.'

'Then I don't want your things in the house any longer. I don't want you coming to the log cabin or anything.'

'OK. I understand. Please just take me to the hotel.'

'Fine,' said Jack through gritted teeth. Things were very far from being fine.

'Not the Miramar,' said Garbo unexpectedly. 'I'm going to move into the Beverly Hills Hotel.'

Jack looked at her, astonished. This most private of people was choosing to live in the most public of hotels. It made no sense. There must be another man. Garbo anticipated his next question.

'There is no other man. I just want a small change of scenery.'

Jack drove her back into Los Angeles and dropped her off at the Beverly Hills Hotel without a word. All the way from Pomona he kept his eyes fixed on the road, refusing to turn his head towards her or even acknowledge her presence. Garbo soon adjusted to the silence. She didn't like the tension in the air but she couldn't have handled him proposing to her again so, frankly, total silence was the lesser of two evils.

Greta would never go near the swimming pool at the hotel and she arranged to have all her meals served in her suite so she would not have to use the dining room either. If she did have to use the lobby she walked through it at great speed, heading directly for the elevator with the brim of her hat pulled down low over her eyes.

Even these precautions were insufficient to completely isolate her from her fans, who soon discovered the location of her new living quarters. The lobby was large and anonymous enough for the most determined of them to sit there all day, waiting for the arrival of the object of their desire. Garbo could spot them at a distance of fifty feet and breezed past their imprecations affecting a selective deafness.

One morning one of them arrived at seven o'clock and took up residence in a chair that allowed her to stare at the ever opening and closing doors of the elevator. After more than five hours her vigil was rewarded as Garbo strode from the elevator, through the lobby and out towards her car, which the chauffeur had waiting for her at the front entrance. The fan pursued her idol, who as usual pretended not to notice her. This one, however, was different. Undaunted by the lack of any reaction, she raced down the long, sweeping drive ahead of Garbo's car and disappeared into the shrubbery.

As the car approached, the fan leaped from the bushes and threw herself into the road. Garbo's chauffeur braked sharply and brought the large car to a screeching halt inches from the prostrate body of the fan. The girl made a rapid recovery, got to her feet and dashed to the window producing a pen and piece of paper from somewhere, which she thrust into Garbo's face.

'Please may I have your autograph?' she asked, the very combination of words that Garbo usually dreaded. This time Garbo was forced into an involuntary reaction.

'Gott!' she exclaimed. 'Are you all right?'

'Oh yes,' said the fan in a tone of voice that suggested that death was a small price to pay for such a highly prized autograph.

'Good. Now you can drive on,' Greta said to her chauffeur as zealous doormen from the hotel seized the girl. She was devastated. She had a good idea to switch her allegiance to Marlene Dietrich.

Garbo meanwhile decided to switch her allegiance from the Beverly Hills Hotel to a small, furnished house Harry Edington had found for her to rent in Chevy Chase Drive. It was a conventional two-storey structure of the Spanish style so popular in California in the 1920s. She remembered with an amused shudder her reply to one of the first questions put to her as she stepped off the train in Pasadena with Moje back in 1925. A reporter asked the traditional question, 'Where do you want to live?' expecting the conventional answer of 'A big house in the Hollywood Hills like Douglas Fairbanks and Mary Pickford', but instead she gave what, given her modest upbringing, seemed to her an entirely reasonable answer, 'I would like to find a room with a nice quiet family,' thereby earning herself instant popularity among those reporters who struggled to create two paragraphs from the standard replies that actresses usually parroted at them.

Now she had her own house but something inside her prevented her from turning it into a home. It had eight rooms and three bathrooms; she had no need of such expansive accommodation so she closed off the upstairs and pretty much lived on the ground floor. There was a living room, a dining room, a kitchen and a library besides the servants' quarters, which were soon occupied by a Swedish couple who were failed actors rather than true domestics. For Garbo, though, their Swedish ancestry was sufficient recommendation.

She moved all her possessions into the house, but they only amounted to one trunk, three suitcases and a few boxes. A single taxi was able to take them from the apartment at the Miramar Hotel to the house in Chevy Chase Drive. She was more interested in the question of privacy and one reason why she had taken the house was that the garden at the rear of the house was shaded by lemon trees, offering some protection for when she chose to sunbathe in the nude. In addition, at the far end of the garden, beyond the swimming pool, there was a rose-covered cement wall, which separated her property from that of her next-door neighbour. She hoped she might be able to persuade her neighbour to erect something just as substantial on his side.

The privacy she sought so fiercely in her domestic environment was given a boost when the studio realised that her absence for three months had actually caused her fan mail to increase and the newspapers continued to write about her even though she wasn't on the same continent. Thalberg tried hard to convince Mayer that MGM could actually profit from Greta Garbo's notorious loathing of publicity.

'It works just as well for us as it does for her,' he explained enthusiastically.

'She won't talk to the magazines or the press or the radio,' complained Mayer. 'How does that work for us?'

'You have to appreciate the angle they've taken. Look at this stuff.' Thalberg spread out on Mayer's desk the three most recent articles, which the publicity department had sent him. 'The Woman Who Lives Behind A Wall' contained an interview with the couple whose property abutted Garbo's, while 'Hollywood's Number One Mystery' and 'The Scandinavian Sphinx' expounded at considerable length on the riddle wrapped in a mystery inside an enigma that was Greta Garbo.

'They just love her and the less she cooperates the more they seem to love her. They don't expect her to cooperate any more, so when she doesn't they don't think she's snooty, they just think she's Garbo and that's what Garbo does.'

Mayer wasn't convinced.

'I liked it better when she did those photos with the USC football team.'

'Track team,' corrected Thalberg, 'and she hated them.'

'Who cares what she thinks? She's an actress, for Christ's sake!'

Despite his studio's claim that MGM had more stars than there were in heaven, L.B. Mayer always resented his studio's reliance on them. Twenty years before, in the early days, when he was desperate to break into the new movie industry and get out of the scrap-metal business, there were no stars. It was his rival Carl Laemmle, founder of Universal Studios, who had started the idea by publicising the real name of Florence Lawrence. She had previously been known only as 'The Biograph Girl', after the name of the company that made the films she appeared in.

Soon it was realised that the stars were what the public came to see and ownership of these actors gave producers power. It was just unfortunate that this power was such a double-edged sword, granting stars who were not afraid to use their own negotiating strength the ability to irritate hard-working, decent businessmen like himself who were just trying to scrape an honest dime. Thalberg looked at the scowl on Mayer's face and knew exactly what he was thinking.

'Don't worry about it, L.B. Trust me. It'll work out. When are you leaving for the White House?'

Mayer beamed at his young colleague.

'Tuesday. We go to the Inauguration Ball and we get to stay over in the Lincoln bedroom.'

'That's great. It's the least you deserve after all the work you did for Hoover.' It was true: Mayer's energetic work on Herbert Hoover's campaign had helped to win the 1928 presidential election for the Republican, and Hoover had recognised that. Even Thalberg was impressed, and emitted a low whistle.

'Can you imagine? Me, Lazar Meir, the peddler's son from Kiev!'

'America is a wonderful country, L.B.'

'Hoover says I'm gonna be the first guy to sleep over at the White House during his presidency.'

'It's great that Washington understands the power of Hollywood.'

'Washington won't be allowed to forget it, let me tell you. That's why I'm not going to be messed around by a Garbo or a Gilbert. They get any more ideas and I'm gonna put them in a crappy talker. That'll finish them off.'

Thalberg knew perfectly well that Mayer would never dare to jeopardise his own investment like that but he knew, too, that Mayer made an unforgiving enemy and that he fought every battle until he felt he had emerged triumphant.

Back at the house on Chevy Chase Drive, Gustaf, the butler, kept his new mistress constantly supplied with the latest fan magazines so she could appreciate the success of her strategy. She lay on her stomach like a young girl, turning the pages of the fan magazines and carefully marking the article 'Why Garbo Has Never Married' by Marcella Burke.

'Gustaf, cut this one out and send it to my mother.'

'A parcel arrived from Stockholm this morning. Shall I bring it, madam?'

'Oh yes, it's the Swedish magazines. My mother always sends me all the articles about me they print in Sweden. What's this?' Garbo held up two identical copies of *Modern Screen*.

'I'm sorry, madam. I must have bought two copies of the same magazine.'

'Then you must take them back to the store and get a refund.'

'They're only twenty-five cents, madam.'

'And while you're there you'd better ask for the money back on this one too.' She tossed a copy of *Silverscreen* at him.

'I only bought one copy of that, madam.'

'I know, but there's nothing about me in it. It's a waste of money.'

Gustaf and Sigrid, the cook, could not understand the extraordinary frugality of Garbo's ways. She gave them a hundred dollars a month for all household expenses including food and insisted on a receipt for every purchase, but when Gustaf proudly showed her the little black book and the accounts which demonstrated that they had managed to spend only eighty-five dollars that month, Garbo complained they had still been too free in their use of her money.

Her eccentricity and her desire to retreat from society grew constantly. In her work she remained as dedicated and serious-minded as ever, but her idiosyncrasies multiplied. The possibility of playing male roles, something she had thought of occasionally before, became a more serious interest. She was fascinated by the thought of Dorian Gray, Hamlet or St Francis of Assisi. She mentioned them to Maria Huxley, who thought her husband Aldous might want to write one of the screenplays, but he demurred, particularly at the idea that Garbo might play the saint. 'Is she going to wear the full beard?' he asked, pondering whether being associated with such an absurdity would be good for his career.

Every summer the actor Basil Rathbone and his wife Ouida hosted the most glamorous fancy-dress balls in Hollywood. During a costume fitting for her new film *The Single Standard*, Gilbert Adrian told Garbo he would design a Hamlet outfit for her if she would agree to accompany him to the next Rathbone ball. Adrian expected the traditional blanket Garbo refusal, but the prospect of going as the Prince of Denmark intrigued her.

'Can I see the costume first?' she asked. Adrian nodded and within days had fitted her for black satin trousers, full-sleeved blouse and circular collar. Garbo loved it and spent the evening toying with the dagger in her belt and causing, just as she had planned, much discussion as to the identity of the slim young man in the costume of the melancholy Prince of Denmark. It was all going swimmingly until she was spotted by Henry VIII and his daughter, Elizabeth I.

'Shit!' said the king. 'It's Garbo.'

'Where?' asked the puzzled Gloriana.

'In the Hamlet costume.'

'That guy?'

'It's not a guy, it's Garbo.'

'How can you tell?'

'I fucked her, for God's sake!'

'You told me you fucked Florence Nightingale and the Empress Josephine.'

'I did.'

'Is there anyone at this party you haven't fucked?'

'Yes. The Hunchback of Notre Dame.'

'Thank God.'

'Come on, I want to introduce you.' He tapped Hamlet on the shoulder. The troubled Dane swung round.

'Hello, Flicka.' There was a pause before the famous guttural voice decided to admit its identity.

'Hello, Yackie.'

'This is Queen Elizabeth, otherwise known as Ina Claire.'

'Please do not tell anyone else. I want to see how long I can keep my identity a secret.'

'If it's any comfort, everyone is talking about you but no one knows.'

'That's why I want to keep it a secret.'

'Well, that's fine, but we have a secret of our own, don't we, Ina?' He laughed rather harshly and steered her away, hoping to have left a devastated Garbo in his wake, but Garbo was used to Jack's ways and continued to enjoy the disguise until she was publicly unmasked by the extrovert lesbian, Lilyan Tashman. After that, much to the irritation of its hosts, the party descended into nothing more than a gossip about Jack Gilbert's obvious attempt to flaunt his latest conquest in front of the woman with whom he was still clearly in love. Hamlet left since there was no longer any point to the evening, and Henry VIII dragged his daughter out to the pool, where they indulged in some entirely inappropriate, indeed positively incestuous, behaviour.

On the following Monday, early in the morning, Garbo strode out to the car and found a newspaper on the driver's seat. Gustaf hurried behind clutching the brown bag containing the lunch Sigrid had cooked for her. Garbo didn't see why she should spend her hard-earned money on subsidising the MGM studio canteen. She picked up the *Los Angeles Herald Examiner* and began to read as Gustaf drove along the deserted Washington Boulevard towards Culver City.

'Is this your newspaper, Gustaf?'

'Yes, Miss Garbo.'

'Do you buy one every day?'

'Yes, Miss Garbo.'

'Have you finished with it by the time you pick me up?'

'Yes, Miss Garbo.'

'Good. Then leave it on the table next to my bed.'

'Yes, Miss Garbo.'

Having devised this plan, which would save her over twenty dollars during the course of the year, Garbo felt particularly pleased with life. Her career seemed stable, she had money in the bank for the inevitable rainy day, she had laid a few demons to rest in

Sweden, and best of all she wasn't being constantly swept off her feet, proposed to or in some way attacked by Jack Gilbert.

She was on her way to Catalina Island for the location shooting of *The Single Standard*, in which she was to play her first American role. She liked the script because it posed a question she thought highly relevant to life in America in 1929: can there be a single standard for both sexes when mothers are judged in a different way from fathers? It was based on a controversial series of articles in *Cosmopolitan* by Adela Rogers St Johns and at Thalberg's suggestion the writers who had adapted them for the screen had added a number of touches that audiences were bound to recognise as being extracted from Garbo's life. The star was so comfortable with her life that she agreed to everything. The boat that her character and her character's lover sail away on is called *All Alone*, and she expresses her desire for privacy in a number of different scenes. Above all, Arden Stuart, the character she was to portray in *The Single Standard*, was a warm and sympathetic one. Garbo thought that at last she had succeeded in convincing Irving Thalberg that she should play 'no more bad womens'.

Yes, life was good, mused the twenty-three-year-old woman with unusual serenity. Idly she picked up her 'free' newspaper and was immediately confronted by the stark shocking headline: JOHN GILBERT TO WED INA CLAIRE. Her stomach was churning. She felt as if she had been hit by a truck. She read on in sickening realisation that she was not over Yackie. She was not over Yackie at all.

Chapter Eleven

~~~~~

Ina Claire was a big star but only on Broadway and to Greta's amazement she was thirty-seven years old. How . . . ? She could barely frame the question, she found it all so upsetting.

It came as a shock to almost everyone, not just Garbo. Jack and Ina had known each other less than six weeks when Jack proposed. By his standards that was quite average, but coming so quickly after the break-up with Garbo, everyone, including the happy couple, was asking if it was for real. Presumably they answered their own question with a rousing affirmative.

Ina had been married to a journalist but had been divorced for a few years. She was slim, blonde, attractive and sophisticated. She mixed easily with everyone and was such a contrast to the moody, anti-social Swede with whom he had been obsessed for the past two and a half years that Jack found himself immediately attracted to her. She was interested in other people and found their company engaging and if she didn't, she was quite capable of acting her way through the encounter. Jack found this urbanity adorable. Ina wasn't part of the silly, trivial crowd of Hollywood actresses with whom he had spent so much of his recent life. Ina read books, not just scripts, and could hold meaningful conversations about matters other than show-business gossip, although she made a pretty good fist of that too. Ina was the child of theatrical parents, just as he was, and her childhood had been just as miserable as his. Their lack of formal education made them both thirsty for knowledge. They made an excellent match, he felt.

The only person in Hollywood who wasn't surprised by the bald announcement in the newspapers was Harry Edington. He was talking about it in his office when the telephone rang. It was a person-to-person call from a Miss Alice Smith on Catalina Island.

164

He knew who that was all right. He had been expecting it since the moment he had heard the news.

'Hi, Greta,' he greeted his most famous client as if it were to be a normal conversation.

'Harry, Yackie is going to marry this Ina person,' came the wail down the line.

'Ina Claire. Yeah, I know.'

'Who is she?'

'She's a big Broadway star, Greta.'

'I mean, who is she that she can marry Yackie just like that?'

'Well, I guess they love each other.'

'But Yackie loves me.'

'*Did* Greta. He did love you. He loved you for a long time.'

'We are lovers. We belong together.'

'Greta, I understand you're upset . . .'

'You have to stop it, Harry.'

'Stop what?'

'The wedding. You have to tell Yackie no, you cannot marry this Ina.'

'Greta, I'm his business manager. I can't tell Jack what to do in his private life.'

'Then who will stop this terrible marriage?'

'I guess the finger points pretty firmly at you.'

'Me?' Greta was shocked.

'You're the ex-lover. If he's gonna listen to anyone, it's gonna be you.'

'But I am shooting *The Single Standard* on Catalina.'

'I know. How's that going, by the way?'

'Harry, please, you can't let this happen.'

'Greta, I'm the best man. We're going off to Las Vegas so they can tie the knot.'

'It will be a disaster if Yackie marries that woman.'

'You're not thinking of doing anything, are you?' asked Edington a little uneasily. It would not help his professional reputation if one of his clients were to burst into the wedding of another of his clients and shoot him dead. However, having shuddered at the prospect for a moment, he started to think that, since there was no such thing as bad publicity and he was representing Garbo for free . . . A shriek down the phone from Garbo interrupted his reverie.

'This wedding cannot go ahead. Yackie loves me and nobody else.' The line went dead.

Harry Edington took the white handkerchief from the top pocket of his jacket and wiped it carefully round his neck. He was dripping with sweat. He had thought the affair between Garbo and Gilbert was finally over. Jack had told him as much and since Jack had always been the one carrying the torch, it seemed reasonable to suppose that he was telling the truth. They had certainly seemed a hot item for many months, but Edington was an experienced observer of the Hollywood scene and he knew that actors who got involved with each other when working together soon found other diversions when they were paired with different actors on their next film.

More cynically, Hollywood couples could also decide to move on once the publicity bandwagon had grown tired of them. He knew that didn't apply in the case of Garbo and Gilbert. Jack had been genuinely, overwhelmingly, in love with her, and she had never wanted the publicity bandwagon to come calling in the first place. So, what was he to do? He was Jack's best man, and they were leaving that afternoon on the train for Las Vegas, Nevada. Garbo was his most famous client, and he didn't want to upset her either.

In the taxi on the way to the railway station he came to a decision. He would say nothing of Garbo's telephone call to Jack. If the marriage to Ina Claire were to have the slightest chance of succeeding then it had to be allowed to stand on its own two feet. Any mention that Garbo was still interested in him and Jack would physically turn the train round on its rails and they'd all be heading back to Hollywood and disaster. No, he owed it to Jack, whom he genuinely liked, to let the marriage go ahead and give him a chance to get over Garbo.

On the other hand it was quite clear that Garbo was the love of his life, not Ina Claire, and now it appeared that maybe he was the love of her life. They were both his clients. He could act Cupid in a way few business managers would ever be in a position to duplicate. The prospect tantalised him until the train drew into Las Vegas.

As the happy couple and the rest of the wedding party emerged from the Las Vegas town hall it seemed as though the entire population of the small Nevada town had turned out to acclaim them. They followed them down the street into the hotel where the wedding breakfast had been arranged. Harry had ordered three dozen bottles of champagne to be served to the guests, but if everyone in town wanted to join in the toast that supply would soon be exhausted.

A reporter asked Ina naïvely what it was like to be married to a great star. Everyone in the wedding party held their breath. This apparently straightforward question was pregnant with ghastly possibilities. A momentary shadow of pain passed over Ina's radiant features before they were frozen dead in a smile of the purest ice.

'I don't know,' she said sweetly to the young reporter with his pen hovering over his new notebook. 'Why don't you ask Mr Gilbert?' There was a pause as everyone waited for Jack's response. Two seconds later came that loud, distinctive laugh and the flashing of his dazzling white teeth. In those two seconds Harry figured the marriage would last between a year and eighteen months. Fortunately the happy couple were not disposed to stay too much longer in Las Vegas and they soon left for the chartered plane that would take them all back to Hollywood and sanity.

Ina had arrived on the West Coast to make sound films. There was a desperate shortage of stage-trained actors in Hollywood, and it was widely believed that their voices would be necessary to save the industry. Ina Claire certainly believed it and she made many helpful suggestions to her new husband as they ran through his lines together.

'You need more of a pear-shaped tone, honey.'

'A what?'

'A pear-shaped tone. You have a white voice.'

'A light voice?'

'No, a white voice.'

'What the fuck's that?'

'It's a thin voice that comes from the throat instead of here.' Ina pointed to her diaphragm.

'Listen, lady, I think you sometimes talk out of your ass, but not out of there.'

'Jack, you wouldn't last five minutes on Broadway with a voice like yours.'

'Thanks, that's a big help.'

'I mean, you have to strain to be heard at the back of the Shubert Theater but you should be OK with a microphone in a studio.'

'Even with a white voice?'

'Well, you can do something about it. That's why I'm trying to help.'

'Look, sweetheart, I'm Jack Gilbert. Women line up in their millions all over the world to see my movies. Why do you think me talking out of my belly's gonna make any more of them pay their quarters?'

'I'm just trying to help.'

'MGM have hired a voice coach for me. I don't need your help.'

'You haven't made a sound movie before.'

'I've made ninety movies and I know every bit of this goddamn business like the back of my hand.'

'Except sound.'

'Nobody knows shit about sound. So how come I'm worse off than any other silent-movie star?'

'I didn't say you were . . .'

'It won't be a problem – it's Tolstoy. They loved me in *Anna Karenina*. You remember that, right? They like me in these wild parts. I've got Eleanor Boardman as the wife and Renée Adorée as the gypsy sweetheart, and Mayer's assigned Lionel Barrymore to direct. Not even you can object to that 'cause he's a famous Broadway star and he knows how to talk out of his ass like you . . .'

'OK, Jack, OK. I really didn't mean to upset you.'

'Why don't you go and learn your own lines?'

'Because I've already . . . That's a good idea,' Ina conceded. 'I have to meet with Harold Grieve. I'll see you at dinner.'

Ina had hired Grieve, a highly successful interior decorator, to remodel the house on Tower Road. Jack had originally built it in a fit of artistic immaturity for himself and Garbo, who as far as Ina could see, had absolutely no taste whatsoever and had done nothing to impose common sense and good taste on Jack. It was up to her to do so. She was already thinking she should persuade Jack to build on another wing so she could still play her piano when Jack was in one of his moods. Even Ina, who knew all about the ups and downs of careers in show business, was starting to become less than enchanted with the extremes of emotion that Jack displayed. A good review would send him soaring into the sort of ecstasy that needed no companion, whereas an unkind phrase could plunge him into a pit where no companion would ever venture.

Ina was determined to sort Jack out. His legendary affairs had never really grown into a relationship of any substance. His first marriage to a Southern belle called Olivia Burwell was arranged quickly in 1917 when he had just been called up to serve in the Great War and he was convinced he was going to die in France. In fact the influenza virus caused his conscription to be delayed until 11 November 1918, after which his services as a soldier were no longer required. The marriage ended shortly afterwards. His second marriage to the actress Leatrice Joy lasted slightly longer but was undermined by her frequent disappearances to star in films for Cecil B. DeMille and by his own promiscuity. Garbo had shown absolutely no interest in anything about the house on Tower Road, despite the annexe and the Swedish forest that Jack had constructed for her. He had never known the bliss of a woman's touch in the home.

Jack was quite happy for Ina to busy herself with domestic matters. He had far too many career worries to preoccupy him. Above all he was concerned about Louis B. Mayer. Jack did feel that MGM had chosen his first sound movie carefully. There was just one significant problem – L.B. Louis B. Mayer had supposedly been on his way out of the studio in March 1929. All the industry gossip had confirmed what Harry and Nick Schenck had told him the day he had shaken hands on his new deal: William Fox was determined to take over MGM and merge it with his own studio. There would be room for the Boy Genius Thalberg in the ranks of the new super-studio's top executives, but not for L.B. Mayer.

Nick Schenck, Mayer's rival in New York, and Harry Edington, who had created the deal that offered Jack a future at MGM without his nemesis, had reckoned, however, without L.B.'s connections in Washington. Perhaps more significantly, William Fox was involved in a terrible car crash that had incapacitated him at the very moment that the deal needed Fox's ratification. The merger collapsed, MGM survived, and Louis B. Mayer strengthened his position there, having achieved a notable victory over Nick Schenck.

When Mayer got wind of Jack's new contract he was burning with rage. Then he discovered that Schenck had also offered Thalberg $250,000 for his silent approval of the merger and the boiler was stoked even more furiously. He had never trusted Thalberg much anyway. Now he knew he was a rat. As for Gilbert, the very idea that his studio was paying that degenerate bum $250,000 for each of six pictures and his lawyers had assured him it was watertight ... Words failed him. If there was one thing he could do to acquire some small measure of revenge for all these slights, it was to destroy Jack Gilbert's career. He set about it with a will.

It was true that Lionel Barrymore had been a Broadway actor, a member of that royal family of Broadway, the Barrymores, along with his brother John and his sister Ethel. However, Lionel liked Hollywood. His siblings merely tolerated it, rather like Ina Claire, as a place in the sunshine they came to in order to make some easy money and snigger at the fools who thought it was difficult. Lionel liked working at MGM and he liked L.B. Mayer.

'Lionel,' Mayer had said, as he took his famous new star on a tour of the factory, 'I love talent like yours. I worship at the feet of talent. You just need to be careful about that stuff you're using.'

'The morphine?' Barrymore was shocked. How did Mayer know about that? 'It's just medicinal,' he blustered. 'I have this terrible arthritis and my wife thought ...' Mayer stopped walking, turned and looked up at the taller man, fixing him with a glare that

Barrymore, for all his technique honed over forty years, could never match.

'I don't care what you do as long as you're not unfit for work at MGM. I'm planning to pay you more money than you've ever known in your life.'

'Well, gee, L.B., it's hard to know how to say thank you when you talk like that.'

'I don't want you to say thank you.'

'Then what do you want?' he asked suspiciously. Lionel Barrymore had been around show-business folks for long enough to know that self-interest lay behind most declarations of devotion.

'I want your loyalty.'

'That's it?'

'That's it. Some day I might need you to do me a favour.'

'L.B., you have my assurance. When that day comes you can rely on me.'

And now that day was here. Mayer had been as good as his word: Barrymore's career had received a sharp boost when he wound up on the MGM payroll. He had played the role of the on-screen director in the balcony scene from *Romeo and Juliet*, which Jack had played with Norma Shearer in MGM's showcase *The Hollywood Revue of 1929*, but now L.B. had a real director's job for him.

'I want you to direct Jack Gilbert's first talker.' Barrymore was shocked.

'Me? I've never directed a movie before.'

'Yes, you have. You directed some movie or other back in 1917.'

'Yeah, before the Russian Revolution. I hoped everyone had forgotten about it. It wasn't a hit.'

'Maybe, but you're a great stage actor. Gilbert's a movie star. He needs your guidance.'

'He needs help with the dialogue maybe, but me to direct?' Barrymore was clearly uncomfortable. Mayer tried to persuade him by referring to the story in glowing terms.

'It's by Tolstoy,' he proclaimed proudly. He knew Tolstoy was a good thing. 'It's called *The Living Corpse*.'

'I've never heard of it.'

'Me neither, but Irving thinks it can be as big a hit as the other Tolstoy we did with Gilbert. You were in that. You remember how big that was?'

'Sure, but that had Garbo in it. Is she in this one?'

'No, we're not ready to let her talk yet. But you've got a great cast – Eleanor Boardman plays the nice wife and Renée Adorée is the other dame. Oh, and Conrad Nagel's her second husband when she thinks Gilbert's dead.'

'Sounds great, but I still don't think you need me.'

'You didn't get on with Jack when you acted with him.'

'Everyone gets on with Jack.'

'That's not what I heard.'

Barrymore didn't know exactly what Mayer had heard and had no idea what Mayer was expecting him to say.

'OK, he can be a little bombastic at times . . .'

Mayer wasn't interested in generalities.

'You remember that time we walked round the studio and I told you that all I wanted from you was loyalty?'

'Sure, I remember. But haven't I always been loyal, L.B.?'

'I'm talking about now. Now's the time I need you. I want to give Mr Gilbert a kick up the backside.'

'You don't need my help for that. You've kicked every ass on the lot at one time or another.'

'Gilbert thinks he's untouchable. He thinks the public loves him.'

'They do. We all know that.'

'They don't know what he sounds like.'

'His voice is fine. We all know how he talks. He's going to be fine.'

'Not necessarily.'

Mayer turned to face Barrymore and waited for the response. Slowly it dawned on the actor what he was being asked to do. He wasn't thrilled.

'You want me to ruin his first talker?'

'Doesn't have to be ruined. He just needs a kick up the backside like I say. If the public don't like his voice when they first hear it, that will give Mr Gilbert a big shock. It might be bad for that movie, but he'll recover.'

'Why me?'

'Because he trusts you. You're a Broadway actor. You know about voices and you'll have the best sound technicians on the lot.'

'I thought you'd want the worst.'

'Oh no!' Mayer's face cracked into a huge grin. 'That's the whole point. Gilbert will know we gave him everything we could – great story, great cast, great director, great sound crew – and it's still a stinker.'

'In which case the only person Jack'll be able to blame is himself,' concluded Barrymore.

'Exactly.' Mayer beamed.

'Does Irving Thalberg know about this?' Mayer's eyes narrowed.

'That sonofabitch!' he screamed. 'Did you know what that Nick Skunk did? He paid the Boy Genius a quarter of a million dollars not to tell me he was planning to sell the studio to Fox. Well, he can take the consequences now. I'm in charge and I'm staying in charge. Are you with me or against me?'

Barrymore knew that he had little choice. If he said 'no' his own career would mysteriously disintegrate. If he helped to destroy Gilbert, at least the good scripts would keep coming his way. He was nearly sixty years old. He had no plans to retire.

'I'm with you, L.B.,' he declared, as convincingly as he could.

Jack was not as thrilled as Mayer hoped he might have been when he learned the identity of the director who had been assigned to his first sound film, now called *Redemption* rather than *The Living Corpse*. He immediately suspected a plot and went straight to his manager. Harry was no more pleased than his client, but he tried hard to calm Jack's fears.

'Sonofabitch Mayer wants to destroy me.'

'Look, everyone's jittery about the impact these talkers will have. Mayer and Thalberg have got millions tied up in you. They want it to work as badly as you do.'

'Not Mayer! He wouldn't care if *Redemption* was a flop if he could use it to break my contract.'

'Exactly. But he can't break the contract. We know that. He has to pay you for six pictures at two hundred and fifty thousand dollars a pop.'

'He could just pay off the contract.'

'Can you see L.B. Mayer handing you a cheque for a million and a half dollars and telling you to go off and have a long vacation at his expense? I don't think so.'

Jack accepted the logic of what Harry was saying but he was still fearful of what that first sound movie might do to his career. He knew that look of implacable cold hatred that Mayer gave him whenever they bumped into each other on the lot. It was not the look of a man who was carefully shepherding his biggest male star through a difficult period to preserve his integrity. It was the look of a man who couldn't wait to see his biggest male star shafted and to hell with the expense.

Lionel Barrymore was so nervous that he was removed as the director halfway through the shooting of *Redemption*. His replacement was Fred Niblo, who had done such a sterling job in similar circumstances when he had replaced Stiller after the latter had been fired from Garbo's second American movie. *The Temptress* had been a big hit and had unleashed the Garbo phenomenon on the world. *Redemption*, on the other hand, was a complete disaster. It was turgid, it was slow and it was boring. Some of its problems were technical. Neither the camera nor the microphone could move. The camera, encased in a booth to stop the noise of its mechanism from being picked up by the microphones strategically placed around the set, was stationary. Actors had to stand near the piece of furniture behind which the all-important microphone was hidden. The motion-picture camera had almost become a contradiction in terms. It was like watching a bad play from the stalls without the benefit of being in a live theatre with actors performing only a few feet away.

Jack watched the finished movie in a small viewing theatre on the MGM lot with growing horror. When the lights went up Fred Niblo sat with his head in his hands and Irving Thalberg sank back further into the folds of his luxurious armchair. Jack decided on a bold course of action. Though he would never give Louis B. Mayer the satisfaction of hearing him say it, he felt guilty for having taken money for such a dreadful movie. It must never see the light of day or the darkness of another projection room. He leapt to his feet.

'Irving, you gotta let me buy it.'

'Huh?'

'I want you to destroy all the prints and let me buy the negative.'

'Why?'

'Why? So I can take it on a boat to Catalina and dump it into the Pacific Ocean.' Fred Niblo took his head out of his hands and spoke up in agreement.

'For what it's worth, I agree with Jack. I don't think I've ever seen a worse picture. Please, Irving, just shelve it.'

'Jack, it's my fault. I shouldn't have gone for Tolstoy.'

'That's good of you, Irving.'

'I'm thinking now your first sound movie should be a comedy, something light-hearted.'

'Got any ideas?'

'I was thinking of *Olympia*.'

Jack looked puzzled. 'The Olympic games?'

Thalberg smiled. 'No, no, it's the title of a play by Molnar, a light comedy about high society in Vienna at the turn of the century.'

'Isn't that kind of stuff out of fashion now?'

'Oh, don't worry, we'll update it.' Thalberg remained upbeat, but Jack was still doubtful.

'I don't know, Irving. Audiences don't go much for that high-society stuff any more. I mean look at *The Big Parade*. They liked me as an all-American doughboy.'

'Trust me, Jack, we'll make it so the plain folks of America love it, not just the snobs on Broadway.'

'What's my part?'

'A dashing cavalry officer.'

'I like it.'

'What about this piece of garbage?' asked the worried director of the piece of garbage.

'We'll shelve it.'

'Thank you, God.'

'Don't thank God,' joked Jack. 'Thank Irving.' Fred Niblo looked at Irving Thalberg with adoration.

'I just did,' he said with feeling.

L.B. Mayer did not display the same gratitude to Thalberg. When he heard what his deputy had done he was incensed.

'You shelved a half-million-dollar production!'

'It's nearer seven hundred and fifty thousand if you take into account Jack's salary and the studio's overheads.'

'We can't afford to shelve it.'

'We can't afford not to,' said Thalberg with some asperity. 'Jack's still a big star, and we need to make that contract of his work for us.'

'I want that picture to play the movie houses.' Mayer's vehemence, particularly with regard to Jack, constantly surprised Thalberg.

'Then let's see what the Molnar picture does first. If they accept his voice in a charming comedy, it might be possible to slip *Redemption* into distribution on the bottom half of a double bill somewhere and not do too much damage.'

'Why are we paying this drunken bum all that money if we have to hide his pictures on the bottom half of a double bill?'

'He doesn't drink when he's working, L.B.'

'Oh, excuse me. He's not a drunken bum, then. But he is a degenerate bum.'

Thalberg knew that further protests were futile. At least he had got Mayer to agree to the Molnar film being Jack's first talker. As long as it was a whole lot better than *Redemption*, Jack Gilbert would survive.

Jack raced into the house on Tower Road and immediately summoned Ina and a bottle of champagne.

'They *liked* it?' asked Ina in wonder. Jack had done nothing for days but drink and gripe about how appalling *Redemption* was and how it would kill his career.

'Of course not. They hated it,' he grinned as he fired the cork deliberately at Carlos, who was carrying two champagne flutes. The Filipino butler, who had been attacked in this manner before, sidestepped the flying cork expertly.

'So why the celebration?' asked Ina, taking the glass and holding it away from her dress as it bubbled up and threatened to pour over the side.

'They're going to shelve it and start over with a new movie.' Ina was relieved. She understood what a financial sacrifice MGM was making and was happy that Jack would receive another chance to make an impact as a star in talking pictures.

'Who's the girl?' she asked, half hoping Jack had put in a plea for her but suspecting strongly that the prospect of their working together did not greatly appeal to her new husband.

'A Broadway broad. Maybe you know her. Her name's Catherine Dale Owen. I never heard of her.'

'Oh, Catherine's a sweetie,' said Ina. 'I knew her at the Academy.'

'The Academy of Motion Pictures? The one L.B. set up?' asked Jack, a little confused. Ina wondered how anybody could leap to this conclusion when the conversation was centred on Broadway.

'No. The American Academy of Dramatic Arts. Where we all trained.' Jack looked at her with some hostility. Ina wished she had held her tongue. She had forgotten for a moment how insecure Jack was. That he had never trained as an actor was a bone of professional contention between them. She tried to rescue the moment with a snippet of information she knew Jack would find comforting.

'Catherine was featured in some magazine article as one of the world's ten most beautiful women.'

'Really?' said Jack, immediately mollified, exactly as Ina had predicted he would be.

Jack's pleasure at the prospect of working with one of the world's ten most beautiful women (he wondered briefly how he could find this list, who else was on it and how many of them he had slept with) was tempered by the announcement a little while later that Lionel Barrymore had again been assigned to direct. He wondered why the studio was risking a repetition of the problems that had bedevilled *Redemption*.

Barrymore himself was equally puzzled when Mayer had told him of his new assignment and tried to decline. Mayer was not pleased.

'I've got a script for you to read. *A Free Soul*. Norma Shearer's playing your daughter. You play a drunken lawyer and if you're as good an actor as I think you are, I can almost guarantee you an Academy Award as Best Actor.'

The Academy Awards were only a year or two old but already they were being eagerly sought within the industry. When Barrymore read the script he knew that what Mayer had spoken was no more than the truth. It was a great role and he was perfect for it. He couldn't miss. All he had to do was supervise a poor job of recording Jack Gilbert's voice. Frankly, he thought Gilbert was a pain in the ass and this time he wouldn't let L.B. down. If it was a choice between L.B. and Gilbert, he knew who paid his wages.

Jack was quite pleased with his work on *His Glorious Night*, as *Olympia* was now called. He always liked wearing a uniform because he knew that he looked good in one. Catherine Dale Owen spoke with that plum in the mouth that Broadway actresses always had, but maybe the combination would be a potent one at the box office. After all, it must have been something of a gamble to pair the moody Swede with the dashing all-American boy in *Flesh and the Devil* and that had turned out pretty well. The dialogue was pretty stilted, but that was the way they were making them nowadays. Jack learned his lines and did his best, making sure that Catherine knew he was the big star. Of course there was always the chance that she would want to rehearse in his dressing room over lunch, just the two of them. That was how the affair with Renée Adorée had started.

The MGM studio was changing its physical appearance in deference to the new demands placed upon it by the arrival of sound. All the stages where the action was filmed had to be reconstructed with thick cement soundproof walls. Miles of recording cable had to be buried beneath the floor and, to the amusement of most employees, balloons were tethered to the roof with the word SILENCE written on them in the vain hope of stilling the noise of air traffic. It was hard to know quite what a passing pilot might do, even one who would like to be cooperative, short of turning off the engine and hoping to glide to a landing at the nearby airport. It was an indication that even the great Metro-Goldwyn-Mayer hadn't the faintest idea of what to do for the best.

On the new sound stage the director of *His Glorious Night* was experiencing much the same emotion. Lionel Barrymore gave his last-minute instructions to the two actors to be sure never to move out of range of the large microphone which was hidden behind the vase of flowers on the table and retreated to talk to the man who tyrannised the entire set – the all-powerful sound recordist. Catherine smiled nervously at Jack.

'Gosh, this feels so strange. Like our feet are glued to the floor.'

'You have a pretty voice, my dear,' said Jack comfortingly. 'The audience will adore it.'

'Thank you, Mr Gilbert. I know the audience is going to love the way you talk as well.' Jack sure as hell hoped so. He heard the new instructions being yelled round the set.

'OK, everyone. Quiet now! Turnover the camera! You OK for sound, Doug? Mark it! And . . . action!'

Jack spoke his lines in a normal tone of voice, but the dialogue was wooden, and the general anxiety in his body made his voice sound strained.

'Sweetheart! I thought you'd never come!' he emoted as the dashing cavalry officer Captain Kovacs.

'Careful, please,' replied the princess whose icy demeanour has been melted for the first time. 'The window's open above.'

The recordist, who was listening to the actors' voices through the sound-recording system, was not greatly impressed by what he was hearing. To him Jack sounded highly artificial.

'But do you know that I've been there for two hours waiting, waiting, waiting?' At this point the camera cut because the operator, trapped in his airless box, was nearly fainting from the heat. He staggered out, sweat pouring from him, his clothes soaked.

'I worked on *Greed* with von Stroheim,' he gasped. 'It was more comfortable in Death Valley when it got to be one hundred and twenty degrees than it is in there.' The sound man had problems of his own and complained to the director.

'Jack's voice sounds really strained.'

'Turn the bass down, then,' ordered Lionel Barrymore. The sound man smirked. God! Why didn't these directors understand the first thing about sound? Still, perhaps it was just as well. Their ignorance was the source of his power and paycheque.

'That's gonna make him sound even worse,' he explained. Barrymore was unmoved.

'Just do it,' he ordered, and returned to check the health of the camera operator, who had fortunately recovered enough to be coaxed back into the sweatbox. The camera turned and the actors continued, but this time Jack's voice sounded a little higher. The recordist turned to the director and raised his eyebrows. Barrymore ignored him. Meanwhile Jack was struggling on manfully with the terrible lines.

'But you could have sent some word. Oh darling, oh darling, oh dearest one, what have I done but wait, wait, wait, ever since I've known you?' Catherine, stiff as a statue, did her best too.

'I beg to remind you that if I hadn't dealt with you that way our little secret wouldn't have remained a secret.'

Now Barrymore was nodding in approval at the actors. Jack was still surprised that he wasn't hearing the director's voice cajoling the right emotion from him as he spoke his words, but of course the arrival of sound had taken away that crutch for the actor for all time. Jack had to place his trust in the lines and he wasn't too sure that he could.

'I don't wish it to be a secret. I love you. I've told you that a hundred times a week. I love you, I love you.' Of course he had been saying similar stuff to actresses since he had first started playing leading roles as the Great Lover but he had previously been secure in the knowledge that nobody outside the set would ever hear the words – except for the occasional lip-reader who would write letters of complaint when he helped himself to language that was a little too robust.

At the end of the take the sound recordist stamped over to talk to the director again.

'Lionel, I'm afraid Jack sounds like a horse's ass.' Barrymore was getting sick and tired of having some lowly technician tell him how to do his job – a job he had never had any desire to do in the first place.

'That's what L.B. wants. Now just go back there and twiddle your little knobs,' he snapped back at him ungraciously.

After the mandatory pause to wipe off the camera operator and allow him to gulp in enough air to normalise his heart rate, the action continued. The blonde ice princess tried to explain her reluctance to run away with the dashing Captain Kovacs.

'But I am betrothed to another!'

'Oh dearest one, you cannot marry him. You couldn't be so cruel. I felt the throb of your blood as it ran in tune with my pulse.' Jack picked up a jug of water and poured out a glass.

At the end of the take the recordist played it back for Barrymore to listen to on a pair of headphones. When Jack poured the water it sounded like he was standing directly under Niagara Falls. Barrymore started.

'Jesus! What's that sound? Is it the water he's pouring?'

'No,' said the recordist, who had realised by this time that there was something very weird going on. 'That's just the sound of Jack Gilbert's career going down the toilet.'

Chapter Twelve

~~~~

Jack and Ina both enjoyed staying at the Georges V Hotel in Paris. It was the only spark of mutual enjoyment they managed on their delayed honeymoon. Ina had been a Francophile for many years and she was anxious to show Jack the glories of the country. Jack, however, soon had his fill of museums, art galleries and cathedrals, although Ina seemed never to tire either of seeing them or of talking about them. This was not Jack's idea of a holiday, and it was certainly not Jack's idea of a honeymoon. Ina revelled in the cultural feast of Paris after the cultural famine of Hollywood. Her friends, who were anxious to meet the Great Lover, shared her view of the difference between French and American culture.

It was ironic therefore that when they visited many of the sights of Paris they were mobbed by movie fans, or at least Jack was. Outside the Louvre and Les Invalides Jack's fans rushed to see their hero in the flesh. He was well acquainted with this sort of frenzy in America, but it rather surprised him that he should experience the phenomenon to the same degree in Europe. He enjoyed bathing in the familiar waters of fan worship until he realised that Ina was feeling, as she put it, 'de trop'. However big a star she was on Broadway, it meant nothing in Paris.

In a desperate attempt to make herself feel better, she dragged Jack to meet all her friends, but it was doomed to failure. She was anxious that he should not disgrace himself as an 'ignorant American' and so she tried to coach him to deal with the probable topics of conversation. Jack fiercely resented her condescension.

'I'm not stupid, you know.'

'I didn't say you were.'

'That's what you think.'

'I'm trying to help you. I don't want people to think you're just a tourist.'

'I *am* a tourist. I don't live here. Of course I'm a tourist.'

After a week of statues and paintings and tapestries and east windows and flying buttresses and people who seemed to drink wine through the nose, of writers who had never written a book or a play or a script and theatre people who had never – or so they proudly proclaimed – seen a movie in their lives, Jack longed for the supposed shallowness of Hollywood.

When they got to the south of France Jack started to drink heavily again, a cause of frequent arguments with his new bride. One morning he staggered onto the quayside in Cannes harbour from the boat on which he and Ina were guests. He was badly hung-over from the previous evening and he sprawled into the first taxi he could find.

'Yes, m'sieur?' asked the taxi driver, who recognised Gilbert and had a fair idea he'd be struggling, like most Americans, with the concept of the currency exchange rate.

'Take me to Paris,' demanded Jack, who had forgotten that he and Ina had taken the train from Paris to Cannes two days ago.

'Paris, m'sieur?' asked the taxi driver in surprise. He had always wanted to go to Paris. The idea of doing so at John Gilbert's expense excited him enormously. Jack was unable to confirm the destination before collapsing in the back seat and snoring. The taxi driver slipped the car into gear and began the 700-mile journey to Paris. He wondered how best to tell his wife that he might not be home for a few days. Still, the way the marriage was at present, she probably wouldn't notice his absence.

Jack woke up as night began to fall and the taxi was entering what was clearly a large city. He was confused. Where the hell was he and what was he doing in the back of this taxi? He vaguely recalled that he was on his honeymoon in France and that they were staying with some friends on a yacht in the south of France, which wasn't much different from Marina del Rey, but he had no idea where his new wife was.

'Where are we?'

'This is Lyons, m'sieur.'

'Lee-on? Where's that?'

'We shall be in Paris tomorrow.'

'Paris? We just left Paris. Where's my wife?' The taxi driver shrugged. Why should he have to speak English all the time? Why didn't these arrogant Americans at least make the effort to talk in the language of the country they were visiting?

'I don't want to go to Paris. I want to go back to Cannes.' Slightly disappointed that he wouldn't be making the trip to Paris with a movie star, the taxi driver was comforted by the sight of the meter. With a sigh he executed an abrupt three-point turn and headed back towards Provence.

On the homeward journey across the Atlantic on the SS *Olympic*, Ina apologised for the unhappiness she felt she had generated on the honeymoon.

'I never meant for either of us to feel like that,' she said as she lay in his arms in their cabin on the final evening.

'I know you didn't.'

'I so wanted our honeymoon to be something we'd both remember.'

'Oh,' smiled Jack, 'I think we'll remember it OK.' Ina kissed him and began to unbutton his shirt. He tried to respond but he knew there was a problem, and not for the first time. It panicked him when he first realised that there was no response below the waist. It happened sometimes when he had been drinking heavily, but he had been relatively restrained in his drinking habits in Europe. Since there was no Prohibition over there, he had not felt the manic need he sometimes did in America to drink in order to prove a point to the federal government.

He lay back and let Ina have her way with him. He had never allowed a woman to take the initiative in lovemaking until he met Garbo. He remembered that first heady romantic thrill they had both felt and mourned its disappearance as he still did most days. They had made love with such a fine fury. None of his other affairs had ever given him quite the same erotic surge. He looked down and saw with wry amusement that Ina had in fact managed to evoke some interest. He had better not tell her it was the direct result of his fantasising about Greta Garbo.

The next morning they docked early in New York harbour. They were met as usual by Hubert Voight, MGM's head of publicity on the East Coast. He was carrying with him all the reviews for *His Glorious Night*, which had just opened in New York the previous week. Jack leafed through them as Voight chattered amiably about the hotel he had booked for them and the interviews he had arranged with the press.

'What are they like?' asked Ina anxiously, determined to focus on her husband's career rather than her own for the moment.

'They're OK,' said Jack slowly, 'not great, but OK. I've known worse.'

'The one in *Variety*'s a stinker,' added Voight unhelpfully, 'and that's a real shame. We could have used a good one there.'

'Where is it?' asked Jack immediately. He knew he shouldn't read it but he couldn't help himself.

'Jack, are you sure?' asked Ina doubtfully, but Jack was already staring at the death sentence in the one paper that everybody in the industry read.

A few more talker productions like this and John Gilbert will be able to change places with Harry Langdon. His prowess at lovemaking . . . takes on a comedy aspect . . . that gets the audience tittering at first and then laughing outright.

'Laughing?' asked Jack dumbly. 'Why? How?'

'Can we go and see it?' asked Ina.

'Sure,' said Voight, regretting his impulsive gesture of including the *Variety* review with the others. He should have let a junior bring the cuttings. 'It's playing at the Capitol.'

They slipped in for the 2 p.m. showing. The Capitol Theater wasn't full, but there was a respectable attendance, not as many as Jack had hoped or expected but a decent-sized crowd. As soon as the film started he realised why it wasn't full. The movie wasn't as bad as *Redemption* but it wasn't a whole lot better. Jack could sense that his own lack of ease during the filming was transmitting itself to the audience and making them just as uneasy. His voice wasn't bad but it wasn't particularly good either. It was just . . . ordinary. He wasn't sure that the Great Lover of the Silver Screen could afford to sound ordinary. Within ten minutes of the opening titles he had something much worse to worry about.

It was during an early scene with Catherine and the words coming out of his mouth were 'Oh, beauteous maiden, my arms are waiting to enfold you. I love you. I love you. I love you.' He remembered querying the speech with Willard Mack, who had adapted the Molnar play, but Lionel Barrymore had assured him it would be all right. He had said something quite similar a hundred times before on the set in response to the director's urging for him to be more passionate. He liked saying 'I love you'. He thought that just by forming the words he gave his acting added verisimilitude. The paying audience, however, had never heard them.

Now he realised that such words seemed to embarrass the audience. He recognised the laugh they produced. It wasn't the laugh of an audience who had discovered something deliciously comic. It was the laugh of an audience who were embarrassed at such displays of open emotion and wished they were any place but in the Capitol Theater. Even Jack and Ina felt uncomfortable watching such full-blooded declarations of love with other people sitting near them. It was something you might want to watch alone or with your lover but not with strangers and to be honest probably not with your parents or your children.

Jack remembered the stories that were told about Joan Crawford when she first came to MGM, stories about the blue movies she had allegedly made when she was still called Lucille LeSueur and had been a showgirl with the Shubert Organisation. One Christmas sixty men had crammed into a small studio viewing theatre to watch what was rumoured to be one of Joan's notorious films. To be frank, it was hard to see if it really was their Joan as the film was permanently out of focus, but that did little to diminish the men's obvious enjoyment of the illicit delights on display. However, what Jack recalled with great clarity, despite the inebriated state he was in at the time, was what had happened in that small theatre when a woman had wandered innocently into the room.

'What's going on in here?' she had said loudly to the men who were watching with the deepest concentration the antics of 'Joan' and her admirers on the screen. Instantly the men became sheepish and embarrassed and, although the woman had left as soon as she had discovered what was happening, the atmosphere had been destroyed and the party soon broke up. Nobody wanted to see the film any more.

He was experiencing something of the same reaction now. *His Glorious Night* was not an especially bad film, despite its poor direction and sound recording. It had some nice lines and the sort of story that might well have succeeded in other hands but with him and the wooden Catherine it was a catastrophe. Both their careers would suffer.

Ina did her best to comfort him when they returned to the hotel. She called room service and ordered a thick filet mignon, plenty of French fried potatoes and a very expensive bottle of red wine.

'It was a matinee,' she started. 'Audiences always sit on their hands at matinees.'

'It's a movie,' replied Jack between clenched teeth, 'not a goddamn theatrical performance. There's no such thing as a matinee. It's the same movie, day or night.'

'But the audience is still different at different times of day and they react differently. Your voice sounded OK to me.'

'To me too.'

'So where's the problem?'

'I'm Jack Gilbert, the Great Lover of the Silver Screen. I can't have an OK voice. I gotta have a great voice.'

'I don't think so.'

'I know so.'

At the same time, 3,000 miles away in Culver City, California, Louis B. Mayer was sitting in his office examining the box-office returns on *His Glorious Night*. They were pretty consistent with the reviews, which had been mixed at best. What was clear was that

Gilbert could not 'carry' a sound picture with his name alone. As a silent star he could. It didn't much matter what the studio put him into, Gilbert's pictures would return a heavy profit. *His Glorious Night* suggested strongly that such days were gone forever. Mayer contained his disappointment and managed a satisfied smile.

Irving Thalberg, who was sitting opposite him, wasn't smiling at all but that was as much the result of his state of health as the figures on the Gilbert picture. Mayer thought it was about time he discovered just how weak Irving's heart really was.

'Well, this one isn't going to make a buck for the studio. How much are we owing on his contract?'

'A million dollars.' The very sound of the figure gave Mayer palpitations.

'We're gonna have to release *Redemption*.'

Thalberg looked pained. 'You can't do that. You know it's worse than *His Glorious Night*.'

'And whose fault is that?'

'It's ours.'

'Don't be such a *chocham*.'

'We rushed these two films into production. We did a bad job and we must accept part of the blame.'

'You're *meshuggah*.' Mayer tended to revert to the Yiddish of his early years whenever he got excited. He had hired Conrad Nagel, who he thought had the best manners and speaking voice of any actor on the lot, and ordered Nagel to teach him to be a gentleman. Like the reviews of the Gilbert picture, the results had been patchy.

'*His Glorious Night* was made in thirteen days,' began Thalberg as he tried to explain the poor response. A veiled attack on Mayer might be the best way.

'We needed something to show to the distributors.'

'That didn't help them, it didn't help the studio, and it sure as hell didn't help Jack Gilbert.'

'We have to pay that degenerate bum a million dollars and *Redemption* isn't going to make a cent for this studio as long as it's sitting on the shelf.'

'We have to work out why they're laughing at his voice.'

'We know why. It records like it's high-pitched, like a cissy's voice.'

'Jack's no cissy.'

'No. He's a drunken, degenerate bum, that's what he is.'

'I mean his voice isn't the way it records. We all know what Jack sounds like.'

'It's one of those sound things, like they explained to us.'

'What sound things?'

'His voice records high. It's technical. There's nothing that can be done about it. We'll just have to cut our losses.'

'If you show *Redemption* straight after *His Glorious Night*, it'll ruin Jack for all time. You know how sensitive he is to just one bad review.'

'I don't give a goddamn how sensitive that bum is.'

'He's my friend, Louis, as well as our employee. It's not right for us to abandon him at this stage. OK, his voice is not what the audience expects, but it's our job to work out why and solve the problem if only so we can protect a valuable asset.'

'Wake up, Irving! Gilbert's not valuable any more. The audience is fickle – we all know that. They change their favourites. We have a new raft of actors coming in from Broadway who know how to speak. One or two of them'll become stars and the audience won't give five cents what happens to Gilbert.'

'Louis, I'm telling you: if you release *Redemption*, he'll never work again.'

Mayer looked at his head of production. There wasn't a glimmer of compassion.

'You gonna fight me about this?'

Thalberg stared at him for the longest time, but then regretfully shook his head. He wasn't strong enough to defy the critics, the public and L.B. Mayer. Jack would have to wait for a day when Irving felt stronger, when he had a plan, for God's sake. All he had at the moment was constant fatigue.

Mayer took great pleasure from that resigned shake of the head. He loved the taste of victory, and a victory over Gilbert, the actor he hated most, and Thalberg, who was inclined to get above himself and whom he would never forgive for taking William Fox's 250,000 pieces of silver – well, that gave him enormous satisfaction. It gave him a feeling of warmth that reached down to the ends of his toes.

'What about Garbo? Are we set on *Anna Christie* as her first talker, or do you still want her as Joan of Arc?' Thalberg saw the smirk on Mayer's face and flushed with anger.

'It was a good idea. If Shaw had sold us his play . . .'

'It was a bad idea.'

'We agreed we'd go for a stage vehicle first just like we did for Norma and for Marion Davies . . .'

'Didn't work for Gilbert.'

'Shaw's not Molnar.'

'Shaw's not O'Neill either. And you want us to give him seven hundred and fifty thousand dollars just because *Anna Christie*'s been on Broadway! Garbo pictures cost five hundred thousand tops!'

'It's cheap, considering how much we've got invested in Garbo.'

'What makes you think the O'Neill play's gonna work for the Swede?'

'Well, the character's Swedish for a start.'

'She's a whore. Audiences won't accept Garbo as a whore.'

'They accept her as a mistress.'

'A whore's different.'

'Why? Because she takes money for sex?'

'No. Because she does it without love. Audiences will forgive a woman anything she does if she sacrifices it all for love.'

'What about *La Dame aux camélias*?'

'What's that?'

'*La Traviata*.'

'Musicals are different. Opera is different.'

'So what are you saying? No to *Anna Christie*?'

'I'm saying don't come bawling to me if it's a flop.'

Thalberg was determined that *Anna Christie* was not going to be a flop. Greta Garbo was the last of his roster of film stars to make a talking picture and he didn't green light the project until he felt that the technicians in the newly founded sound department were comfortable about protecting their highly prized asset. He surrounded Garbo with reliable actors who would not deflect from the lustre of the star. George F. Marion, who had played Anna's father in the 1921 original Broadway stage production and in the silent-movie version two years later, reprised the part for MGM; the hard, rough Irish sailor Matt who falls in love with Anna was played by the solid Charlie Bickford, who had scored a success in *Dynamite*, Cecil B. DeMille's first talkie; and the old woman, Marthy, who was effectively the light relief, was played by the talented comedienne Marie Dressler, who had been out of fashion for ten years.

On the technical side, the lighting was in the capable hands of Bill Daniels, and Frances Marion, who had written *Love*, adapted the screenplay from the play. Yet again she provided a happy ending for Hollywood audiences, which, despite making a mockery of the original, proved ultimately successful. The direction was entrusted to the ever-reliable Clarence Brown.

It was Brown who gave Greta the one direction she had reasonably supposed she would never hear.

'Greta, can you make your accent a little more Swedish?' he said after the first reading of the script. Garbo burst into laughter. MGM had been coaching her for months on how to lose her Swedish accent and now, playing the part of a Swedish woman, she was being asked to exaggerate it.

'I want you to sound exactly the way the audience would expect a Swedish woman to talk,' Clarence Brown explained. Garbo nodded. It made sense. One of Jack's problems was that the audience had expected him to sound differently from the way they actually first heard him. Garbo had to give the audience a voice that matched her screen persona, but it was a struggle to sound Swedish and yet at all times be comprehensible, particularly to the American ear, which didn't much care for any kind of foreign accent.

Alma, her maid, and Billy, who helped to look after her hair and make-up, both looked ashen with worry as Garbo left her dressing room and began the long, slow march to the sound stage – or the scaffold, as it felt like to her. She could hear the gathering nightmare of the fourth movement of Berlioz's Symphonie Fantastique in her head. That orchestral music led to the nightmare climax of the Witch's Sabbath. What black magic awaited her?

She walked past the series of photographs of MGM stars that lined the corridor on the way to the sound stage. The one that always jumped out at her was the photograph of her and Jack, taken on the set of *Flesh and the Devil*. She was lying on her back with her face turned away from his and towards the camera. Although Jack was theoretically in the dominant position, the art of Clarence Brown's composition and Bill Daniels's lighting ensured that it was her face that dominated the photograph. Was Jack permitted to remain on public display because it was a photograph of Garbo rather than Gilbert?

What a bitter irony for poor Yackie if the relationship that had meant so much to him was one of the main reasons that his career had gone into a tailspin. It seemed as though when the two stars had met Garbo had absorbed so much of Gilbert's heat that his star had begun instantly to wane. The intention on MGM's part had certainly been to create two stars where there had previously been only one, but instead, the high profile of their celebrity love life had rendered that outcome impossible. It was clear to all who observed Garbo and Gilbert in 1930 that she had eclipsed him permanently.

On the march of doom Garbo couldn't help wondering if she too would join the lengthening list of casualties in the war against the microphone. Jack might have been the highest profile victim of the sound process but he was by no means alone – Emil Jannings, winner of the first Academy Award for Best Actor, had returned to Germany, along with Pola Negri, who had starred in Moje's only Hollywood hit, *Hotel Imperial*. One of Jack's former lovers, Renée Adorée, had gone, as had the Hungarian beauty Vilma Banky, and her husband, Rod La Rocque. And it wasn't just the foreign stars who had failed the test – Corinne Griffith, Clara Bow and the Talmadge sisters had decided to take early retirement. One of the latter had walked straight from the cinema where her sister's first sound film was playing into the nearest Western Union office and wired GET OUT NOW WHILE YOU STILL HAVE YOUR

LOOKS AND BE GRATEFUL FOR THE TRUST FUND
MOTHER SET UP.

Greta had rehearsed her opening move a number of times. As the
door to the ladies' section of the waterfront saloon opened she
paused and looked around. Her appearance was pallid, her clothes
unremarkable, and she carried a battered suitcase. This was Garbo
as no movie audience had ever seen her. She dragged her weary
body over to the table. Sitting down she opened her mouth and
uttered the words that were to add significantly to her legend.

'Gimme a viskey. Ginger ale on the side. And don't be stingy,
babee.'

Three short sentences but they were enough. Clarence Brown
exchanged delighted looks with Doug Shearer. At the end of the
take everyone gathered together to listen to the playback. Garbo's
voice had a deep melancholia that perfectly matched not just the
character of Anna Christie, who had been abandoned as a child,
raped by a cousin and ended up as a prostitute, but also the world-
weary woman who had been doomed to helpless, hopeless love
affairs since her first appearances in *The Torrent* and *The Temptress*.
Greta was thrilled with the sound of her own voice.

'Do I really sound like that?' she asked shyly, as if not daring to
believe the evidence of her own ears. Clarence Brown grinned and
nodded his confirmation. There was a spontaneous burst of
applause and cheering from the loyal crew on the set. Alma gave
thanks to the Lord.

Thereafter the filming proceeded confidently and quickly. The
only major problem came two and a half weeks into shooting when
the rumour flew round the studio that the stock market had crashed.
The rumour turned out to be the truth, and it soon became apparent
that the Era of Wonderful Nonsense was over. It had seemed as if
the stock market went only one way. People bought stocks and
shares in the sure expectation that they would be able to cash them
in for large profits whenever they wanted. Black Tuesday, as 29
October came to be known, disabused them of that notion.

Ironically, 'Everything that happens, happens for the best in the
best of all possible worlds' had been a popular saying of the day,

encapsulating the mood of well-being that had gripped the United States of America in the 1920s. Garbo and Jack had been a symbolic part of that feeling, for the motion pictures and in particular those made in Hollywood had made themselves into a central feature of most people's lives. What had been a working-class indulgence in the 1910s had become a fact of everyday life in all sections of society in the post-war decade.

The new President on his campaign trail in the autumn of 1928 had promised voters 'A chicken in every pot, a car in every garage', but on Tuesday 29 October 1929, while Anna Christie and her father were burbling on about 'that old devil sea', all that came to an end. Suddenly it wasn't so clever to have borrowed on margin when frantic stockbrokers were ringing to tell you that unless you paid what you owed you'd lose everything. Garbo listened that night on the radio to Eddie Cantor telling jokes about his uncle who had just died.

'Poor man, he had diabetes at forty-five. He should worry. I had Chrysler at a hundred and ten.'

Self-lacerating jokes were common among show-business people. Garbo and Harry Edington worked out that she had probably lost $100,000 in the devastation on Wall Street. Garbo was shattered, although Edington pointed out that she was one of the lucky ones. She had a contract that was paying her $5,000 a week. She would survive and prosper. It was the people who lost their savings and their earning power at the same time who would really suffer. Garbo was not among them, but that was not the way she felt as she first absorbed the news. She had come to America as part of the migration of poor people to the golden land. The main reason for being in Hollywood as her sister died, as Moje died back in Stockholm, was that she was making money to protect her from the poverty of her childhood for the rest of her life. Now, suddenly, it had been taken away from her.

Not without trepidation, MGM finally decided to release *Anna Christie* in the spring of 1930. Although the studio felt it was a good showcase for Garbo's talents, there remained the tricky task of selling what was essentially a downbeat and unglamorous story about a disappointed waterfront prostitute to what was still in large part a simple-minded audience that went to the movies to forget their problems. Frank Whitbeck, the advertising executive in charge of the West Coast theatres, was given the task of inventing a slogan to introduce Garbo to the public in her new guise.

He brought the layout for the poster, which emphasised Garbo's haunting beauty, to Thalberg's office and arranged the series of drawings on the chairs that lined the room. When he had finished his presentation, Thalberg rose from his desk and prowled around the room with his hands behind his back, studying the campaign. He was unconvinced. He shook his head in frustration.

'It's OK but it's not what I was looking for.'

'Well, what *are* you looking for?'

Thalberg shrugged helplessly. 'That's just it. I don't know what I want. I'll be able to tell you when I see it but I can't tell you.'

They sat and talked dejectedly for nearly two hours, while outside in the notorious Thalberg outer office, distinguished writers, producers and directors waited to see the MGM wunderkind with a patience they would have exhibited for no other movie executive. Finally Whitbeck picked up a used envelope from Thalberg's desk and sketched on the back of it the proportions of a twenty-four-sheet billboard, six blocks long and four blocks high. He pencilled in two words and showed them to his employer.

Thalberg stared at the envelope. The two words in king-sized lettering read:

GARBO TALKS

Rarely in the history of advertising and show business had two words had such a powerful effect.

'That's it!' cried Thalberg. 'I knew I'd recognise it when I saw it.'

The campaign was a huge success. People liked the film and they liked Garbo in it in particular. Her first entrance was cunningly delayed until the film had been running sixteen minutes, so that all the audience could think was 'Where's Garbo?' That first insouciant look and those three short staccato phrases were almost enough in themselves to win over the eager cinemagoers.

It certainly worked with the critics, who were as fascinated as the audience by the prospect of Garbo talking. It was to one of them 'the voice of a Viking's daughter, inherited from generations of seamen who spoke against the roar of the sea and made themselves heard'. *Picture Play* called Garbo's vocal performance 'the voice that shook the world'. The playwright Robert E. Sherwood had initially queried why the MGM publicity department was now calling Garbo 'the greatest living actress'. After seeing *Anna Christie*, Sherwood admitted in print that all he could do was to agree.

Garbo's was the one dissenting voice. She never watched the daily rushes, so she had no idea what the film was really like until she saw it in a Beverly Hills cinema with two male friends, one from France, one from Sweden. After the first few scenes had been played, Garbo started to sink lower and lower in her seat. Clarence Brown's direction that she should play a more stereotypical Swede than the character she had first imagined bothered her greatly. She shook her head and groaned softly, 'Isn't it terrible? Whoever saw Swedes act like that?' The others agreed, and well before the end they left the cinema in misery.

Even it becoming a smash hit, setting weekly box-office records everywhere, didn't convince Garbo that the film was any good. When Frank Whitbeck was introduced to her on the MGM lot as the man who had invented the slogan 'Garbo Talks', she merely asked him, 'Aren't you ashamed?' Whitbeck felt sure he could discern a twinkle in Garbo's eyes as she said it, but, like every other man, he was captivated more by the startling blue of her eyes and those extraordinary eyelashes than by the words that came out of her mouth.

America and Hollywood, however, didn't much care what Garbo thought privately. *Anna Christie* had been as much a triumph as Jack's sound debut had been a failure. Just as Jack appeared to have a voice entirely different from what audiences had suspected and paid the penalty, so Garbo had one that sounded entirely like the one they had been imagining for four years. Just as Jack was handicapped by the choice of an old-fashioned play with stilted dialogue, so Garbo benefited from the extra nine months of refinement in recording techniques, complete executive support and the choice of a play with relatively naturalistic dialogue. Just as Jack had started to act differently when he was cast in a talking film, so Garbo had scarcely altered her style. Jack's florid, emotional performances went out of fashion as soon as Al Jolson ad-libbed, 'You ain't heard nothing yet.' Garbo's modern way of acting, drilled into her by Moje Stiller, gave her a technique that effortlessly made the transition to sound.

Sound thrilled audiences. Car tyres screeching and machine guns firing particularly delighted them and the gangster film quickly became the most popular kind of movie for audiences keen to hear as well as see their idols. In the wake of the depression, men who took what they wanted, even at the point of a gun, were the new film heroes. Warner Brothers, who had pioneered the sound film, soon became the acknowledged masters of this new genre, and for *Little Caesar* and *The Public Enemy* they imported two young men from the Broadway stage – Edward G. Robinson and James Cagney, who became stars with their first films. They were of the streets, of their time. Jack Gilbert and his costume romances were not.

Jack Gilbert, the man who looked most at home in a tuxedo or the gold-braided uniform of an officer in some East European or Ruritanian army, was yesterday's hero, and there seemed to be nothing he could do about it. Where once he would have played a round of golf before lunch, followed by a swim and then a long, competitive game of tennis, now he mostly sat at home and brooded.

Ina hoped that her plans to re-design the house might comfort Jack and shake him out of his inertia. Her first contribution was the creation of a bedroom suite that owed more to contemporary fashion than to the monk's cell from *The Merry Widow*. Then Ina extended the servants' quarters, because of course she had to have her own maid and her maid could not be expected to share living accommodation with Carlos. Then, while the builders were already there, she became very excited at the prospect of building a Venetian bridge to the swimming pool. As it was going to be a big surprise for

Jack, she scheduled for work on the new bridge to begin when Jack was away from the house for most of the day.

Jack had finally been persuaded to have a long and probably uncomfortable conversation with Harry Edington about money, for Harry was only too aware that the bills were starting to mount up.

'Jack, you've got to realise that you're no longer earning ten thousand dollars every week.'

'I'm getting more. That's what you and Nick Schenck said.'

'Yes, in theory.'

'What do you mean "in theory"?' asked Jack, rather worried.

'The new contract, though more profitable overall, contains a clause whereby MGM don't have to make the first scheduled payment of fifty thousand dollars until the first day of principal photography on your new picture. Thereafter you get fifteen grand every week until they reach a quarter of a million, but right now there's bupkiss.'

Jack's anxieties increased. 'Harry, you know Mayer's in no hurry to rush Jack Gilbert into another picture.'

'You have to ignore Mayer. I told you: he'll never stop hating you. That's the way he is.'

'It's not Mayer that bothers me. It's Irving. I can't get in to see him.'

'Well, Irving's notorious for being evasive if it's a meeting he doesn't want to take.'

'But I thought Irving was my friend.'

'Me too. That's why these bills concern me. Your last two movies have been disasters as far as Metro are concerned. I suspect L.B. is going to spend a long time searching for the right property while you stay at home.'

'Staring at the bills, you mean.'

'And those bills are starting to eat into your savings.'

He came home to find the courtyard filled with stonemasons building a Venetian bridge, in addition to the general melee of builders, plumbers and carpenters. Jack exploded in anger.

'Get the hell out of here!' he screamed at everyone.

'Don't you want the Venetian bridge?' asked the stonemason,

who had been looking forward to applying his art to the creation of something permanent at the house of his wife's favourite movie star.

'No, I don't. Now scram!' Hearing the raised voices, Ina came running out of the house.

'Jack, it was my idea. Mine and Harold Grieve's. We thought it would be fun to surprise you.'

'Well, I'm surprised OK. Surprised you didn't see what a stupid idea it is.'

'A man who put a monk's cell into a guest bedroom shouldn't be too surprised at a Venetian bridge leading to a swimming pool.'

'I don't want it and I don't like it and I can't afford it.'

'Money? Is that it, you cheap sonofabitch?' hissed Ina, suddenly conscious of the audience of builders and labourers who were watching them as if they were rehearsing scripted dialogue.

'Me? Cheap? Are you crazy?' yelled an outraged Jack, who had been accused many times and with some justification of being a spendthrift but never of the reverse. He, unlike his new wife, had no problems with arguing in front of the help.

'I'm going inside,' said Ina sharply and turned on her heel. Jack followed her. He was looking forward to the argument. After biting his tongue at the studio and with the press, it felt good to let rip. Ina was the one standing in the way when he vented his anger and she took the full force of his verbal attack straight between the eyes. Jack didn't stop until he had reduced this strong woman to tears.

Next day Ina emerged with two packed suitcases – straight into the waiting mob of press journalists and photographers. After the reports they had received the previous night, they knew perfectly well that this would be the next step. In procession they followed Ina and her suitcases and servants down the hill and into a hastily rented house on Linden Drive.

'Is the marriage over, Mrs Gilbert?' asked one reporter. Ina stared back and then gave the reporter the full benefit of her iciest smile.

'Not at all. We are building a new wing on to the house, as you probably know. Mr Gilbert is supervising it, so I'm renting this place to learn my lines while the house is being remodelled. It's quite straightforward.'

'So you are going to live together again?'

'Oh heavens, yes. In fact Mr Gilbert and I are having dinner together at Chasen's tonight. I'm sure you'll find us there around eight o'clock.' Ina disappeared indoors to telephone Jack and inform him that unless he wanted their marriage to be pronounced dead in tomorrow's newspapers he had better meet her at Chasen's at 7.45 p.m.

Jack agreed and returned to the couch to stare dully at this month's *Photoplay* magazine. He hadn't dared to discuss it with Harry or Ina or anyone, but he was sure they both knew about the article, which was headlined 'Is Jack Gilbert Through?' Ina had felt sorry for him when she had read it, and he couldn't stand her pity. Harry was too frightened for himself to think of Jack: the article had virtually accused him of taking money from MGM as well as from his client because the studio had provided a well-paid job for the powerful business manager.

The more Jack looked at the article the more he suspected that, although it was written by a feature writer called Katherine Albert, the impetus and the information for it had come from Mayer or Thalberg or both. *Photoplay* would not have dared to risk alienating the affections of the biggest studio in Hollywood. He knew perfectly well what MGM was up to. They wanted to get out of the contract Nick Schenck had signed with him and they would use any means to do so. He had hit the skids in the most painful and public way and he had no idea how he was going to arrest his precipitous descent. He picked up the telephone and called his friend Buster Keaton.

'Doing anything tonight, Buster?'

'Drinking,' replied Buster in characteristically laconic fashion.

'Mind if I join you?' asked Jack politely.

'Be my guest,' replied Buster. 'I usually start at the Starlight Club in Santa Monica around seven in the evening and finish in the gutter on Hollywood Boulevard about four in the morning.'

As Ina was shown to her empty table at Chasen's at 7.50 p.m. her soon-to-be-ex-husband was setting up the third whisky chaser of the night in a speakeasy ten miles to the west in Santa Monica.

'We are going to have a great evening,' announced Buster to Jack grandly. 'I am going to explain to you how Natalie and Joe Schenck persuaded me to sign with MGM, who then destroyed my career and my marriage.' Buster tossed back the chaser and signalled to the barman to bring the bottle and leave it.

'No, you're not.'

'I'm not?'

'No, you are going to listen to how MGM destroyed my career and my marriage. I was the biggest earner in movies.'

'I had my own film unit.'

'L.B. Mayer stuck me in the worst films he could find.'

'He sent me writers and directors who weren't funny to make my comedies.'

'Flicka left me, you know, and now Ina's gone.'

'Natalie's left me, taken the boys and kicked me out of my own house.'

'I love women, but they all leave me. Why?'

'It's all I want to do, make people laugh.' Buster fell backwards off his chair. Nobody laughed. Nobody noticed. Not even Jack. The familiar warm fog was descending on him. Buster picked himself up and climbed back on his stool.

'I've known comedy since I started in vaudeville when I was three. Where do these guys at MGM get off telling me how to make people laugh?'

'I loved Flicka. I still do. I think about her all the time. How can I get her back?'

Buster thought about the problem briefly.

'Let's see who can drink a whole bottle of Jack Daniels quicker. If I finish first I get Natalie and my film unit back.'

Jack grinned. He signalled for two full bottles.

'That's a great idea. If I win I get a great script from MGM and I get to marry Greta Garbo!'

He raised his glass in salute to his friend, the great comedian and philosopher.

'Skol!' Jack drank deeply. Buster looked at his glass.

'Of course it's cold. It's been in the icebox.' Buster drained his glass, but Jack was already filling up his next.

Chapter Thirteen

Anna Christie was such a success that MGM immediately re-made it in German with a different cast and director but with the same star shining brightly at its centre. This time even Garbo was pleased with the result. The director was her friend Jacques Feyder, and the part of Marthy was played by Salka Viertel, who was to become one of her closest friends for the next ten years. Even though she was less familiar with German than English, Garbo worked so assiduously at it that the rest of the cast, who had been imported from Germany, told her that her German was practically without any accent at all. This time, when she saw the final result she did not walk out of the cinema before the end.

Contrary to all expectations, she, a Swede who spoke English badly, had made the transition to sound movies successfully, while her former lover, indeed the world's former lover, Jack Gilbert, had plummeted from the highest position on the Hollywood totem pole to its very bottom in just a few months. She shuddered whenever she thought about it. Her Yackie, the brash, self-confident man who had taken her under his wing when she had first arrived because he knew everything and everybody and by virtue of his power and success, was virtually inviolable was now, by all accounts, a helpless, drunken wreck.

Garbo heard at the end of August 1930 that Jack and Ina had legally separated and were planning to sue for divorce. She was sad but hardly surprised. She did wonder whether she should call Jack and offer him a friendly shoulder to cry on but she was pretty sure that he would not be content with just her shoulder and before too long she would be fending off yet another proposal of marriage. That was the trouble with Jack. He had been in Hollywood so long he believed in the ethos of the happy-ending stories he had always played in.

If Garbo arrived on his doorstep or even picked up the phone, he would immediately assume that she had come back to him. It would be the fulfilment of all his fantasies, and she did not wish to be Jack's fantasy. She was already the fantasy of millions of men all over the world. She knew it because her mailbag was now the biggest in the studio – nearly fifteen thousand fan letters a week. Maybe she should ask Harry to negotiate a new contract for her on the basis of a dollar for every fan letter she received. Except of course MGM would cheat and lie about the number. Currently, the studio's postman just piled them in the corner of her dressing room every day until the end of the week when Alma, her maid, prevailed on him to take them all away unopened rather than deliver any more.

'Who are these people?' Garbo asked rhetorically as yet another unwanted sack was delivered. 'Why do they want my autograph? Why do they want my photograph? I am not their relative.'

Garbo returned to work on her next movie, knowing that another big success would result in yet more fan mail, more requests for interviews and more demands from L.B. Mayer for public appearances and cooperation with the studio's voracious publicity department. She shrugged it all to one side and concentrated on preparing for her second sound film.

It was called, with typical MGM subtlety, *Romance*, and it was again lit by Bill Daniels, directed by Clarence Brown and adapted from a stage play, this time a play by Edward Sheldon about the life of an opera diva called Lina Cavalieri. Despite being reunited with the technical team that had served her so well on *Anna Christie*, Garbo felt instinctively that *Romance* lacked the same cohesion. Partly it was the result of casting her as an opera singer. She worried that her fans might not accept her as such, but Brown ensured that she would never be seen in shot actually singing or even miming to the pre-recorded voice of a proper singer.

When she remonstrated with Irving Thalberg, he acknowledged that the play from which the script had been adapted was an old warhorse.

'But it's a proven popular success and with you as the star, Greta, it'll be even more popular.'

'I do not want you to use my popularity to support a bad film.'

'It won't be a bad film. I've seen the dresses Gilbert Adrian has designed for you. They are fabulous.' Garbo was only partially mollified. Adrian's spectacular dresses would not be a successful camouflage for a poor script.

What *Romance* needed was Jack Gilbert, maybe not the alcoholic wreck of contemporary legend, but a new Jack Gilbert, a young Jack Gilbert, someone with whom she could create a spark of creative fire. Clarence Brown and Irving Thalberg cast instead an unimpressive, unknown young man from Kentucky, who was injured in a car crash on the first day of shooting.

Buttressed by the success of *Anna Christie* and secure in the knowledge that her fan base was increasing after they had heard her talk, Garbo carried the picture almost single-handed. At the end of the year she was nominated for the Academy Award for Best Actress for her performances in both *Romance* and *Anna Christie*. Unfortunately the two nominations split the vote, and Norma Shearer, Irving Thalberg's wife, won for her appearance in the lachrymose *The Divorcee*.

Perhaps more significant than the response of the film industry to Garbo's growing stardom were the financial returns on *Romance*, which was never going to be a major work in the Garbo filmography. The cost of its production was less than $500,000 and it earned, both home and abroad, well over $1 million. After deductions for the cost of prints and advertising and studio overheads, the final result was a profit of $287,000. MGM realised that they could stick Garbo into almost anything and it would return a healthy profit. This realisation would not help Garbo's anxious search for better scripts. As far as the studio was concerned, better scripts did not necessarily mean bigger profits.

As ever with Garbo, the greater her stardom grew the more frantic were the attempts of her fans to track her down and the more paranoid she became. Mary Pickford, who, along with her ex-husband Douglas Fairbanks, had been the royal family of

Hollywood until Gilbert and Garbo knocked them off their perch, still entertained royally. When Lady Mountbatten arrived in Hollywood, it was Mary Pickford who hosted the formal dinner welcoming her. Among the guests to be invited was Greta Garbo. She declined with thanks. Lady Mountbatten was not one to take 'no' for an answer and she prevailed upon her hostess to write a long letter to Garbo explaining precisely why it was so important that she attend the dinner. Garbo ignored it.

Lady Mountbatten's next hostess was Marion Davies, but Davies's invitation to dine with Lady Mountbatten was also declined. The indefatigable Englishwoman was not to be denied. She arranged to be given a tour of the MGM studios. Louis B. Mayer always had time to show off his studio to distinguished foreigners, especially if they were women with first-class social connections.

'Do you have a particular desire to meet one of my stars?' he asked, hoping he would not get the usual response. He did.

'Yes,' said Lady Mountbatten, 'I should really like to meet Greta Garbo.' Mayer sighed. He summoned his chief aide, Eddie Mannix.

'Eddie, send word along to the Garbo set. Tell her Lady Mountbatten is on the lot and would love to stop by for a minute and meet her.' Mannix looked askance at his boss but trotted off to do his bidding just the same. They were on the set of a *Tarzan* film so that the distinguished visitor could admire the body of Johnny Weissmuller, the erstwhile Olympic swimming champion and now hero of the Tarzan movies, when Eddie Mannix came scurrying back.

'I'm very sorry, Lady Mountbatten, but Greta says she is very sick and it will not be possible to meet her.' At this point even the redoubtable Lady Mountbatten admitted defeat.

Sometimes Garbo's social maladroitness extended to her own friends as much as to strangers. She would almost never agree to meet anyone in advance. She far preferred to hint that she might drop round the following evening for dinner, and many were the evenings on which dinner had been prepared after receiving such a hint but Garbo never arrived. When the friend rang the Garbo house, the telephone was always answered by Gustaf, who parroted the message given to him by his employer that Miss Garbo was not at home, he had no idea where she was and no idea when she might return. As for the possibility that Greta would agree to meet her friends' friends, well, it was never going to happen. Robert Montgomery, who acted alongside Garbo in *Inspiration*, the film she made after *Romance*, remarked sourly that even starring in a film with Garbo did not appear to constitute a social introduction.

Gradually the identity of the owner of the house in Chevy Chase Drive became known ever more widely. She was horrified when she came down to breakfast one morning and found a dozen fan letters clearly addressed to her at 1027 Chevy Chase. She was convinced that her neighbours – who could see into her garden from their upstairs window – were spying on her. She started to get up at 5 a.m. to take a swim or wait until after night fell. Eventually this stratagem started to pall, and she decided to move to another house in Beverly Hills, on Camden Drive. The rent was $600 a month but, although it afforded more privacy, she soon discovered that the proximity of the trolley cars kept her awake at night. Within a few weeks she was on the move again, ever westward, this time to a house on San Vicente Boulevard in Brentwood. Finally she appeared content, for the house was completely hidden from the street by huge cypress trees.

During her pilgrimage in search of security she lost the services of Gustaf and Sigrid. Garbo was not an easy woman to work for, and they finally admitted defeat in their attempts to please her. They rarely received a word of praise or thanks but were always on the receiving end of criticism when things did not go exactly as Garbo wanted. To replace them she hired a black chauffeur to drive her and an elderly woman from Alsace who was to do the cooking and the general housekeeping. Her cooking seems to have been a little less than exceptional but her discretion and tolerance for Garbo's many foibles were outstanding. For Garbo discretion was not only the better part of valour; it was the main virtue she demanded from anyone who had regular contact with her.

The Swedish contingent that had shared her early years had now mostly left Hollywood and returned home. Stiller of course was dead, Seastrom had decided that the attractions of Stockholm outweighed those of Hollywood, and Lars Hanson never gave himself the chance to make the transition to sound films, believing it was a hopeless cause. To replace her Swedish friends and her ex-lover Jack Gilbert, Greta Garbo became particularly friendly with two talented women of very different temperaments. One of them was Salka Viertel, the classic European intellectual in exile in California who had played Marthy Owen in the German-language version of *Anna Christie*. The other was a remarkable, tempestuous bisexual by the name of Mercedes de Acosta. The latter was so adept at spinning stories about herself and her origins that it is hard to be precise as to where factual evidence finishes and pure fantasy begins.

It appears that she was born in the United States to Spanish-Catholic immigrant parents. Her mother was allegedly descended from Spanish nobility, and her father was a lesser-born poet. She claimed to have been raised as a boy until she was seven years old when she was confronted with incontrovertible evidence to the contrary. It seems unlikely to be true but to someone like Garbo, whose own sexuality was a constant source of speculation, it was probably an endearing story. Both women had lost their fathers when they were young and both had suffered the premature deaths of siblings.

Mercedes was five feet three inches tall with jet-black hair setting off her pale, almost translucent skin. She wore men's trousers long before Garbo and then Dietrich became fashion icons for doing so. In her autobiography Mercedes reveals a penchant for outlandish dressing that Garbo must have admired – pointed shoes with large silver buckles, a full skirt covered by a full-length black coat with huge lapels and on her head a Cossack hat. Her outfits provoked either admiration or scorn but invariably they attracted comments from the people whom Mercedes was out to impress. Tallulah Bankhead took one look at her frequently bizarre combination of hats and coats and likened her to a mouse in a topcoat.

Among those who seem to have been particularly impressed were

Cocteau, Diaghilev, Nijinsky, Stravinsky, Picasso, Matisse, Robert Frost and Dorothy Parker. Mercedes de Acosta was what became known as a 'star fucker', in her case, literally so. She wrote some small books of poetry and two plays, one of which, *Jeahanne d'Arc*, was produced in Paris and the other, *Sandro Botticelli*, was produced by the Players Company at the Provincetown Playhouse in New York. Both starred Mercedes's very close friend of the time, Eva Le Gallienne.

It was Salka Viertel who brought Mercedes and Garbo together. Salka, who was fifteen years older than Garbo, had been born to reasonably wealthy Jewish parents in Galicia, then part of the extreme eastern end of the Habsburg Empire. She became an actress in Vienna, where she met Berthold Viertel, a rising young theatre director. Eventually, after after working together in Leipzig, Dresden and Munich, they married and became part of the fashionable arts scene in Berlin in the 1920s. They followed the distinguished silent film director F.W. Murnau from Berlin to Hollywood, where Berthold was commissioned to write a screenplay for him.

The Viertels settled happily in a house on Mayberry Road in Santa Monica. This house, soon to be widely known as 'Salka's salon', hosted meals and conversation for the many European exiles in Hollywood, where discussions ranged from politics to philosophy to contemporary trends in the arts. Sunday afternoons would see the convivial company of Thomas Mann, Bertolt Brecht and Aldous Huxley and their wives devouring Salka's strudel, by common consent the best strudel west of the Pennsylvania station. It was all very different from the Sunday brunches at Jack's house, and Garbo was thrilled to be a part of it. It took her back to those early, bewildering but stimulating lessons at the hands of Mauritz Stiller.

Garbo looked particularly stunning the day she met Mercedes at Salka's house. She was dressed in a white jumper and dark-blue sailor trousers. She wore no shoes and her lustrous hair, freed from the attentions of the MGM make-up artists, hung straight down to her shoulders. She wore the visor in which she usually played tennis, shading her piercing blue eyes. It was an insouciant look that could have been designed with the sole objective of making

Mercedes fall in love with her. After lunch they pushed back the carpet and danced together to records on the phonograph.

'Which one do you like?' asked Mercedes, looking through the collection.

'This one,' declared Garbo, handing her 'Daisy, You're Driving Me Crazy'. Mercedes put it onto the turntable and dropped the needle. As the music started the dancing began. When the music finished Mercedes flung herself onto the couch.

'I love your voice,' she said simply.

'Is that all?' asked Garbo coquettishly. To her surprise Mercedes found herself colouring. It was quite clear that it wasn't just Garbo's voice that Mercedes found overpoweringly attractive. Before she could stammer an answer, Garbo had dropped the needle onto the record again and pulled Mercedes back onto her feet. It was to be an exhausting afternoon. They waltzed to Rudy Vallee singing his big hit of the moment 'Goodnight, Sweetheart' and they tangoed to 'Schoene Gigolo'. Garbo felt the pull of instant attraction for the first time since Jack Gilbert had overwhelmed her on the set of *Flesh and the Devil*.

Afterwards she took her new friend back to her new house at 1717 San Vicente Boulevard, much to the surprise of the Alsatian housekeeper, who was more used to Garbo fending off visitors than inviting them into her house without warning. Mercedes, who was expecting the Brentwood house to be in keeping with the traditional image of a glamorous movie star, was shocked to see how gloomy and sparsely furnished the place was. Although Garbo claimed to live in her bedroom, like a struggling unemployed actress living from hand to mouth in a bedsitter, the room contained little other than a bed, a desk, a dressing table and several hard, uncomfortable chairs all fashioned in the same heavy oak. The only object that appeared to give its owner any pleasure was a slim but somewhat dead-looking tree out in the courtyard which could be seen from the bedroom window.

'I call it my winter tree,' she said rather sadly. 'It reminds me of home and the probability it would soon be covered in snow if we were in Sweden. Now I have to change.'

Mercedes was wrong-footed again. Garbo had invited her to see her bedroom. That usually suggested a woman who was already open to the suggestion of sexual intimacy. At least that was how it had always worked in the past. Nothing was certain with Garbo. She understood that she was not expected to remain in the room when Garbo was changing. That was obviously a step too far at this stage. Mercedes duly walked downstairs and waited in the nondescript living room. Presumably the outfit Garbo chose to put on would indicate how the rest of the evening was likely to go.

When Garbo came down the stairs twenty minutes later, she was dressed not, as Mercedes was hoping, in something low cut and slinky but in a black silk dressing gown and men's bedroom slippers. In the time it took to dress, Garbo's whole demeanour seemed to have undergone a radical change. When Mercedes looked surprised, Garbo quickly justified the odd choice of footwear.

'Everyone thinks I have large feet.'

'But you don't!' cried Mercedes quickly.

'Size 7AA. Anyway, I like these slippers. They are comfortable.'

'Are we going to bed?' asked Mercedes hopefully but with considerable trepidation. Garbo shook her head. Mercedes couldn't understand how she had misread the signals so badly.

'I thought . . .' She had no idea how to continue. She was used to taking charge in sexual matters both with male and female lovers. Garbo's bewildering mood changes threw her. Her hostess knew exactly what her guest was thinking and tried to explain.

'This afternoon. It was fun. I enjoyed it.'

'I'm still enjoying it.'

'It is evening, soon it will be night. I do not sleep well.'

'I'm the same,' sympathised Mercedes. 'I've never had a good night's sleep in my life, I don't think. Still we could do things to keep awake until we were really tired.' Mercedes felt better as she tried to regain the initiative, but Garbo shook her head sorrowfully.

'In the morning I have to go to the studio again.' Mercedes knew a brush-off line when she heard one.

'Do you want me to leave?' Garbo looked as if she couldn't care less.

'Let's not talk. It is useless to talk and try to explain. Let's just sit here and not speak at all.'

'Shall I talk, and you can just listen? Maybe I can send you to sleep. I could recite a list of Argentinian politicians. That should do it.'

'Yackie understood. He drove out to the beach one day to find me. He stood next to me for an hour. He knew when I did not wish to speak.'

The mention of Jack Gilbert was like a slap in the face to Mercedes. Maybe it was true after all what they said – that Jack Gilbert was the real love of Garbo's life and that she had never found anyone to match up to him. So for an hour Mercedes sat next to Garbo and looked at the darkening sky and the emergence of the stars until she mumbled an excuse and left. She did think, however, as she drove home, that she had never remained as silent for as long as that in her whole life and she had never enjoyed a spell of protracted silence as much as she had enjoyed that hour of no words with Garbo. Mercedes was in love, and she was not going to rest until the object of her affections, like everything else in her life, was firmly under her control.

Mercedes had heard all the rumours about Garbo's sexuality. It was clear to her that Greta was pretending to be conventionally heterosexual, as she herself had been, because anything else for a movie star who was also a sex symbol was out of the question. Garbo, like Marlene Dietrich, harboured homosexual inclinations, she was sure of that, and she determined not only to press her own suit but to encourage Garbo to admit to her lesbian tendencies even if only to that privileged, sophisticated circle of like-thinking women in Hollywood, many of whom were bisexual. Salka Viertel was alleged to be of their number, as was Aldous Huxley's wife, Maria, and of course Mercedes herself had experienced heterosexual marriage at an early age. The Swede, however, had never been attracted to any social grouping, and the prospect of joining the 'sewing circle' of Hollywood lesbians with Mercedes as its unofficial president was far from overwhelming.

Marlene had dressed as a man in *Blonde Venus* a full six months before Garbo was to do the same in *Queen Christina*, but Garbo always thought that she and Dietrich were quite different, for all that the press and public were constantly trying to tie them together. Dietrich seemed to like the controversy she stirred up when she dressed in a tuxedo. Garbo liked to wear men's clothes occasionally because she found them comfortable and practical.

Mercedes loved the fuss she and the Swedish star made when they were photographed striding down Hollywood Boulevard.

'Have you seen the papers?' she asked, pointing out the screaming headline GARBO IN PANTS! over the photograph of the two of them.

'I don't wear pants to get into the newspapers,' stated Garbo matter-of-factly.

'Then why do you wear them?'

'Have you ever tried to get out of a car in a skirt with half a dozen photographers snapping away?'

'Is that the only reason?' asked Mercedes, a little disappointed.

'I wore pants when I was growing up in Sweden.'

Garbo knew perfectly well that Hollywood regarded her dress sense as eccentric, but this knowledge could not persuade her to forego the pleasure of wearing a man's old coat and shoes and riding on horseback to watch the setting of the sun over the Pacific Ocean. Mercedes's attempts to identify Garbo's penchant for men's clothes with a statement of her sexuality met with fierce resistance.

'It's just what I like,' protested Garbo. 'I like wearing men's clothes. I like not wearing jewellery and make-up. I like my house the way it is. I know people make fun of me but I don't care.'

'They think you're a les, you know,' said Mercedes.

'They can think what they like. I am me, that's all.'

Marlene indulged her taste for sex with men and occasionally women because her sex drive took her into those places. Garbo did not seek sex so much as protection. Moje had been her first love and he had been homosexual. She didn't mind the fact of his homosexuality, indeed if anything it made her feel safer with him. Yackie was her first lover and there might have been a future with him, but he wanted too much to show her off and, though she was an actress, parading herself before a gawping world was a prospect that filled her with dread.

The world was still in love with her, even if the emotion was not reciprocated. She was the only star who could refuse interviews with the press and still generate endless publicity about herself and her films. Jack's fall from grace was so rapid that he was still making pictures under his old contract when he was being totally ignored by the press that had previously swarmed all over him. It appeared that whatever magic he had possessed (and was increased when he and Greta fell in love so publicly), she took with her when the relationship ended. Garbo thought many times how she could repay the debt she felt she still owed Jack, but then a new movie would start and all her energies would be concentrated on the problems created by her latest role.

As Garbo sat in the back of her second-hand Packard on the way to the studio to begin work on *Susan Lenox: Her Fall and Rise* she dismissed such thoughts from her mind. She had enough to worry about without heaping the problems of Jack Gilbert on top of them. This latest film did not boast a great script, with its story of a girl escaping respectable foster parents to become a famous courtesan. She felt she had played this role many times before ('More bad womens,' she had complained to Salka, who was already thinking that she could do as good a job as Garbo's scriptwriter as any of the hacks the studio assigned to her films), but she recognised that this kind of woman was now particularly popular with the public.

In the 1920s, women had largely been nice girls or vamps. In the depths of the depression the range of stereotypes had expanded to include women who sold their bodies as an economic necessity. All the female stars were playing such parts these days, even the saintly Norma Shearer – who Garbo and most of the other MGM actresses believed was getting an early peek at all the good roles by virtue of her privileged position as the wife of Irving Thalberg. Shearer's roles in *A Free Soul* and *Strangers May Kiss* were not so different from Joan Crawford's in *Possessed* and Constance Bennett's in *The Easiest Way*. Garbo did not like being lumped in with all the other female stars on the lot. She thought she was certainly different, if not better, and as such she shouldn't have to follow the trend because it was temporarily profitable for the studio.

Now they had paired her with the guy with the big ears who the studio thought was the coming man, what was his name again, oh yes, Clark Gable. A few years ago, Garbo couldn't help thinking, as the Packard drew up outside the gates of the studio in Culver City, such a role would have automatically gone to Jack Gilbert. Whenever she thought about Jack she became melancholy.

Garbo got out of the car and began the short walk to her dressing room with her hat pulled down low over her forehead in an attempt to avoid making eye contact with any of the MGM workers. She thought back over the films she had made since *Anna Christie* – *Romance*, *Inspiration*, *As You Desire Me*, adapted from the Pirandello play, and now *Susan Lenox: Her Fall and Rise*.

She turned into her dressing room where the faithful Alma was waiting for her. Garbo handed her the brown paper bag that her housekeeper had placed in the car for her that morning. Despite her increasing wealth Garbo continued to believe there was no point paying inflated prices in the MGM commissary for food she didn't particularly want. It was far more sensible to have a lunch that she did like in the solitude of her dressing room.

She sat in the make-up chair and closed her eyes. This was one of her favourite moments of the day. The make-up artists were told never to talk to her unless she initiated the conversation. The patting of the cream onto her face was like a facial massage. She thought back over the reviews for her recent films. Mostly they cared less for the movie than they did for her and, though she was probably her own severest critic, mostly Garbo agreed with this assessment. If she was in a bad film, she herself escaped unscathed. When Jack Gilbert was in a bad film, he was excoriated.

Gilbert again. It happened so often. He was gone from her now she knew that. She knew she was destined never to marry, but the very concept of marriage brought Jack back into her mind even more firmly. She didn't feel guilty it was over – after all, he was the one who had run off and got married so impetuously – but, even if she didn't dare to pick up the telephone and call him, she still worried about Jack and particularly how he was coping with his present crisis. She hated to see him pilloried in the press, dreaded the casual conversations that told her he was drinking himself into oblivion. Maybe it would be better for Yackie if he just retired from the screen. He couldn't go on absorbing the blows of this constant criticism.

In self-imposed exile in his Moorish house on Tower Road, Jack Gilbert read the reviews of his succession of weak movies and was coming to the same conclusion. For Garbo 1930 was the year of her triumph in the two versions of *Anna Christie*, but for Jack it was the year when he sat at home with nothing to do other than drink. He used to drink because he enjoyed the taste of liquor and because it made him uninhibited at parties. He liked people who drank: they were his kind of people. Now he drank because the alcohol temporarily deadened the pain.

The doctor he went to about his stomach pains said he had the beginnings of an ulcer. Jack had been somewhat inebriated even for this 10 a.m. appointment.

'I don't get ulcers, I give 'em,' retorted Jack. The doctor looked puzzled.

'L.B. Mayer used to say that to me all the time,' he explained.

'How are you sleeping?' asked the doctor. Now it was Jack's turn to look puzzled.

'On my side, I think. How would I know? I'm asleep.'

'I meant how well do you sleep?'

'Oh, I see. Pretty badly to be honest.'

'That's all a result of the drinking, I'm afraid, Mr Gilbert.'

'Baloney! I've been drinking since I was fifteen.'

'Exactly. It's all caught up with you. If you go on at this rate you could suffer liver failure and that would be the end.'

'Oh, come on, doc.'

'Do you have impotence problems?'

'Me? The Great Lover of the Silver Screen?'

'Well? Do you?'

It was true that he was no longer erect in the morning, but he had assumed that that was because he was sleeping alone much of the time. There had been that embarrassing occasion when he got that pretty blonde chorus girl back to the house and found he couldn't perform. But that wasn't the norm . . . apart from the time with the waitress who hid in his car and offered her services right there in the car park – but he thought that was because the girl wasn't attractive.

'Only once,' he said.

'Mr Gilbert, you have to stop drinking. Your health is deteriorating rapidly.' Jack decided to find another doctor.

The insomnia and the pains in his stomach just got worse, and he was also aware that his heart was beating in an irregular rhythm. The cardiologist asked him almost the same questions.

'Do you exercise, Mr Gilbert?'

'I used to play tennis. I could play thirty-six holes of golf before lunch . . .'

'Now, Mr Gilbert? What about now?'

'Not so much now.'

'And how much alcohol do you consume?'

'You tell the government what I say?'

'A doctor-patient conversation is entirely confidential.'

'A couple of bottles a day.'

'Beer?'

'Beer, scotch, rye, gin, who's counting?'

'Mr Gilbert, if you continue drinking at this rate your heart will give out in a few years.'

'Well, as long as I get a decent part before I go . . .'

'How do you sleep?'

'On my side. OK. Thanks, doc, I get the message. Send me the bill.' He got up and left. These doctors were all obsessed with taking away from him the only pleasure he had, the only thing that made life bearable these days.

He sat on the couch that night and slowly unscrewed the top of the bottle of Jack Daniels and poured himself a double. He tossed it back in one gulp and waited for the familiar burning sensation at the back of his throat. He picked up the current edition of *Photoplay* from the coffee table and thumbed through it. There was no mention of him anywhere in it. He remembered when there were two or three articles a month and ever so many references to him in the gossip columns, noting his smiling attendance at premieres and nightclubs and restaurants. He hurled the magazine across the room in disgust. *Photoplay*! They were responsible for everything that had gone wrong in the past two years.

That traumatic article by Katherine Albert in *Photoplay* – 'Is Jack Gilbert Through?' – had been the precursor of many similar features. They all seemed to think there was something wrong with his voice, even though many of the journalists had talked to him many times and knew that there wasn't. James Quirk, who had once been happy to write articles praising the Great Lover, had, unaccountably to Jack, jumped on the bandwagon. He had asked the boffins at the phone company American Telephone & Telegraph whether there was anything that could be done to make Jack's voice more palatable to the human ear and he had been told that there wasn't. Just as the camera loved Jack's face, so the microphone hated his voice. The article was utter garbage scientifically of course, but by the time he had read to the end Jack was starting to believe it too.

At first Jack decided to brave it out by going to the studio every day and sitting in his palatial bungalow specially constructed in a corner of the lot, holding court to any friend, actor, executive, writer or technician who wanted to stop by, have a drink and share a joke. As it became clear, however, that Irving Thalberg was not going to ride to the rescue, they all realised that Jack's situation was hopeless. He could fight Mayer if his movies made money and Irving Thalberg was on his side, but when his movies failed and Irving was nowhere visible then calling in to see good old Jack became a bad career move. MGM employees who still wanted a future at the studio entered his dressing room at their peril. Eventually the knocks on the door stopped altogether.

Those of Jack's friends who did not abandon him as a matter of professional self-preservation continued the increasingly difficult task of attempting to keep his head above water. One night in the Brown Derby restaurant Jack saw the unprepossessing figure of the journalist Jim Tully, who had written one of the worst personal attacks Jack had ever experienced, a scurrilous article entitled 'John Gilbert – the Screen's Most Romantic Hero Has No Glamour For Hollywood's Severest Critic' in *Vanity Fair*. It was, by the standards of the time, extremely cruel and frequently untrue. Jack had never met the hustler who claimed to know him well enough to pronounce judgement on him. Tully called him 'a strutting ham', 'a minor talent', 'not gifted' and, worst of all, 'a coward'. He also castigated him for having no sense of humour and then revealed that, quite unknown to Jack, his biological father John Pringle was working as an extra in Hollywood for $10 a day. Jack, at the time, was making $10,000 a week.

As soon as Tully's presence was pointed out to him, Jack was on his feet and walking purposefully towards him. He couldn't get anywhere near Mayer or Thalberg but he was going to beat the living daylights out of this creep. It wouldn't solve a damn thing in the long run – he knew that perfectly well – but it would make him feel a whole lot better in the short run. Fancy this creep having the temerity to call him a coward. Well, everyone would soon see exactly who the real coward was.

'I'm Jack Gilbert. Get on your feet, creep.' Tully, not surprisingly, looked nervous. He showed no signs of moving, indeed he looked round the restaurant, as if hoping that someone would come to his rescue. Jack was standing for no more of this prevarication.

'You heard me, creep. Now get on your feet, or are you too cowardly to take what's coming to you?' Very slowly Tully got to his feet. While Tully had done quite a bit of research on Jack for his article, Jack had done no research on Tully and so did not know that this unimpressive figure was a former prizefighter. As he rose from the table Tully's right fist shot straight out in front of him and made contact with Jack's jaw. The crack of fist on jawbone resounded round the restaurant as Jack slumped to the floor, dead to the world. It was yet another rapid fall for the Great Lover.

Chapter Fourteen

Greta Garbo's restless search for privacy continued as she tried to catch up with the latest productions on Broadway. She registered at the Hotel St Moritz in Manhattan and ordered her tickets through the concierge at the hotel, always asking for two seats on the aisle in an attempt to ensure she had nobody sitting on either side of her. She would invariably time her arrival at the theatre to coincide with the rise of the curtain and disappear as it came down. While the audience demonstrated their approval of the performance, Garbo would be out of the theatre and into the first available cab.

One Wednesday she slightly mistimed her arrival at the theatre to see Katherine Cornell, who was starring in *The Barretts of Wimpole Street*, the smash-hit play by Rudolf Besier about the life of the poet Elizabeth Barrett. She was dressed, as usual, in a long coat with its collar turned up and a hat pulled down over her forehead. She sat in her usual centre aisle seat with her head down, staring at the floor, willing the curtain to rise, but her hopes were dashed by an usher who, slightly alarmed by her strange behaviour, asked if she was all right.

The usher was shocked to realise that the object of her sympathy was the most famous movie star in the world. She told the doorman, and within seconds the news had filtered backstage. The actors came racing out of their dressing room and started pushing each other aside to peek through the curtains at the most advantageous spot and see if it really was Greta Garbo sitting in the third row on the centre aisle seat. The curtain went up twenty minutes late with the whole cast still unsure if it really was Garbo or not.

At the end of the performance Kit Cornell was taking off her make-up when her dresser came racing in.

'She's asking for you!'

'Who is?'

'Garbo!'

'That's not Garbo. It's just some young woman who wants to look like Garbo. They all do that nowadays.'

'They don't all come backstage afterwards and ask to see you.'

'Did she leave a name?'

'No, but you wouldn't expect her to, would you?'

'Well, maybe not Greta Garbo, but she could say she was a friend of my husband or of Irving Thalberg. That would be a clue.'

'Aren't you going to see her, then?'

'No. It's not Garbo anyway. It's some practical joker.'

'What shall I tell her?'

'Tell her I want to be alone.'

'Oh, I can't do that!'

'All right, just tell her I'm really tired after the show and I never see strangers. If it is Garbo, she'll identify herself.'

Early the following morning Garbo emerged from the hotel wearing her now trademark dark glasses, a pair of sensible flat shoes and a coat with its tweed collar turned up so it reached her ears. She liked to take an early-morning walk through Central Park because such bitterly cold but bright days like this reminded her a little of January days back home. Unfortunately by now the press had caught the news and they were in the lobby in large numbers.

A horrified Garbo bulldozed her way through the throng and dashed outside, grabbing the first taxi she could find that would take her to the park. Unfortunately for her there were plenty of cabs around that morning, and the newspaper reporters and photographers simply followed her vehicle, stalking their prey. Arriving in Central Park at 72nd Street, Garbo thrust a dollar bill at the driver and started to run across the park as the dozen following taxis screeched to a halt and their occupants began to race across the grass in close pursuit. Garbo was quite fit and managed to outpace her hunters for some time before they cornered her. She turned to face them and the traditional chorus of banal, shouted questions.

'I can say nothing. I am not in love with any man. I do not want to marry. I just want to be left alone.' At that moment a cab driver stopped to observe the scene of thirty journalists and photographers surrounding one thin, frail woman. The woman took one look, turned tail and ran towards it. She leaped into the taxi and ordered it to stop outside the Hotel St Moritz at the employees' entrance. So ended Garbo's futile attempts at going out for a walk at 7 a.m. Depressed, she opened the door to her suite. There on the floor was a handwritten note from Kit Cornell, apologising for her rudeness the previous night and inviting her to lunch.

On the Super Chief from Chicago to Los Angeles she stared out of the window as the majestic landscape of the western United States rolled past. She saw it but she took no comfort from it because her restless mind would not give her a moment's peace. Her contract with MGM was due to expire in a few months' time and she had no idea what to do. She was rich now, richer than she had ever dared to dream was possible the day she and Moje had arrived in New York. She had earned more than $1.3 million since that day. Low income-tax rates and prices depressed because of the economic situation, combined with her own undiminished instinct for frugality, meant that, at the age of twenty-eight, she did not need to work for financial reasons. Indeed, she might never need to work again, but that prospect brought no happiness in its wake.

It was Irving Thalberg who finally persuaded her to sign a new contract and return to the screen in a project the studio had nursed by injecting $15,500 into a Broadway production of an adaptation of the Vicki Baum novel *Grand Hotel*. Garbo was to play the part of the Russian ballerina Grusinskaya and to receive first billing, which was particularly important since Thalberg had persuaded Mayer that it made sense to pack the movie with star names including Joan Crawford, Lewis Stone, Lionel Barrymore, Wallace Beery and Jean Hersholt. To play the part of the man with whom she falls in love, Baron Felix von Gaigern, the handsome and debonair aristocrat who is trying desperately to persuade the world that he is rich when he is in fact a flat-broke thief, Thalberg came up with an interesting idea but thought, for safety's sake, he had better talk to Mayer about it first.

'Gilbert? Are you crazy?'

'I think it's great casting.'

'He's a bum.'

'No, he's not. He's sitting there taking our money till the end of his contract.'

'He has no voice.'

'Now, L.B., you know perfectly well what happened to Jack's voice.'

'The public doesn't care about him any more. He's all washed up.'

'That's what I worry about it, but Garbo and Gilbert were a great team.'

'*Were*, Irving, were a great team. Now there's Clark Gable and Jean Harlow, William Powell and Myrna Loy, Fred Astaire and Ginger Rogers.'

'OK, OK, maybe you're right. I'm worried that Jack just sits home drinking himself to death.'

'Hey, this is MGM. We're not a hospital. Let him go somewhere else if he has to dry out. Besides I can think of a better Gaigern.'

'Go on then, who?'

'John Barrymore.'

'He also likes a drink.'

'He's a great actor, a great stage actor with a wonderful voice. I think Garbo'll like him.'

'More than Gilbert?'

'She hates that bum. Why do you think she kept leaving him at the altar?'

In the house on Tower Road Jack had heard all the stories about *Grand Hotel*, how it was going to be a new kind of picture with lots of different stories and lots of stars. He had heard that Irving was thinking about him for the part of Baron Gaigern and he hadn't been able to sleep at night with worrying about it. He would kill for a part like that, a big juicy starring part, playing with the top-rated stars in the studio and – most important – playing opposite Flicka again. He thought about contacting her, getting her to plead his cause to

Mayer and Thalberg but decided against it. He didn't want her, more than anyone, to see how far he had sunk in the world. After weeks of hoping came the news he dreaded. Barrymore had got the part. That made a brace of Barrymores whose sole purpose in life appeared to be to destroy him.

Garbo was triumphant in the movie, easily winning the battle of the egos and justifying her first position on the credits. She and John Barrymore conducted a professional relationship of the highest mutual respect. On the morning of their first scene together he showed up surprisingly early, and she showed up surprisingly late. It transpired that Garbo had been waiting patiently outside the sound stage to escort her new leading man onto the set. Barrymore was touched particularly when Greta Garbo made a public pronouncement at the conclusion of their first love scene: 'You have no idea what it means to me to play opposite so perfect an artist.'

She went further and covered up for him on those days when he was too hung-over to start work on time. She certainly showed no sign that she was regretting the fact that Barrymore had replaced Gilbert in the part, and the response of the audience to the pair of them as lovers was equally positive, despite the twenty-three-year age gap between them.

Just about the time that Garbo signed a new contract specifying no more than two films a year and that she was to be paid $250,000 for each one, so Jack Gilbert's contract (which it resembled somewhat, if only because Harry Edington had negotiated both deals) was coming to an end. For many months he had comforted himself with the prospect that, though he knew MGM would not offer him any kind of a renewal, he would now be free to pursue all those dreams that the golden handcuffs of MGM had made him put to one side. He could direct as well as act for other studios. He could also write, because if anyone knew a decent movie script when he saw one it was Jack Gilbert. But as the dreaded day of freedom, 31 July 1932, approached, he started to panic. He hadn't been in a decent film for years. His public was no longer there. They had found other gods to worship.

He was now suffering from painful, bleeding ulcers aggravated by the alcohol he consumed. A single whisky could now have the effect that three doubles used to have. He needed the booze as a way of dealing with his insomnia. In the small hours of the morning he felt his loneliness to be overwhelming and the whisky helped to get him back to sleep.

When the alcohol didn't work its magic, Jack summoned his friends. King Vidor was getting used to hearing his phone ring at 3.30 a.m. He knew who it was of course and he hated the trips to the house up the hill because this frightened, paranoid creature was no longer the Jack Gilbert who had been his best friend half a dozen years ago. For a start, there was the matter of the gun that Jack had started sleeping with under his pillow. Frankly, King Vidor thought, it would be a lot safer if he just slept with a different girl every night, but he was no longer as interested in sex as he used to be.

One night he was over at Jack's at the usual ungodly hour, slumped in a chair watching Jack until finally he heard the welcome sound of snoring. King got up and walked into the bathroom, which he'd been desperate to use for half an hour. When he returned to the bedroom he saw Jack kneeling on the bed with the gun levelled at King's chest. Now he'd seen this scene any number of times in the movies, he'd directed one of two of them himself and he knew Jack had been in some as well. What passed rapidly through King's mind was that in his current mental state Jack might be unable to distinguish reality from the movies. God knows he could be like that when relatively sober. He had clearly forgotten that King was in the house and thought he was an intruder. With Jack's shaking finger hovering near the trigger, this was going to need the best piece of direction of Vidor's life.

'Jack,' he said very calmly, 'it's just me, King. Put the gun down. Jack, can you hear me?'

'King?' came the wavering, uncertain voice of his friend.

'Yes, it's me, King,' he repeated as firmly as he dared. 'I'm going to walk towards you. I want you to give me the gun.'

The gun trembled in Jack's hand, his finger hovering over the trigger, as King, heart pounding, walked towards him, not knowing if Jack might be tempted to pull the trigger just to see what would happen. Sober, Jack would never pull a gun on him but in this context he knew he was risking his life as he took those six paces towards the friend who could easily murder him with the slightest movement of his forefinger. The director almost cried out with relief when he felt Jack loosen his grip and he took the gun into his own hand.

'Sorry, King. I didn't realise you were here. When did you come over?'

Next day Vidor was in Irving Thalberg's office repeating the story. 'You've got to do something, Irving. He's in a bad way.'

'I'm sorry.'

'You can do better than that. He really thought he was going to get the part in *Grand Hotel*.'

'I never mentioned it to him.'

'He heard.'

'Who from? The only person I told was L.B. Oh.' It didn't take long for them to trace the origin of the rumour.

'His contract's nearly up. Come on, Irving – he's a decent guy and he's had a raw deal.'

Thalberg opened his desk drawer and took out a script with Gilbert's name on the front cover as its writer.

'This is something Jack brought to me about four years ago.'

'When he was good, you mean.'

'When we had Erich von Stroheim here. They'd had a good working relationship on *The Merry Widow* and Jack wrote this script for Von to direct but then . . .' It didn't need putting into words. Erich von Stroheim's career had gone in exactly the same direction as Jack's and at much the same speed. As far as Thalberg was concerned, they had both committed the cardinal sin of making pictures that had lost money.

'Is it any good?'

'It might be in the hands of a really good screenwriter.'

'Jack knows a good script when he sees one.'

'So do I. But that doesn't make me a writer either.'

'What's the story like?'

'It's OK. It's a black comedy called *Downstairs* about the lives of aristocrats and their servants in Vienna.'

'I can see why Jack wanted Von to direct it.'

'It was difficult for me to tell Jack what I thought of his writing, but I've given it to Lenore Coffee to work over. If I like the job she does I'll give it to Jack to play.'

'And to direct?'

'You want to do it?' asked Thalberg. King Vidor grimaced. Much as he loved Jack, or at least much as he had loved him before he went weird, directing him at the moment wasn't something he was looking forward to. Thalberg smiled. He knew exactly what was going on in Vidor's head.

'It's OK. I'm going to offer it to Monte Bell.'

Thalberg liked Coffee's re-write, and Jack was duly informed that his last picture under his current extravagant MGM contract would be *Downstairs*, adapted from his own script. He was thrilled, soon swallowing the disappointment of seeing that his script had been heavily re-written by another writer. He had been around MGM long enough to know that this was standard studio practice and he threw himself into pre-production. Paul Lukas was cast as the butler to offset Jack's crowd-pleasing, villainous chauffeur, a boisterous Casanova figure that Jack had carefully marked out for himself. It was the sort of role Jack felt comfortable in, far removed from the Great Lover parts that had been his downfall. He knew he was on his way back and was anxious to tell everyone who would listen exactly that.

The stalwart actors Reginald Owen and Olga Baclanova played the baron and the baroness, the 'upstairs' characters in *Downstairs*. For the part of Anna, the young maid who was going to be the female lead opposite Jack, Thalberg and Bell chose a very pretty blonde woman in her early twenties from North Dakota who had started her Hollywood career as a Goldwyn showgirl but who had previously been seen in a small role in Ernst Lubitsch's well-liked musical comedy *The Love Parade* at Paramount. She looked nothing like Garbo, but Jack soon felt the old fires of honest lust burning through his loins. A great part, a script he had originally written himself, a beautiful young blonde hanging on his every word – Jack Gilbert was back, and the world would soon recognise the fact. He even cut down a little on his alcohol consumption. After all, there was nothing that compared with the high of actually being on top in Hollywood.

Jack had always lived his parts to the full. In *The Big Parade* he *was* that doughboy soldier, in *Flesh and the Devil* he inhabited the skin of the army officer besotted by Felicitas, the character played by Garbo. Audiences always respond to a truthful performance, and Jack took his characters home with him. In *Downstairs* his character, Karl, is redeemed by his love for the virginal and beautiful Anna. In life Jack soon felt much the same way about Virginia Bruce.

Virginia certainly reciprocated those feelings. She had grown up in North Dakota sitting entranced in the movie theatre watching John Gilbert make love to Greta Garbo and Renée Adorée and Mae Murray. She had longed to be in their place, to feel the passion of his kisses on her lips and within days of meeting Jack Gilbert she was in the house in Tower Road experiencing it all, just as she had imagined it. Jack had been so beaten down by Hollywood that this fresh young woman seemed to offer him a new start in life.

'You're young and pretty. You're everything Hollywood likes,' he murmured as his lips travelled down her neck towards her delectable breasts.

'Me?' gasped Virginia, not entirely sure of the protocol at this moment. She felt it would be impolite if not hypocritical to remove his hands and lips from her body entirely but she didn't want him to think she was 'easy'.

'Aw shucks, I'm just lil' ol' Virginia from North Dakota,' she protested. Jack helped her out by coming up for air.

'Well, that's better than being lil' ol' North Dakota from Virginia.' She laughed. He seized the chance to kiss her again. This time it was less urgent and more tender. He took her face in his hands and looked directly into her eyes. Even as he did so he knew the gesture was one he had learned from Garbo.

'You're so fresh and naïve. They're going to eat you alive.'

'Who are?' asked a worried Virginia. Nobody had ever mentioned cannibalism in all the warning stories she had heard about Hollywood.

'The jackals and jackasses who run this town. Why don't you go back to North Dakota and save yourself?'

It was apparent from the passion with which Virginia kissed him that she had no intention of taking Jack's advice.

'I never want to leave this house. I sure as hell don't want to go back to North Dakota.' Jack was pleased. This girl made a pleasant change from the cynical sex he had been having recently with whores, who at least wouldn't nag him about his drinking. He wanted to take her to bed, but some inner voice of decency was telling him that he hadn't yet made a full declaration of all the risks she was running.

'I have a bad reputation. If you're seen around town with me, it'll be bad for your career.'

Virginia was puzzled. To her, being seen around town with Jack Gilbert was going to enhance her career.

'We're making a picture together. Why should anyone object?'

'Trust me, they will. I'm a broken-down washed-up alcoholic wreck with a questionable past and a non-existent future.' Virginia wondered why he was so down on the movie. It read like a good script to her. MGM were making it and they were the biggest and best studio in the world. What was he talking about?

'You don't think this movie will be a big hit, then?'

'I think it's great, but you look at my other sound movies and you wonder if this one will be lucky to get released on the bottom half of a double bill in Poughkeepsie.' Virginia breathed a sigh of relief. It was a good movie. The poor boy was just being down on himself.

'I don't care. I think you're the most handsome, witty, intelligent man I've ever met.'

'But of course you come from North Dakota so what would you know?' teased Jack.

'Oh, you're so rude!' protested Virginia playfully. She opened her mouth and let his tongue find hers.

'Sure I am,' smiled Jack, 'but in a handsome, witty and intelligent way.' They both laughed. His hand started to lift the hem of her skirt. Virginia clamped her hand over his and impeded its progress.

'I want to ask you a question.' Jack sighed. He had done all the small talk, he had told her that he would understand it if she wanted to run away but now he would very much have liked to have brought the conversation to a halt.

'OK, you can ask,' he said with his best Groucho Marx leer, 'but I'm not a virgin, so you'd better prepare yourself.' Jack knew exactly what was coming. He'd had this conversation so often it bored him to tears.

'I'm so fascinated by her. What was she like?'

'Who?' There was the slightest ray of hope that she might have an original thought.

'You know who. Garbo, silly. What was Garbo really like?' Jack paused. He did want to get this girl into bed as quickly as possible but the very mention of Flicka sent a spasm of hurt and anger through him and he could feel his sexual interest dwindling.

'She was a pain in the ass. No, really, she was. And not as beautiful as you.'

'How can you say that?'

'Because it's true.'

'But Garbo is the most beautiful movie star in the world.'

'Oh sure, she is. Garbo in the movies is a magical, enchanting enigma, but Garbo in the living room is a pain in the ass.' Virginia was puzzled. Garbo and Gilbert, they were the most famous, most romantic couple in the world. She had wallowed in their fame and their romance.

'I thought you loved her.'

'Oh, everyone loves Garbo,' agreed Jack. 'Especially Garbo.' Virginia looked disappointed. Jack pulled her to her feet. 'Come upstairs with me. It's the most fantastic sight you've ever seen – the whole of Los Angeles spread out before you.'

Virginia allowed herself to be guided out of the living room with no show of reluctance. As they climbed the stairs Jack couldn't help thinking of Garbo's response as a twenty-one-year old, younger than Virginia now, when he had tried the same line on her.

'I think I know what it is you want me to look at. And it is not Los Angeles.' English wasn't even her first language, yet she spoke it more intelligently than this dumbbell from North Dakota. Or was it South Dakota? Oh well, he shrugged, he wasn't looking for intellectual stimulation.

Garbo herself was thinking about Jack Gilbert at just about the same time that he was thinking about her. She had been watching screen tests of young lovers for days now as the studio sought a new leading man for her latest picture. *Queen Christina* was based on the real-life seventeenth-century queen of Sweden who scandalised her court by wearing men's clothing and abdicating in order to live anonymously. Although she had no desire to marry, she was allegedly the object of the affection of dozens of lovers. She rewarded her favourites lavishly and during the course of her ten-year reign she disposed of half of the lands held by the crown.

It was Salka Viertel who had encouraged her to read the biography of the monarch because she could see so many links to Garbo's own life and interests. The studio was happy to commission a script and when they agreed to put it into production Salka Viertel's career rose to new heights. Clearly the end of the queen's life presented some problems. The real Queen Christina abdicated at the age of twenty-eight and died in obscurity in Rome. Nobody would believe that Garbo could live in obscurity, not even Garbo – and she was trying very hard to do so. The solution reached by the producer, director and writer was that Garbo should leave with her Spanish lover to live in his house, high on a cliff. Unfortunately he is mortally wounded in a duel, and she sails away into the unknown – a better ending for a Garbo picture.

The search for the actor to play the part of the Spanish envoy, Don Antonio, with whom the queen falls in love and for whom she sacrifices her throne, was not going well. Garbo had originally wanted Leslie Howard but he had turned it down, then they thought of Nils Asther, the Swedish actor with whom she'd made *Wild Orchids* and who had recently starred successfully as the hero of Frank Capra's tragic tale *The Bitter Tea of General Yen*, but eventually it was decided that two actors talking 'funny' – as Americans always termed foreign accents – would not be a strong commercial proposition. Joan Crawford's current husband, Franchot Tone, who had defected from the left-wing Group Theatre in New York to live the life of a Hollywood star, was also a possibility, but Garbo rejected him, as she did Fredric March, Victory Jory and the man who was getting all the parts that would have previously gone to Yackie, Clark Gable. Ronald Colman was offered the part but, like Leslie Howard, he declined with thanks. The studio toyed with the possibility of linking Garbo with John Barrymore again, but eventually the age gap of over twenty years caused so many doubts that he fell out of favour.

The day after the decision went against Barrymore, Garbo drove over to Salka's house in Mayberry Road. It was unseasonably cold in Santa Monica that day: the temperature gauge barely reached sixty degrees. The two women put on coats and scarves and strode off together to walk alongside the Pacific as the normally placid ocean suddenly took on an unusually angry appearance. The European exiles exulted in the weather. Garbo breathed in deeply.

'Isn't this wonderful? It reminds me so much of Sweden.'

'Look, Greta! Look around. There's not a native to be seen! They're all inside shivering with the heat turned on.' They laughed but the anxiety Salka was feeling brought the laughter to an abrupt end. She worried that unless they cast *Queen Christina* soon Mayer would get bored, force Garbo into any one of a number of scripts that were lying around the studio and cancel her own writing contract. They had to find the right Spanish envoy soon.

'Do you think if we approached Ronald Colman again . . .'

'He's already turned it down.'

'But if you were to talk to him yourself . . .'

'Before he cast Barrymore in *Grand Hotel*, do you know who Thalberg wanted?'

'No.'

'Yackie.'

'Oh.' Salka's mind was racing. Jack Gilbert? That old dinosaur? She couldn't be serious, could she?

'He's a wonderful actor.'

'Well, he was, of course,' admitted Salka slowly. 'But is he right for this? And you know how the rest of the industry regards him.'

Garbo glared at her. She was the only one allowed to criticise Yackie. She hated it whenever anyone else did so.

'Well, if you really think so . . .'

'I do really think so. He is a wonderful actor. I saw his last picture, *Downstairs* . . .'

'Oh, but wasn't that a terrible failure?' Salka was quick to interpose the general response to every Gilbert picture since *His Glorious Night*.

'Did you see it?' asked Garbo bluntly.

'Well, no, but I heard . . .'

'Well, I did,' interrupted the actress. 'Yackie was very good.'

'Are you sure you're not doing this because you feel sorry for him?' asked Salka shrewdly.

'He is a very good actor,' insisted Garbo. 'He will make a very good Don Antonio.'

'Are you still in love with him?' asked Salka.

Garbo walked on without answering, lengthening her stride and forcing the shorter woman almost to start running in order to keep up with her. Eventually Garbo stopped and turned to her friend.

'And what if I am?' she asked quietly.

Salka desperately needed the credit of having written a Garbo picture. If that meant taking on her ex-boyfriend she would just have to swallow her fears. She hadn't heard Garbo talk about Gilbert for months. She thought the affair was long since over and done with. It was slightly disconcerting that she had kept these passionate feelings so well concealed from her. Maybe she didn't know Garbo as well as she had thought.

'What I feel for Yackie is my business. As far as MGM is concerned the only question is, would Yackie be good casting as Don Antonio? I think he would.'

'Are you going to tell Mr Mayer?'

'Oh no!' Garbo smiled. 'That would never do. We have a long way to go before Yackie can be mentioned to Mr Mayer. He tells me he has made a wonderful new discovery and I must sit and watch a movie with him tomorrow morning.'

At ten o'clock the following morning, Mayer ran a movie for Garbo in his private screening room starring Gloria Swanson and an up-and-coming English actor called Laurence Olivier.

'This Laurence Oliver guy is gonna be a huge star,' pronounced Mayer as he settled back into his chair and picked up the telephone to tell the projectionist to roll the film. At the end of it Mayer was pleased that his instincts, as usual, were quite right.

'Well, he's a *faygele*, but I guess he'll do.' To Mayer any British actor who talked like he had a matzo ball in his mouth and a *gefilte* fish stuck up his backside was a homosexual. Garbo thought hard about what she had seen. She saw the talent of the young Olivier, but it was as yet unformed. Could she risk raising the Jack Gilbert issue now? She thought, on balance, she couldn't. Not yet, anyway. Something needed to happen before Mayer and Thalberg could be persuaded. She rose to her feet and thanked Mayer politely for allowing her to see the movie.

'So *nu*? Do we go with the *faygele*?'

'OK,' said Garbo. Mayer was astonished. She'd turned down all those famous actors and now she was taking this unknown Britisher without a struggle. Maybe she didn't fancy the competition. Mayer had a fairly basic appreciation of actors' egos.

'You mean it?' He certainly wasn't going to sign a contract with Laurence Olivier unless he was absolutely sure that Garbo was happy.

'OK,' she repeated and marched out of the theatre. It was not possible to tell if Garbo was happy. Thinking back over the eight years he had known her, he wasn't sure if he'd ever seen her happy, so how would he know what it looked like when she was?

Garbo zipped up her baggy tracksuit top, stepped out into the dazzling California sunshine, slipped on her sunglasses and pulled the brim of her hat down low over her eyes. It was pointless as a disguise. Everyone knew the identity of the tall lady who marched round the lot by herself dressed in such a fashion. It was lunchtime and, as she strode towards the extras, they sprang to their feet from their positions lying on the grass, finishing the remnants of their cardboard-box lunches, like so many pigeons leaving their bread-crumbs and fluttering into the air at the approach of humans. They stood in respectful silence, watching the most famous movie star in the world as she performed the difficult and unusual task of walking towards her car. Coming the other way was the familiar loping walk of Groucho Marx, replete with cigar and painted moustache. He stood in front of her, blocking her way, and stooped to peek under the brim of the hat. Garbo fixed him with the iciest stare she could manage.

'Pardon me, ma'am,' said Groucho jovially. 'I thought you were a fellow I knew in Pittsburgh.' Garbo strode on. Harpo and Chico came laughing out of a nearby dressing room and ceremonially each of them handed Groucho a dollar bill.

Garbo drove home to find a note from Rouben Mamoulian under the door suggesting a lunch to discuss the script of *Queen Christina*, which Bess Meredyth and H.M. Harwood had polished after Salka Viertel's early drafts. Garbo had originally wanted Ernst Lubitsch or Victor Seastrom to direct, but the latter had not wanted to leave Sweden to work again in Hollywood and Paramount would not release Lubitsch. Mamoulian, however, was a good choice as far as Garbo was concerned, and she drove to the Paramount lot on the corner of Marathon Street and Melrose Avenue with considerable anticipation. She had spent much of her last Swedish vacation doing research on Christina, visiting the castle at Uppsala, the scene of the abdication, and making quick, clever sketches of costumes, furniture and embroidery from the appropriate period. At one point she toyed with the idea of claiming a credit as 'technical consultant', but she feared it might attract quite the wrong sort of publicity. Still, *Queen Christina* felt like 'her' film in a way that no previous production had, and Mamoulian was the kind of serious, innovative director who would, she felt, do justice to it.

Rouben Mamoulian was a tall, sensitive, bespectacled Armenian who had already made a name for himself in the theatre before he came to Hollywood as the studios began their relentless search for talent that would not be cowed by the advent of sound. Popular belief ascribed to Mamoulian the invention of the microphone tied to a fishing rod so it could move with the actors, thereby freeing the camera from the static positioning that had so badly affected the pictorial quality of the early talkies.

Over lunch Garbo listened entranced as the director talked of the influence of Stanislavski and the Moscow Art Theatre. She felt as though she were back with Moje again. For all the strength of her own will and the conviction that she was born to play the part of Christina, she also knew that she liked a strong director, someone who knew his business and was both technically imaginative and responsive to his actors.

Garbo had recently seen Mamoulian's *Love Me Tonight*, a delightful romantic musical comedy with Maurice Chevalier, Jeanette MacDonald and Myrna Loy. What she liked most was the way Rouben had used sound and music to move the story along. The Rodgers and Hart song 'Isn't it Romantic?' is sung first in Paris, picked up by people in the streets, then by passengers on a train, until finally a troop of marching soldiers carries it to MacDonald dreaming at the window of her chateau. Garbo almost fell in love with Mamoulian during that number: that creativity was exactly what she hoped he might bring to *Queen Christina*. The lunch did nothing to dispel that feeling.

'How did you feel about the Olivier test?'

'L.B. Mayer calls him "Oliver".'

'I know. He thinks he's a homo as well.'

'He thinks all Britishers are homos.'

'And Armenians?' Mamoulian couldn't help asking.

'He only knows you.'

'And he doesn't know me as well as you do.'

'I don't know you at all.'

'I think you do, Greta.' He was right. Garbo could feel herself slipping under his spell.

'I think Olivier will be fine.'

'Just fine?'

'It's there but he is young. I made a mistake like that before.'

'He's only two years younger than you are.'

'In movie terms he is a child and I am a very old lady.'

'I never went for old ladies before I met you.'

He took hold of her hand. She let it rest there for a second before withdrawing it. In her mind she heard the sound of a hundred flashbulbs going off. Later, there might be time for that, but right now it was time for work.

While Garbo was over at Paramount, work was going on at Metro inside and outside Jack Gilbert's bungalow. Irving Thalberg had agreed to be the best man at Jack's wedding to the lovely Virginia Bruce. It was the least he could do. There had been a number of skirmishes between the two old friends when Jack had thought he had a part under lock and key and Irving came and took it away from him. *Grand Hotel* was bad enough, but *Red Dust* had been worse. The part was that of a tough adventurer playing opposite the new platinum-blonde star Jean Harlow.

Thalberg's first thought was Jack. It was obvious really. It would be a nice change of pace for Jack after the well-received but commercially uninspiring *Downstairs*, but as he thought about it more deeply and heard the reports from his spies on the studio floor that Jack was looking older, sweating profusely and lacked the sparkle of old, Thalberg realised that he couldn't afford to risk casting Jack in such a part. Clark Gable was the new all-action MGM star, and he had to go with what the public wanted.

It had been an awkward meeting with Jack but thankfully the rejuvenating effect of a love affair with the very beautiful and very young Virginia Bruce had so improved Jack's mood that the meeting ended with Jack accepting Thalberg's decision and inviting him to be the best man at his wedding. Thalberg agreed quickly. From his point of view it was a great deal and he gave the approval necessary to turn an empty sound stage into a temporary wedding venue.

The night before the wedding was to take place Jack had a bizarre conversation with the man who was about to become his latest father-in-law.

'Jack, you can't marry Virginia.'

'That's not what she thinks.'

'Are you a man of honour?'

'Haven't you seen my movies?'

'Where is the protection you are offering this young woman?'

'You want to see a gun?'

'I want to see a will.'

'Whose?'

'Yours.'

'You want to see my will? Why?'

'I want to see your will written so that you look after your family.'

'I don't have a family.'

'You will have tomorrow.'

'You want me to write Virginia into my will?'

'And her family.'

'Who is her family?'

'Her family. Me and my wife and our other children.'

'And in return?'

'In return,' replied Virginia's father with due seriousness, 'I will guarantee to you that my daughter is a virgin.' Jack did his best to avoid bursting into laughter, but it was obvious to him that the old man was serious. To humour him and because he thought it was a fun thing to do, Jack re-wrote his will in favour of Virginia and her family that night.

As the newly married Gilberts left for their honeymoon in Europe and Virginia's father hugged himself with delight at Jack's new will, *Queen Christina* began pre-production under the direction of Rouben Mamoulian. The director had turned out to be exactly the sort of man Garbo had been hoping for, and her professional relationship with him was being complemented by an increasingly rewarding life together away from the studio, on the tennis court or hiking in the hills.

She told Rouben all about Moje, from the day she had met him as he was casting for *Gösta Berlings Saga* to the trip she took back to see his grave in the Jewish cemetery in Stockholm. Mamoulian smiled when Greta told him about her confrontation with the Jewish mourner who had corrected her behaviour when she had arrived with an armful of lilies. He also listened intently when she described how she had behaved when she went to the storage room full of Stiller's possessions and remembered where each of them had been bought. There was a scene in *Queen Christina* in which he could use that pattern of behaviour.

The two of them decided to take a brief vacation together before shooting started. It was a good way for them to get to know each other well, which would be of considerable benefit once they were on the studio floor and under pressure of time and money. It was hardly original: directors and actresses had been doing this for years and they were both single people. They did not go out of their way to advertise their plans. Who could object?

They decided to drive to Arizona and see the Grand Canyon at dawn, just the two of them, alone against the rising of the sun in this place of great solitude. It didn't quite work out like that. In Las Vegas they were recognised and thereafter relentlessly pursued by reporters, photographers and the Arizona and Nevada branches of the Garbomaniacs club. Mamoulian soon realised they had made a mistake even supposing they could remain undetected, and two hours after arriving at the Grand Canyon they were on their way back to Hollywood.

Mamoulian could also tell on the first day of shooting that they had made a mistake in casting Laurence Olivier as Garbo's lover. She was just devouring him and she looked stiff and uncomfortable in the scenes in which she was supposed to look relaxed and happy. He could feel her whole body tense as Olivier attempted to embrace her and the result was an embarrassing, juvenile fiasco. The eyes that had enslaved millions registered nothing but a stony, expressionless stare.

For his part, Olivier knew he was overacting and seemed unsure of how to convey emotion so that it registered through the lens of the motion-picture camera. Olivier was a stage actor, schooled in the old-fashioned ways of the English stage. He was pretty enough but he lacked 'weight', and the whole picture suddenly looked unbalanced. Queen Christina wouldn't have abdicated her throne to go off with this callow youth.

Olivier knew he wasn't delivering the goods and tried very hard to let Garbo know that he would do anything to make good. One morning as they were changing the lights round to shoot the reverse of the shot they had just taken, Olivier made a big effort to talk to his co-star who, surprisingly, had not retreated to her dressing room as soon as the bell was rung indicating the sound had been cut. He talked and she listened – for about five minutes. Eventually Olivier ran out of conversation, like a car running out of petrol on a deserted country road at night. He was miserable and there was nowhere to go. Garbo took pity on him.

'Oh vell,' she sighed, 'life is a pain anyway.' It was her philosophy in a nutshell. Later that day, on instruction from above, Walter Wanger, the producer, took Olivier into his office and fired him, initially for being too small.

'What?' ejaculated Olivier. This was a new excuse for him. 'I'm a perfectly standard height.'

'Well, that's the trouble. Miss Garbo is tall and you're barely taller. We need someone a bit . . . taller,' finished Wanger lamely.

'Are you kidding?'

'Then there's the accent.'

'I'm supposed to be Spanish.'

'But you're British.'

'Is that worse?'

'Americans can't understand that lah-di-dah accent of yours.'

'And Ronald Colman? And Charlie Laughton? And Basil Rathbone?' Wanger was getting irritated that Olivier was not taking the hint.

'You might never make a movie actor, Mr Oliver, but I think you have talent. Maybe you should stick to the British stage for a while.' Grateful for the generous payoff, 'Mr Oliver' agreed that this was a sound piece of advice, which he would endeavour to follow. He left the office to some extent relieved that the excruciating experience was finally over, but very conscious that MGM might be right – he was no movie actor. The camera had detected that right away and the producers had just obeyed its dictates – and the wishes of Greta Garbo, who had known before anyone else that he was never going to make it. He returned to London and a certain measure of fame, but it would be six years before he made another attempt to conquer Hollywood.

Garbo and Mamoulian dined together in some gloom that night. It was the same meagre meal that the director was becoming used to whenever he went to Garbo's house. He understood how Garbo managed to retain her svelte figure, although he would have been surprised had she told him about the insecurity bred by Mayer's and Stiller's constant attempts to rid her of what they considered to be the excess weight she had carried as a teenager. Mamoulian liked Garbo very much, but he was wary of star power and he was unsure quite who Garbo had in mind as a replacement for Olivier. When the suggestion came, he couldn't have been more astonished.

'Jack Gilbert!'

'I tank he play the role very well.' Mamoulian's first thought was that Gilbert was past it, an old ham who belonged in a museum; the second was that Garbo was still in love with him.

'Greta, I think it's an interesting idea but he's . . . you know . . .'

'Know what?'

'You must have heard the stories about his drinking . . .'

'Jack has always been a drinker.'

'He's not twenty-one any longer, Greta.'

'Neither am I.'

'L.B. will never go for it. I don't know how I could begin to persuade him.'

'You don't have to. I will do it.' Mamoulian nodded. On the one hand, he was grateful he was not going to have to brave the wrath of the all-powerful Mayer. On the other hand, he had again been made only too aware what a lowly position he held on this production, even though he was the director. He couldn't help feeling threatened not just by his disempowerment but also by the thought that Garbo had brought Gilbert back for a reason and it would have to be something more significant than just wanting to do a good turn for an old boyfriend who was down on his luck.

'Are you still in love with Jack Gilbert?' Mamoulian would never normally have asked such an intimate question, but Garbo had bewitched him as she had bewitched so many before him. She looked at him with some contempt.

'That is my business.'

Mamoulian nodded. It was clear that if she were not actually in love with Jack Gilbert she retained feelings for him that were stronger than those of mere friendship. Realising this, he felt his fledgling relationship with Garbo to be under more pressure than ever. Still, it was not going to be easy for Garbo to break the news to Mayer and it was by no means a foregone conclusion that Mayer would simply give in to her demand. In fact Mamoulian felt there was a more than even chance that she wouldn't get her way for once. It was rare he took the side of the studio executive against that of any creative person, but just this once he hoped that Mayer would send Garbo off with a flea in her ear.

Mayer too had seen the rushes, so he hadn't been exactly surprised when Garbo told him that she and Mamoulian wanted to fire Olivier.

'So the *faygele* didn't work out.' He shrugged. 'What a surprise. Who d'you want now? You turned down every available male lead in Hollywood.' Even though she had been preparing for this moment for weeks, Garbo wasn't looking forward to the imminent explosion.

'Chief,' she said, deliberately using the nickname Mayer liked to hear himself called, 'I want Jack Gilbert.' The eruption was instantaneous.

'Gilbert! Are you a *meshugganah*? That degenerate bum cost this studio over a million dollars!'

'Gilbert or no one.'

'I'd rather burn the studio to the ground than give the part to that degenerate bum.'

'Gilbert or no one,' repeated Garbo and left the room. The sound of breaking glass followed her down the corridor.

Chapter Fifteen

Mayer continued to rage at Garbo for days. He threatened and blustered, but to no avail. Garbo was a big star with a cast-iron contract.

'I can put you on suspension, you know.'

'With all those sets standing idle and all those technicians on salary?'

'I told you before, I'll start a Garbo lookalike contest.'

'Yes? Well, good luck with that, Mr Mayer. I am sure you find another Garbo in Idaho.'

He never really had this problem with anyone else. The East Coast money men and the stockholders would not take kindly to his cancelling Garbo's contract or putting her on suspension. Neither would the audience, and when he accepted this Mayer knew he was beaten.

A disbelieving Gilbert was given the good news and his spirits soared. He had been around long enough to know that Greta had engineered this situation deliberately. He had taught her well in those early days. She was negotiating from a position of strength, and Mayer knew she could be just as bloody-minded as he was. If Greta wanted him as the Spanish envoy, he would get the job. He raced to tell Virginia, who was less enthusiastic than he hoped she would be.

'You don't want me to do this job?'

'Of course I do, honey, but . . .'

'But what?'

'Well, everyone knows about you and Garbo.'

'Oh for God's sake, that was all five years ago. I've been married twice since then.'

'You promise me there'll be no . . . funny business.'

'Me and her? Don't be silly. I'm a married man with a baby on the way.' He pulled her to him and tried to pretend a sexual passion for her he no longer felt. That stomach and the thought of what was growing inside it he found repulsive. Besides, he already had a daughter with Leatrice and frankly, as much as he loved the eight-year-old girl, he wasn't cut out to be a father – not a proper, conscientious, full-time father, which was what young Leatrice needed and what Virginia and her grasping family clearly wanted from him.

It was fortunate that the studio and the new job claimed all his attention. Virginia knew that a working Jack was a happy Jack and a Jack who might even cut down on his drinking. She just wished the job had been with anyone but Garbo.

Harry Edington showed him the contract that MGM had sent round. It was the standard-issue seven-year contract that all featured players signed. The last one had been for millions of dollars. This one was at a tenth of his previous rate. It was a shock, but the humiliating, soul-destroying effects of his long months of unemployment did not permit Harry to negotiate a better deal on his behalf. Jack signed his name and looked forward to a new start at his old studio. Mayer and Thalberg might be out to destroy his career, if not his life, but he held no grudge against the low-paid technicians and support staff whom he saw every day. The grips and the prop men, the make-up girls and the secretaries, they all liked him for the man he was, not just because he was a big movie star. They would all be thrilled to see him again and they wouldn't care that he was being so cruelly underpaid.

'Hi, Jack! Good to have you back again!' He could already hear their voices ringing in his head.

Jack had fought his way to the top before – and that was when he had no influential friends to help him. Sitting by the pool and downing a celebratory bottle of champagne, he thought he could do it again – and with Greta Garbo to star with him he felt certain he could do it again. Harry reasoned that if the picture was a hit, a big hit, he could perhaps tear up the contract and re-open negotiations, on the basis that it was the team of Gilbert and Garbo that had caused this miracle and that his client was from now on a major star again and must have what major stars deserve. On the other hand, if it were a flop, MGM would hardly hold him to the seven-year demands of the contract. They had already paid him for being a flop once; they wouldn't do it again. They would be delighted to toss him out on his ear.

Jack couldn't help thinking that if Greta just wanted an actor to play the Spanish envoy she could have had her pick of the available young men in Hollywood. No, she had chosen him for a reason and the reason could only be that she still had feelings for him, just as he had always retained feelings for her. He wanted to race to the top of Benedict Canyon and shout his love for Flicka across the hills to the ocean. Instead he ran all the way to King Vidor's house, which nestled in the valley below. It made a change from lobbing empty whisky bottles onto Vidor's roof, an activity that could occupy Jack for an entire afternoon.

Vidor had already heard the news on the studio grapevine. The director sat back on his reclining seat by the swimming pool and indicated that Jack should do the same, but his old friend was far too worked up to sit quietly. He told Vidor all the news that the director had known about for a day and a half.

'She's quite a gal, King.'

'You're telling me,' agreed King cordially. It was good to see Jack was so happy and animated – and not through the good offices of Jack Daniels.

'L.B. went berserk,' continued Jack smiling. 'He was screaming, yelling. The whole studio knew in five minutes.'

'That's right.'

'So she still loves me.' King was alarmed. This was not a healthy conclusion to draw.

'Now, Jack,' he warned, 'don't go getting any funny ideas.' But Jack was oblivious to anything other than his own good fortune.

'I knew she did. Deep down. What we had was special, real special. You can't act that.' Vidor thought he had better try to keep a lid on Jack's emotions before he got hurt even worse than he had been already.

'Jack, she's just doing you a favour. She knows how badly L.B. and Irving have treated you and she wants you to have a break. That's all.' Jack would have none of it.

'She's giving me co-star billing!' he pointed out. In Hollywood everyone knew that billing was what really indicated what the world thought of you.

'Yes, like you did for her on *Flesh and the Devil*. I told you, this is payback time.' Jack was hurt.

'Why are you being so negative? This is the biggest break I've had in years.'

'Because you're a married man. You don't want this marriage to Virginia to go the same way as all the others.'

''Course not. So what?'

'So lay off Garbo.'

Jack was ready for him. He sat down in the chair and, with a flashing smile that reminded Vidor of the Jack of old, said quietly, 'I said she loves me. I didn't say I'd do anything about it.'

King smiled in some relief. Maybe they weren't all heading for disaster. Maybe Jack really had grown up.

'All you have to do is give the greatest performance you've ever given in the movies.' It was just banter, something Jack should have volleyed back over the net with ease, but to his surprise Jack said nothing. Vidor looked up from the script he was reading for his latest production, *Our Daily Bread*. Jack's face was entirely different from what it had been only moments before. He looked haunted.

'That's the thing, you see,' he finally admitted. 'I haven't worked for so long, I don't know if I can. I just don't know if I can do it any more.' Vidor could see that Jack meant it. For the first time in his acting career Jack had serious doubts about his own ability.

Driving to the studio for costume fittings, Jack was particularly nervous. It was a journey he had made almost every day for eight years, yet he felt it was his first day on a major film. He had been told that Garbo was likely to be around and he was unsure of his feelings, unsure of what to say to her when he met her again. It would be their first meeting for about three years, in fact since the night he and Ina had seen her dressed as Hamlet at Basil and Ouida Rathbone's fancy-dress ball. Should he thank her for her generosity or would that be too spineless? Should he affect a certain disdain, as if he couldn't care less? Should he embrace her, like old colleagues reunited on an exciting new project? Of these options he preferred the last. That way he could judge from her physical reaction exactly how the land lay between them.

Inevitably the meeting didn't go anything like the way he had been agonising over. He drove onto the lot and saluted the guard at the west gate with his usual friendliness.

'Hi, Robert. Miss Garbo in yet?'

'Welcome back, Mr Gilbert. No. I don't think she's coming in today.'

Jack drove on, very disappointed. No Garbo, after all that build-up! He felt cheated but he knocked on her dressing-room door just to make sure.

'I don't think Miss Garbo's coming in today,' said a passing wardrobe assistant carrying half a dozen changes of costume on their hangers. There was no answering sound from inside. He turned the handle, but the door was firmly locked.

He wandered down to the wardrobe department and started trying on the costume they had picked out for the Spanish envoy. Every time the door opened he jerked his head in that direction, but it was never Garbo who entered. By the end of the afternoon he was plunged into despair. He was sure that she knew when his costume fitting was. She had obviously changed her appointment to make sure they did not meet. Yet she had engineered his casting on the movie. What was she playing at?

As he returned to his car and drove sadly towards the west gate he saw the Packard driven by her chauffeur turn off Washington Boulevard and stop by the barrier. He sped towards it and braked sharply as he drew up alongside. Garbo was sitting in the back seat reading a magazine.

'Flicka!' called Jack with as much controlled cheeriness as he could muster. Garbo looked up immediately. A momentary, fleeting look of panic passed over her face before she smiled her welcome.

Was it because she knew it was him or because she hated to be accosted by anyone in that manner? he wondered.

'Hello, Yackie. Everything OK?'

'Everything AOK,' he confirmed, frustrated by his inability to come up with a sparkling line of dialogue that would cause her to produce one of those Swedish peals of laughter that he remembered so well.

'See you on set,' she said evenly as the Packard slipped into gear and moved away.

He turned round in his seat and watched her leave until another car drove up behind him and honked. Reluctantly he drove out of the gate and turned east on Washington. So, that was it, the big reunion. What in God's name was he supposed to make of it? He thought he detected in that 'Hello, Yackie' the hint of something special. He knew, too, that she could hardly be seen to be displaying any grand emotion for him in public. Besides, it had never been her way: she hated open displays of affection. As he drove north on Beverly Glen, his spirits began to lift. Garbo had chosen him above all other men to star opposite him. She had taken on Mamoulian, who wouldn't have wanted him – he was one of those snobs from Broadway – and he knew well enough how hard she would have had to battle L.B. Mayer. She had done it because she wanted him. He luxuriated in the warmth of his new conviction.

He knew that he shouldn't make too much of this anti-climactic day of fittings. Just wait till I take her in my arms and kiss her on the set, he said to himself. Or better still, on the lips. Then he would know exactly how she felt about him. There would be no disguising the way her body responded to his. That was obviously what she meant by that enigmatic comment, 'See you on set.' He revved the engine as he waited at the traffic lights. It all made sense now. As the lights turned to green he roared off in a rush of adrenaline, happiness and petrol fumes.

Unfortunately it all began disastrously. He had stepped into the shower at 5.30 a.m. on the first day of principal photography, just as he had always done when he had to be in make-up at 7 a.m., but he felt lousy – heavy-limbed and light-headed. He was coming down with flu or something. Nevertheless he was a pro. He dragged himself into work, but by the time he stood up and looked at himself in full costume and make-up he not only felt lousier, he thought he looked lousy.

He complained to the director, not as a star but as a featured player.

'Rouben, I'm not sure about this make-up.' Mamoulian was instantly wary. If Gilbert thought he was a big star who could throw his weight around, he was in for a shock.

'What's the matter with it?'

'I think I look ridiculous.'

'We've had period researchers on this project for weeks. That's how a Spanish envoy to the court of Queen Christina would have looked.'

'I think I look like Lucifer in a vaudeville sketch.'

'You look fine, trust me. Now if you go and sit at that table under the stairs, we'll start as soon as Miss Garbo arrives,' and he moved away to talk with the continuity girl.

There was concern on Garbo's face when she looked at Jack.

'Is there something wrong, Yackie?'

'No, it's just the make-up.'

'You're sweating. Have you been drinking?'

'Damn it, Flicka, no! I haven't touched a drop since they told me I had this part.'

'Then what . . .'

'I have the flu. I woke up with it. I'm sorry. I didn't dare tell anyone. I thought they might replace me. And I didn't want to let you down. You above all people.' Garbo nodded and touched his hand.

After the first shot had been completed, Garbo took Mamoulian into a relatively unpopulated area of the studio.

'That was good work, Greta. Perfectly pitched. I don't have a comment.'

'Rouben, I am sorry.' Mamoulian looked alarmed. Was this to be the preface to her firing him as well?

'About what?' he asked defensively.

'I have the flu. I cannot work any longer.'

Mamoulian breathed a sigh of relief. Within the hour shooting on *Queen Christina* was halted.

Mayer was furious and the studio indulged its love of gossip. Garbo was well known for being indisposed for political and personal rather than properly medical reasons. On the set of *As You Desire Me*, the previous year, she had been sick on exactly those days when Erich von Stroheim was unable to work. Von, like Gilbert, had been attempting a nerve-wracking comeback at a studio that had fired him – in his case for the capital crime of being undisciplined with budgets – a second life which, remarkably, Garbo had also engineered. When Garbo went down in synchronisation with Jack, experienced Garbo-watchers knew exactly what was going on. In fact Garbo was also suffering from insomnia and nervous exhaustion, but she did nothing to discourage the studio gossip that she had taken a dive to help her ex-lover.

Back at the house on Tower Road, Virginia had abandoned her previous hostility to her husband working with his old flame. She knew how MGM would regard Jack's indisposition. Garbo or no Garbo, if Jack could no longer cut the mustard then his career was over, not because Louis B. Mayer hated him but because the unofficial blacklist would keep him out of every studio in Hollywood forever.

Next day Jack still felt nauseous. A trail of reporters tracked him into the Good Samaritan Hospital where he received a chlorine treatment for his nose and throat. Dried out and dosed up with vitamin C, Jack dragged his protesting body into the costume and make-up that had been designed for him – a horrible goatee beard and slicked-down hair. He still hated it, but he was too weak both physically and politically to confront the make-up designer, and the director had already indicated his reluctance to so much as discuss it.

Mamoulian was even prepared to jeopardise his blossoming relationship with Garbo. Confronted yet again by a display of star power, he decided it was time for his directorial ego to assert itself.

'I never rehearse,' said the star.

'You do on my movie,' said the director.

'My first take is the best. Everything after that will be bad.'

'I need to rehearse.'

'Not on a Garbo film,' said Garbo. Mamoulian shrugged and called for the first scene to be shot. Garbo did it her way.

'Cut!' shouted Mamoulian at the end.

'You like it?' asked Garbo, knowing that it had gone well. Mamoulian looked at her.

'Do you?'

'Yes, of course,' she said defensively, aware that this reaction suggested he disagreed. 'Why? Don't you?'

'No. I need you to rehearse it for a while. Then we shoot it. Tomorrow you can look at what we shoot and you can decide which take we use. If you choose take number one, I will never ask you to rehearse again.' They reached take eight before Mamoulian was happy. Garbo smouldered, feeling she was no longer in control of the scene and that she was merely carrying out the director's instructions without contributing anything creatively herself. After so many mediocre directors in recent years she was reluctant to abandon herself entirely to anybody else's ideas.

At eight o'clock the next morning, in full Queen Christina make-up, Garbo sat in the comfortable armchair in the screening room watching the first take and the eighth take. It was blindingly obvious that the eighth take was superior to the first take. The lights went on again. Garbo ran from the room onto the set and straight into her grinning director, who knew exactly what she was going to say.

'Please don't use take one.' Rouben Mamoulian could have kissed her, but he was no more a demonstrative man than Garbo was a demonstrative woman. Besides, they were about to shoot the scene that everyone had been waiting for.

A snowstorm has caused the Spanish envoy's coach to stick in the mud and he is forced to take shelter for the night in a nearby inn. Owing to a shortage of rooms the innkeeper apologises that he will have to share a bed with Queen Christina who is disguised as a nobleman – until he/she unbuttons her outer coat to reveal the figure of a beautiful woman. Now it is 'the morning after'.

Jack watched, enchanted, as Mamoulian brought out a metronome. He set it ticking and demonstrated what he wanted.

'Greta, I want you to move in time to the ticking of the metronome so when we score the picture this scene will have a choreographed feel to it.' Greta caught on very quickly. Jack, lying on the floor, hugged himself. He was in a great picture with at least one great star and a great director. *Queen Christina* was going to be a huge hit. He was back. Mamoulian put his arm round Garbo in a proprietary manner and walked her into a relatively quiet corner of the busy sound stage. Jack watched them go with pangs of jealousy eating away inside him. He was surprised to be so afflicted. He had never felt that way when he had seen Clarence Brown talking quietly to Garbo in a similar situation.

'You remember you told me how you went to see Mauritz Stiller's possessions after his death?'

'Of course,' Garbo nodded.

'And you touched the suitcase because you remembered where he bought it and then the paintings and so on because everything in the room reminded you of him? Well, that's what I want you to think about as you're moving round this room.'

When Mamoulian called 'Action!' Garbo moved slowly round the room touching and stroking objects – the walls, the mantelpiece, a spinning wheel, the pillow on the bed – and then she hugged the bedpost, pressing her body against it as if it were a lover. Jack looked at her and then asked in the deep voice he was cultivating so that nobody would ever mention his so-called high-pitched voice again, 'What are you doing?'

'I have been memorising this room,' came the reply, exactly as she had spoken to Moje's lawyer Hugo Lindberg in the storage facility in Stockholm. 'In the future, in my memory, I shall live a great deal in this room.'

Jack felt he was in the presence of greatness. All right, he wasn't being great himself, but he loved what they were all doing – making a wonderful movie. At the end of her movement Greta came over to

Jack and kissed him, just as the script demanded. Fired with lust, much as the script implied, Jack seized her and pressed his lips forcibly to hers.

'Cut!' cried Mamoulian. A bell rang and the silent studio floor was a bustle of noise again. Jack lay back and inhaled the familiar lingering scent of the divine Garbo. How he had missed it these many years. She was no like other woman. It was still alive between them: he could feel it. It was all he could do to prevent himself from singing out loud.

Mamoulian was surrounded by people asking questions. Garbo pushed her way through the throng.

'Rouben, I must talk to you.' The director waved away the pressing bodies.

'I need to talk to Greta. Hey! That worked, didn't it? I'm so pleased you told me about going to see Moje's grave. Oh, and I've been thinking about the last shot of the movie. What I want you to do is to clear your mind, clear it completely, make it a total blank . . .' Garbo looked impatient. 'Sorry, what was it you wanted?'

'This love scene with Jack.'

'We can go again, if you want.'

'I think Jack is still in love with me.'

'Are you sure?'

'I am sure. I can tell by the way he holds me, the way he kisses me.'

'OK, you go to your dressing room. I'll call you when we're ready. Jack!'

Jack bounded up to the director like an eager puppy.

'Rouben, this scene is great. Just to work on a script as good as this with a director like you, and of course Greta is just the most amazing actress . . . What?' Mamoulian was clearly not responding to the compliments.

'I know you and Garbo were close, but that was five or six years ago now.' Jack tried to pretend as if he did not know what was coming.

'Look, that out there, that was all acting,' he started to bluster, but Mamoulian cut him short.

'Jack,' he said bluntly, 'you're a married man.' He did not feel he needed to continue. Jack decided to change tactics and instead of blustering or laughing he stood on his professional integrity.

'I'm an actor, Rouben! Surely you can tell what's acting and what's for real.' It was probably not the smartest thing to say to a perceptive director.

'You're right, I can,' he snapped. 'And, what's more, so can Garbo.' Jack looked embarrassed. He stared at the floor and ran the point of his right shoe round in a figure eight.

'It was a big affair, you know,' he admitted finally. 'It was the biggest of my life. You can't expect it all just to die away completely. And she's never found anyone . . . Oh I see . . .' Mamoulian was looking at him blankly, rather as he had just been instructing Garbo to do in the last shot of the movie. His belief was that if you stare fixedly ahead, the audience, desperate to read the actor's thoughts, will project their feelings onto that blank canvas.

He was right. When Mamoulian didn't react to Jack's protestation that Garbo had never found anyone to replace him, Jack knew immediately that Mamoulian was 'involved' with her. How deeply he wasn't sure. Maybe they had gone to bed together, maybe not. Garbo was weird, or at least unpredictable, about sex at the best of times. He didn't like to think of the two of them lying in bed together, naked bodies intertwined. Why was his mind going down that road?

Mamoulian saw the hurt in Jack's face and his own features softened. He took off his glasses and wiped them, replaced them on his nose and ran his fingers through his thick, bushy hair.

'I'm sorry, Jack. I didn't want to hurt you. Neither does Garbo.' Jack nodded and tried to smile bravely.

'Sure.' A quotation flashed through his mind. 'Backward, turn backward, O Time, in your flight.' Mamoulian looked at him oddly but decided to keep the whole matter on an even keel.

'Just ease off a little in this scene, that's all. Think of Virginia and the new baby, OK?' Jack smiled his acceptance. How could he not? But the dagger had pierced his heart. It was all a sham. Forcing the studio into casting him as Don Antonio was just a way for Garbo to make herself feel better. It was charity not love that had brought him back to MGM. After everything that had passed between them, she just felt sorry for him.

It was difficult for him after that. He did his best. He was a professional actor after all. He knew his lines and he spoke them beautifully. Everyone said so.

'Jack, what's all this crap about your voice?' someone said to him almost every day. There was nothing wrong with his voice, and everyone wondered why all their friends believed there had been. He couldn't have changed his voice in the last few years, could he? Maybe it was just a trick of the microphone after all and it was now fixed. But if that were the case had it been fixed too late for John Gilbert to re-establish himself as a movie star?

When Harry Edington had told him he was now just a featured player on the lot where he had once been its biggest star he was hurt, but he had expected the blow and he barely missed a step. He was the supporting player to Garbo's star, but it was still the male lead and Garbo had campaigned for him to get it – and he believed she was still, to some degree, in love with him. When Mamoulian told him that he had been mistaken, it was as if all the air was being squeezed out of a balloon. He did his best with the rest of the picture but he felt abandoned by Garbo. She was always professional, courteous and well prepared, just as he had remembered from their silent films together, but she went off to her dressing room to have lunch and never invited him in. The belief that he could get 'it' back disappeared and now he thought he could see feelings of pity on the faces of the crew and the regular extras he had known for ten years. Oh, they all pretended he was brilliant, and scarcely a scene was completed when a grip or a spark didn't say, 'That was great, Jack' or 'It's so good to have you back, Jack.' He would nod and smile and sign autograph books for their nieces and nephews, which instantly made him more popular than Garbo, who as a matter of policy never signed anything, no matter how overwhelming the reason.

The one question he didn't want to hear was 'What are you doing next?' It was meant harmlessly, and in the old days he would have been able to tell them with perfect honesty the titles of his next two or three pictures. Now all he could do was mutter, 'I'm still trying to decide', which, as they all knew in the business, was code for 'I haven't got a job.' Whereas before *Christina* he had felt at least that his slow, sad decline had to come to an end some time, now he felt that he had had the chance and he had missed the opportunity.

One day the writer Hans Kraly, who did a lot of work with Lubitsch, started chatting to him as if he had known Jack all his life.

'I'm working on a script for you.'

'You are?' Jack eyes widened.

'It's a re-make of one of your old successes.'

'Which one? There were so many,' he sighed with fake sincerity.

The writer laughed. '*The Merry Widow*.'

'Is Von going to direct it?' Jack could scarcely believe his luck.

The writer laughed some more. Jack was hurt. Von Stroheim was a great director and because he had fallen out of favour in Hollywood Jack sympathised with him.

'You know that picture turned a profit of three quarters of a million dollars for this studio?' said Jack aggressively.

'Sorry, Jack, I didn't mean to upset you. I thought you knew it was for Ernst.'

'Ernst Lubitsch wants to direct *The Merry Widow* for MGM?'

'Sure. He's talking to Mayer and Thalberg about it now.' The problem of the next part was solved. The character of Count Danilo was perfect for him. With his featured role in *Queen Christina* followed by a co-starring role in *The Merry Widow*, it would be just like old times. He had to do something about it. If he got that part he'd be back on top again, and then he wouldn't need Garbo. He would have everything that came with being a major star and this time he would value it all so much more than he did the first time around. But he had to get that part in *The Merry Widow*.

The decision he came to was his alone. He couldn't discuss it with Harry; he knew exactly what his old friend would say. He couldn't discuss much of anything with Virginia any more, and there was no point in going to Garbo about it. He would have to explain to her about the charity and the pity, and it was not a conversation he felt able to sustain. So he went to see Louis B. Mayer by himself one lunch hour. L.B.'s faithful secretary, Mrs Koverman, was not at her desk in the outer office. He had no idea whether L.B. would be in his office or busy with someone else but he knew if he made an appointment either Mayer would refuse to see him or he himself would lose his nerve. He had to do it when Mayer wasn't expecting him and when he himself wasn't drunk or petrified by nerves. He knocked lightly on the door of Mayer's inner office.

'Mrs Koverman?' Mayer sounded slightly surprised. Drawing a deep breath, Jack turned the door handle and went in.

'Hi, L.B., it's me!' he said brightly, as if dropping in on Mayer was something he did every other day. 'Sorry. Mrs Koverman wasn't at her desk.'

'What do you want?' Mayer did not look thrilled to see him.

'I just wanted to say . . . I know we've had our disagreements . . . I know I'm not your favourite actor . . .' Mayer snorted. Well, at least I got that right, Jack thought. 'I just wanted you to know that I'm really grateful for *Queen Christina*,' he went on. 'I think it's a great movie . . . I hope you like my performance . . . my voice and everything . . .' Mayer continued to stare at him. It was getting unnerving. Why didn't he say something and put him out of his misery? 'It's wonderful to be back here again, L.B. I've signed the seven-year contract because I really want to work for MGM. I just want to put the past behind us and make some great movies together. Like the old days.' That was it. He had spent some time composing the speech, trying hard to get all the salient points in that would tick Mayer's boxes. He felt reasonably sure he had managed that.

Mayer nodded slowly, as if contemplating whether or not to offer him ten or twelve thousand dollars a week from now on, but then his face darkened and his eyes narrowed. Jack knew that he wasn't going to get ten thousand dollars a week.

'You dumb degenerate! You think I wanted you back here? I got you to sign that seven-year contract so you'll never work again!'

'OK, L.B., I get the message.'

'You took a million dollars out of my pocket, you drunken bum! I know all about your drinking. You defiled that beautiful young wife of yours with your drinking.'

'Hey, you leave my wife out of this . . .'

'You think I need you? You think Garbo needs you? Get out of my office and don't come back. I never wanna see your ugly mug again!'

Jack left. There didn't seem much point in trying to argue his case rationally.

The production finished shooting several days overdue and at a final cost, before prints were stuck from the negative and advertising expenses were added, of $1.14 million – it was Garbo's most expensive picture to date, and by some distance. Mamoulian was a careful, sensitive director, always feeling he could do better, and Garbo and Gilbert had both had days when ill health had prevented their working, but still, a negative cost of over a million dollars meant a lot of hard work and good luck if it was going to turn a profit. One thing was sure, observed Jack as he examined the poster the studio was going to release with the film, they weren't going to be selling it on his name. He had thought he was going to get equal co-star billing with Garbo, but that never materialised. He would have settled for her name above the title and his name in first position below it. That would have shown a proper sense of modesty, he thought. Instead he called Harry Edington in a rage when he saw what the MGM publicity department had prepared.

'You got a magnifying glass there, Harry?'

'Why's that?' asked Edington with a sigh. He knew exactly what was coming when his clients began conversations with that question.

'Because you'll need one to see my goddamn name on the poster MGM have cooked up.'

'Jack, only people in the business look at the credits. Audiences don't care.'

'They won't know I'm in the picture.'

''Course they will. Word of mouth, Jack. Best publicity there is, and not even MGM publicity department can buy or stop that.'

'What happened to all that pre-production publicity about Gilbert and Garbo together again?'

'You went to see L.B.,' said Edington sharply. 'Against my advice.'

'L.B. is an asshole but he knows how to sell a movie.'

'Exactly right, he sure does.'

'So he needs my name up there with Garbo's.'

'He doesn't see it that way. And he's taken any mention of your name out of the trailers for the movie theatres.'

'What! You're not just going to let him do that, are you?' There was a long pause, and then Jack could hear the sound of another telephone ringing in the distance. With some relief in his voice, Edington disengaged himself as quickly as he could.

'I gotta go. I have another call holding.'

'If it's Flicka, say thanks for the memories.'

'Jack, if you've done a great job, the reviewers will notice and the public will find you. Trust me.'

'I always have, Harry.' He replaced the phone and thought back to the time when Harry was putting the phone down on other clients to take his calls. He remembered how he had introduced Garbo to Harry, how he had leant on Harry to take her on as a client, how he had pleaded that she was only earning $350 a week and he shouldn't take his usual percentage from her. Now, apart from him, who remembered those days? Well, maybe Harry was right and the public would find him again if the movie turned out the way he was hoping.

Queen Christina was a good film – certainly Garbo's best talkie – and the studio was optimistic when the first reviews appeared. Jack scanned them all eagerly, desperate for a sight of his name in conjunction with his ex-lover's, desperate also for a word of praise that would restore his shattered self-confidence as an actor and raise him back to the pinnacle of the industry he still loved. The *New York Times* seemed to damn him with faint praise: 'Mr Gilbert's make-up may be more than slightly extravagant, but there are scenes in which he acts very well,' while the acerbic critic Otis Ferguson launched a scathing attack: 'It reaps no profit from the fact that under the ambassadorial mustachios you can perceive the lineaments of Mr John Gilbert, made up like the devil in a musical comedy.'

Most of the reviewers pretty much ignored him. The direction was uniformly praised, as was the performance of the star. It was, as Jack had always recognised, Garbo's picture, and it was understandable that she should take the lion's share of the reviews. He shrugged off the disappointment. Now it was all about the public. Would they come back in their numbers to see the re-teaming of those legendary lovers John Gilbert and Greta Garbo? In Jack's mind that was always the correct order of the billing. Man first, woman second, established star first, newcomer second.

It was a question that troubled Louis B. Mayer as well. He had done his best to ensure that Gilbert was almost invisible on the posters. If the picture succeeded triumphantly, he wanted to make sure that it was only Garbo who gained the kudos, but it bothered him that he couldn't control the public as well as he would have liked. He could, however, control the dissemination of information about the box-office figures. He called in his chief assistant, Eddie Mannix, his most loyal lieutenant, the man who had pulled Jack Gilbert off his boss in that notorious brawl on the floor of Marion Davies's bathroom.

'Eddie, I want Gilbert to think *Queen Christina* is a failure.'

'It's a great picture, Chief. All the critics agree.'

'Box office, I mean. I want Gilbert to think the picture hasn't made a nickel.'

'How we gonna do that? He can read the grosses in *Variety* same as we can.'

'Who tells *Variety* what the grosses are?'

'We do. At least Loews Theaters does.'

'Exactly. I want you to keep two sets of books on this one. One for the real gross receipts and one for the public.'

'Just for Gilbert?'

'Mostly for Gilbert – but that arrogant Swedish bitch needs a good spanking too. She thinks she can walk into my office and tell me who to cast in an MGM picture. Well, she wanted that degenerate bum and if she thinks having Gilbert as her co-star has cost her at the box office that will be just the lesson she needs to learn.'

Mayer's little scam worked perfectly. Official box-office records eventually revealed that *Queen Christina* made a profit of $632,000 but, as far as public and industry opinion went, it was a failure. The old magic wasn't there. That was the end of Garbo and Gilbert as a pair of fabled screen lovers.

Eddie Mannix brought the final figures into Mayer's office at the end of a long day. Mayer picked up the books and scanned them quickly. His face broke into a beaming smile. This was exactly what he had wanted: large profits in the MGM coffers and the end of John Gilbert's short-lived comeback.

'So, it worked,' he said, pouring out two generous whiskies and carrying them over to the large comfortable white sofa. They clinked glasses.

'Something there you need to look at, Chief,' said Mannix, tossing back his drink.

'What?' asked Mayer, examining the final accounting figure again with evident relish.

'First time ever. Look at the domestic gross.'

'Seven hundred and sixty-seven thousand. Pretty good. What was *Susan Lenox*? Eight hundred grand?'

'Eight hundred and six. And the foreign was seven hundred, giving us a profit of three hundred and sixty-four thousand dollars.'

'So the big change is the foreign earnings.'

'Not big – huge. It's a huge change. One million, eight hundred and forty-three thousand dollars on foreign earnings. I think Garbo might slip from her high position domestically. That little girl Shirley Temple at Fox earns more than Garbo does for us here, but Europe is just huge for Garbo.'

'So we need to give her exclusively European roles.'

'Yeah, big stories, classic stories. The foreigners like those kinds of pictures, and she looks great in period costume.'

'When she's not playing a man.'

'Oh sure, but she can't do that again. *Queen Christina* was special.'

'Irving thinks we should remake *Anna Karenina*.'

'With Jack?' Mannix was stunned. Mayer was horrified.

'Are you *meshuggah*? Gilbert will never get another part as long as I am head of this studio.'

'I heard he was being considered for *The Merry Widow*.'

'That's what I wanted him to hear.'

'And for Clarence Brown's *Sacred and Profane Love* with Joan Crawford.'

'Let's get him all excited so when he sees that *Christina* is a terrible failure and he'll never get either of those two roles he'll blow his filthy brains out.'

'Who are we going to get for *The Merry Widow*?'

'Lubitsch thinks Maurice Chevalier and Jeanette MacDonald.'

'You're borrowing the whole lot from Paramount?'

'No. I want MacDonald to sign a long-term contract here and maybe Chevalier too.'

'You know nobody much cares for Chevalier.'

'Eddie, I was talking to Jack Warner last night. He tells me Eddie Robinson is a pain in the ass. "The Thinking Actor" they all call him, but they keep renewing his contract because his pictures make money and if Chevalier makes money for this studio, well, I don't care what kind of a sonofabitch he is, I'll hire him. And that goes for any actor who makes me a profit.'

'Except Jack Gilbert.'

'Of course. Except Jack Gilbert.'

'Even though re-teaming him with Garbo seemed to work? I mean, you could argue that the big European grosses were the result of them wanting to see Garbo with Gilbert again.'

'You could, but we ain't gonna. Gilbert's finished.'

'We've got a seven-year contract with him.'

'At a thousand dollars a week.'

'You're willing to blow off fifty gees a year just for the satisfaction of knowing Jack's sitting at home?'

'Not just sitting at home. Sitting at home, drinking.'

'L.B., this isn't right . . .'

'Oh, stop worrying. I guarantee that after six months he'll throw in the towel.'

Mayer was right. When Jack realised that his comeback had been a failure he turned instantly to the comforting presence of the bottle. Virginia, now with the additional responsibility of the baby Susan Ann, was horrified by how Jack was behaving and especially by the tone in his voice. Everything that was wrong with his life he seemed to blame on her.

She was carrying the baby into the living room one morning soon after breakfast when she overheard the end of one of the interminable conversations with Harry Edington that were now almost a daily feature of Jack's life.

'Nothing? After a co-starring role with Garbo? . . . OK, feature role . . . But what about other studios? I mean, if we get an offer, MGM will let me go because they'll get me off salary for the time I'm on loan . . . Nothing? Not even RKO? . . . Fine, you do that.' He banged the phone down, reached for the bottle of Jack Daniels and poured. Virginia knew the day was virtually lost from this moment.

'Oh, Jack. It's not ten o'clock in the morning yet.'

'I don't need your permission to drink.'

'You know, you've been sick ever since I've known you. If you stopped drinking . . .'

'If I stopped drinking – what? You'd make love to me?' Jack was angry with Virginia for pushing him away at night, but in fact he had been badly affected by another outbreak of impotence. The Great Lover of the Silver Screen could no longer achieve a sustainable erection. Virginia understood how badly bruised his ego must be because of what had happened at the studio and this latest physical humiliation but she didn't see why she should take the blame. And she was glad he couldn't paw at her with his breath stinking of alcohol.

'We have a baby. I'm up nights feeding her. Maybe if you just cut down on your drinking, made yourself presentable again . . .'

'What then? MGM would assign me a decent role? Any role?'

'Jack, it's exhausting looking after a baby.'

'You have a maid and a nanny. You don't need to do it all yourself.'

'I need to feed her myself, so I don't get proper sleep any more.'

'That's your excuse, is it? Or am I so repulsive, so drink-sodden, you can't bring yourself to touch me?'

'Jack, you're passed out half the time . . .'

'Or don't they drink in South Dakota?'

'North Dakota,' said Virginia dully. She was fed up having to defend the state she came from.

'Well, there's nothing else to do in that godforsaken part of the world.'

Virginia tried to change the subject. 'Maybe they're just waiting for the right script to come along.'

'The right script came along. The remake of *The Merry Widow*. My great triumph of 1925.'

'That's wonderful.' Virginia didn't sound too thrilled because Jack didn't sound too thrilled. There had to be a catch somewhere.

'It *is* – for Maurice Chevalier. They borrowed him from Paramount to make it. King Vidor told me about this action movie *Chained*. It's gone to that sonofabitch Clark Gable – that dumb ox with the big ears. And the part in the Joan Crawford picture Mayer's given to Bob Montgomery.'

'I'm so sorry, Jack.'

'Sure you are. I guess that solves everything.' Virginia watched as Jack reached once more for the bottle.

'Jack, please don't . . .' Jack swallowed down another shot in one gulp. The back of his throat must be burned away by now, she thought. Jack looked at the disapproval that seemed to him to be now permanently etched on to her pretty face.

'You know Garbo was never like this.' He was spoiling for a fight. He couldn't get to Mayer or Thalberg or even Garbo or Harry, so he settled for the closest target to hand.

'I've been waiting for this,' Virginia said.

'Waiting for what?'

'For you to compare me to Garbo. How can you?'

'I can't. She's incomparable. Garbo was the sun and the moon to me.'

'And me?' asked Virginia, setting herself up for the final insult. 'What am I?'

'You? You're North Dakota. Now get me another bottle.' He hurled the empty one into the cavernous fireplace. It was a gesture he seemed to remember making in *The Cossacks* – or was it *Love?* Ah, yes, *Love*. Gilbert and Garbo in *Love*. God, how long ago that now seemed. What was it? Five years ago? Six?

Virginia left the room and, effectively, the marriage.

On 20 March 1934 readers of the trade paper *The Hollywood Reporter* were surprised to see emblazoned on the back page a privately paid for advertisement. It read:

Metro-Goldwyn-Mayer
will neither
offer me work
nor
release me from
my contract

Jack Gilbert

Chapter Sixteen

Jack worked out a simple divorce settlement with Virginia. He was an old hand at it by now. Virginia got two insurance policies, property worth $42,000 and $150 a month to provide for the support of Susan Ann. Jack went off by himself to Hawaii on board the SS *Monterey*, staying in his cabin during the voyage and waiting there until the boat was empty before taking a taxi to the hotel. It was a matter of hours before the press discovered he was there. It wasn't a great vacation.

When he returned to Hollywood, he found that his admission of abject failure had worked. MGM had agreed to release him from his contract, but his days now seemed endless as he stared at the telephone, willing it to ring.

One night he was sitting drinking with King Vidor, who had divorced Eleanor and was involved romantically with his script girl, Elizabeth Hill.

'Are you going to marry her?'

'Maybe.'

'What's the point? You'll only find some other girl you like better.'

'So what's your suggestion?'

Jack smiled as he remembered the fateful words, now seven years distant.

'Why don't you just fuck her and forget about it?' King smiled as well. How Jack's life had changed on the back of those words. They were quiet for a moment. The sun had lost its fierce noonday heat and was sinking rapidly in the west, though not over the ocean as he always expected it to do. The sun seemed to set to the north, somewhere up by Malibu rather than due west in Santa Monica.

There was a nip in the air, and Jack shivered. King thought Jack looked dreadful. They had drifted apart in the past few years, as they probably would have even if Jack had remained a star. King had had the traumatic end of his marriage to Eleanor and the vicissitudes of his own career to consider. The continuing decline in Irving Thalberg's health made King's position at MGM much more unstable. Mayer was anxious to take charge completely and freeze out Thalberg, whom he had still not forgiven for what he regarded as the betrayal over the proposed merger with Fox.

'Have you seen the new Garbo picture?'

'*The Painted Veil*?' Jack shook his head.

'It sounds terrible,' said Vidor, trying to introduce a lighter note into the conversation.

'What about this affair with George Brent?'

'That's just studio gossip. Can you really see Flicka and Brent getting together?'

'Maybe *she* should just fuck him and forget about it.' Jack laughed, but it was a hollow laugh. They were kidding each other. Everyone knew that Garbo had ended her relationship with Rouben Mamoulian after the premiere of *Queen Christina* and begun a new one with the co-star of her latest film, a dull adaptation of a Somerset Maugham short story about a doctor's wife in the disease-ridden Orient.

Despite the added frisson of the two actors' personal relationship, there was no explosion of interest in the newspapers. Unlike Jack, Garbo's new lovers were not particularly newsworthy in themselves and they knew that if they wanted to keep the relationship going they had to ensure that they kept a very low profile when they were with her. The lack of newspaper gossip strengthened the studio's realisation that nobody much cared for *The Painted Veil* – not in the United States at least, where Garbo's domestic grosses continued to tumble. Once again, however, a strong return from sales in the rest of the world saved her and the film crawled into profit.

Rouben Mamoulian had the intellectualism that John Gilbert lacked, George Brent shared Garbo's obsession with privacy, and Mercedes de Acosta offered a physiological choice that no man could compete with, but none of them made the impact on Greta

Garbo's soul that John Gilbert had. She knew it, but she feared to acknowledge it openly. Jack knew it, but realised that Garbo would never admit as much to him or to anyone. She dealt with the emotional connection between them by doing her best to ignore it. Jack dealt with it by constantly picking at the scab.

'Any idea what Flicka's doing next?' asked Jack, affecting a casual air. Vidor wasn't too sure how to answer, since he suspected the knowledge would cause yet more pain to his friend.

'I think Thalberg's bored with her.'

'Well, God knows, Irving does tire of people.'

'I think Flicka's going to join David Selznick's production unit.'

'The son-in-law also rises.' It was the standard reference to David Selznick in Hollywood since he had married Irene, L.B. Mayer's younger daughter.

'That's the one.'

'Has he announced something for Flicka?' Vidor started to shift uncomfortably in his seat. Jack saw what was going on. 'What? For God's sake, King, just tell me,' he said aggressively.

'They're thinking of remaking *Anna Karenina*.'

Jack smiled. 'So that's it. Who's up for Vronsky this time?'

'Freddie March.'

'She'll be using the garlic on that one.'

'You've lost me.'

'When she doesn't like her leading men and she wants to stop them getting too close to her, she slips a clove of garlic into her mouth and chews on it. Works every time.'

'She never tried it on you, then?'

'Me? Why would she do that? She loved me.'

'Selznick likes all those classic novels. Ben Hecht told me he did all his reading before he was twelve.'

'Are they going to change the title again?' Vidor shook his head. 'I don't know. Why would they?'

'That's right. I mean, there'd be no sense in calling it Garbo and March in *Love*.'

'It wouldn't sell a single extra ticket,' said Vidor, offering the traditional Hollywood reason for every decision.

'And it wouldn't be true,' added Jack softly.

'What about you?'

'What about me?'

'Are you just going to sit here and wait for the phone to ring?'

'You got a better idea?'

'Go to England.'

'Why?'

'You speak the language. They like you there. They make movies over there.'

'I belong here, King. What would I do in England? Eat fish and chips and wear a bowler hat?'

'Then direct.'

'I want to direct. I directed Garbo in *Love*. You remember . . . when Eddie Goulding couldn't . . .'

'I remember. So get Harry to call the other studios.'

'He did.'

'And?'

'They think I'm dying.'

'You're not dying.'

'I know that and you know that, but I had that heart problem so now Paramount and Fox and Warners think I'm dying. Anyway they won't hire me.'

'So you're just going to sit here?'

'I still get sent scripts. I read them all very carefully. If I could find the right one . . .'

'Don't wait for the script to come in the mail. Write it yourself.' Jack's eyes brightened for a moment but then he shook his head sadly. As a boy he had dreamed of being a writer but he was always insecure about it, fearing that his lack of formal education would cause his work to be laughed at. He believed that Thalberg had only let him make *Downstairs* because Lenore Coffee had re-written it so extensively, which reinforced his fears. He confessed as much to Vidor, who told him not to worry.

'You should see the badly written crap that lands on my desk every morning.'

'You really think I could do it?'

'I know you could do it.'

Jack got very excited by the prospect of being a writer. He turned the guest bedroom into his study, then he bought a solid upright Underwood typewriter and a box of foolscap paper. One afternoon he obeyed the first rule of writing, which had been explained to him by a smiling Plum Wodehouse in the MGM commissary one lunchtime: 'Apply the seat of the pants to the seat of the chair.' Unfortunately that was as far as he got. He carefully rolled the paper into the machine and typed 'UNTITLED by John Gilbert'. Then he stared at the typewriter keys for the next thirty-seven minutes, but nothing came into his head. How did writers do it? he wondered.

He got up, wandered over to the window and looked out. He thought he ought to think of a story before he started the actual script and he didn't have to be sitting at his desk to do that. He could think of a story sitting by the pool. He went downstairs and flopped onto the long, low chair he lay on when he wanted to sunbathe. Shortly afterwards he was snoring gently in the afternoon sunshine. When he awoke it was cocktail hour and none of the writers he ever knew worked through cocktail hour. He went upstairs to shower, not too depressed that his first day as a writer could not be judged a triumphant success. It was the first day after all. Something would happen. Something did.

In 1934 Columbia was still considered a Poverty Row studio. It had almost no stars, and the films that originated from Columbia were invariably handicapped by low budgets, every penny of which was grudgingly authorised by Columbia's president, the vulgarian Harry Cohn. That year L.B. Mayer had decided to punish a surly, rebellious Clark Gable by loaning him to make a film for Columbia. The resentful MGM star complained bitterly to his friends that he was being 'sent to Siberia'. To everyone's surprise the result was Frank Capra's *It Happened One Night*, which won Gable an Oscar as Best Actor. Harry Cohn was ecstatic.

Metro-Goldwyn-Mayer had long been regarded by other studios (and particularly by Columbia) as the House on the Hill, the one which all the others secretly envied. 'Metro had white telephones,' commented one producer acidly. 'Warner Brothers had black telephones.' For Harry Cohn to show Louis B. Mayer that he could take an MGM actor and win him an Oscar was a source of enormous satisfaction and now that he had done it once he thought he could do it again. One evening he was sharing a drink in his office with Lewis Milestone, who had directed the big Universal hit picture *All Quiet on the Western Front*. They were discussing the merits of a new project, *The Captain Hates the Sea*, when Milestone suggested John Gilbert for the leading part of the newspaperman who embarks on a sea voyage in order to stop drinking so that he can write a book. Cohn was surprised.

'Gilbert? I hear he's all washed up.'

'Well, you have to admit this part isn't much of a stretch for him – and he's always been a good actor.'

'*Was* a good actor.'

'Once a good actor, always a good actor.'

'He's a drunk and he's sick.'

'That's just studio gossip.'

'It's good enough for me.'

'He's cheap, though. That million-dollar contract is long gone, and what would L.B. Mayer say if we hired Gilbert and *The Captain Hates the Sea* turned into another *It Happened One Night*? How many times can Harry Cohn make Louis B. Mayer look like a *chocham*?'

As ever, the appeal to Cohn's ego won the day, and he agreed to look at a test if Milestone could get Gilbert to make one for free. Milestone travelled hopefully to Tower Road, but Jack was initially reluctant. He wanted to get back to work all right, but Columbia . . . He had been the biggest star in Hollywood – it was getting to be a well-worn groove in the record. Milestone continued to wheedle.

'Listen, Jack, if you want to show everyone in this town that you're not washed up then you've got to do this. If you're embarrassed coming into Columbia during the working day, and I understand that, I'll shoot the test at six in the morning. You can be back here by eight.'

Jack was still reluctant. The truth was, though he was unwilling to confess as much to Milestone, Jack was terrified of making a test in case it was bad and even more terrified of making it in case it was good, he got the part and then maybe couldn't deliver the performance on film that everyone wanted from him, as he now believed had been the case on *Queen Christina*. Besides, he was feeling ill again every morning and his stomach ulcers were causing him constant pain.

Eventually a date was set for the test and, somewhat to Milestone's surprise, Jack showed up on time, having learned his lines. Both Milestone and Harry Cohn liked what they saw and Cohn called him into his office to congratulate him in his own distinctive way.

'Listen, you keep your nose clean and stay sober and do your work and I'll go to bat for you in every studio in town.'

'You mean you'll get me off the blacklist?'

'What blacklist?'

'The blacklist that you studio bosses circulate between yourselves.'

'There is no goddamn blacklist. I don't know where you got this idea from.' There was a short pause as Cohn added softly, 'But if *The Captain Hates the Sea* is a success, I'll see that you're off it.'

The Captain Hates the Sea was not a success. For the first week Jack did as Cohn and Milestone had requested, but then the lonely evenings began to take their toll as Jack's demons invaded his mind. Was the script good enough? Was he good enough? Was this just more ritual humiliation? Alcohol anaesthetised the doubts. The more he drank, the less worried about it all he became, but of course the less he was able to work. He might drag himself onto the set but he was frequently in no condition to act. Ina Claire had persuaded Carole Lombard to look after Jack and stop him drinking by any means possible. The good-hearted Lombard had a dressing room close to Jack's and responded to Ina's request with predictable generosity, barging into his dressing room without knocking whenever she suspected he was looking for the bottle.

'A drink – oh God, that's wonderful. Here, let me.' She took the bottle from his trembling hand and poured two singles. She drank the first one quickly and then went and sat next to Jack on the day bed, holding the other one in her hand.

'You are such an attractive man,' she whispered as erotically as she could, despite being shocked by the alcoholic fumes coming from his mouth. It was difficult to shock Carole Lombard, the archetypal man's woman, but Jack's condition was worse than she had anticipated. Jack looked longingly at the glass in her hand. Remembering her promise to Ina Claire, Lombard grimaced but swallowed it. It only delayed the inevitable though. She couldn't nurse him twenty-four hours a day. At home after studio work had wrapped for the day Jack was suffering from bleeding ulcers and fevers, which caused him to start hallucinating.

Milestone got the cast as quickly as possible onto the rented ship, which was docked in San Pedro Harbor, south of Los Angeles. Despite a strike that was currently in force, the director persuaded the union to permit him to sail the ship out of the harbour for filming purposes. Once they were on board Milestone felt he would be able to supervise Jack's destructive drinking.

Unfortunately the rest of the cast included such equally doughty drinkers as Walter Connelly, Victor McLaglen and Walter Catlett. When the actors had to drink alcohol on film they were supposed in fact to be drinking cold tea, the standard industry substitute for whisky. However, as Milestone soon discovered, the actors were very good at substituting real alcohol for the cold tea that was supposed to be the alcohol.

The amount of film shot each day declined as the ship sailed fruitlessly under unexpectedly leaden skies in search of the sun. Even when they found the sun the actors, particularly the star, were rarely in a state in which they could perform. Less and less celluloid dribbled off the ship into the Columbia laboratory. Harry Cohn looked at the daily production reports and grew increasingly irate. In desperation he wired Milestone: HURRY UP THE COST IS STAGGERING. Milestone wired back briefly: SO IS THE CAST. It was a last hurrah for Jack Gilbert, and a disappointing one at that.

Chapter Seventeen

The reception of *The Captain Hates the Sea* was a blow to Jack but it was hardly the worst he had received. The disasters of *His Glorious Night* and *Redemption* were much harder to bear, and neither of those two was as bad as *Queen Christina*. He had known that those first two talking pictures had scripts that weren't particularly good and, technically, nobody seemed to know what they were doing. *Christina* was different. The script was solid – Thalberg would never have let it proceed to production if it hadn't been – and it had had a first-class director in Rouben Mamoulian. Above all it had Garbo, the greatest star in the world.

Jack had been around movie sets all his life. He knew a great picture by its smell, by that indefinable chemistry created by the combination of script, director and star. He felt certain *Queen Christina* couldn't miss. Yet somehow it had. Like everyone else he had read the box-office figures that *Variety* printed. *Queen Christina* had been a commercial failure. If he couldn't make it with a great script, a great star and a great director then he really was all washed up. *The Captain Hates the Sea* merely confirmed it.

There were still friends who wouldn't let him go. Cedric Gibbons, MGM's top art director, was one of them. He was married to Dolores del Rio, the beautiful Mexican actress with dark, flashing eyes, an oval face and jet-black hair. It was impossible not to respond to her beauty or to Cedric's loyalty, so when they invited him over for dinner, he allowed himself to be cajoled into going. There he met the woman whom Hollywood had always set up as a rival to Garbo – the woman with her own parallel legend, Marlene Dietrich. Cedric had invited Marlene because he knew Jack would find her attractive and anything that kept him away from the bottle was a commendable course of action. His wife had a shrewd idea that Marlene, in her role as a German *hausfrau*, just might find Jack to be a project that was worth pursuing. Dolores del Rio, it transpired, was not just a pretty face.

She was just in time. Adela Rogers St John had rung Dolores to warn her of a confrontation she had just had with the ex-Great Lover. He was driving erratically from Tower Road down towards Washington Boulevard in his open-top car when he drew up at a set of traffic lights next to Adela.

'Jack!' she called in friendly greeting, but Gilbert didn't appear to hear her. 'Jack!' she called again. The face that turned to hers was frighteningly otherworldly.

'Hi, Jack. Where are you off to?' she asked.

'I'm off to kill L.B. Mayer,' he said, his voice a somewhat robotic monotone. He roared off before the lights changed.

Adela caught up with him at the next lights.

'You gotta gun?' she asked lightly, hoping that he hadn't. Jack stretched over and opened the glove compartment, from which he extracted the gun he usually kept in the drawer in his bedside cupboard.

'I'm gonna shoot L.B. Mayer, then I'm gonna shoot myself.' He then roared off again through the red light.

To her relief, Adela saw a police car approaching in the rear-view mirror, flagged it down and explained the situation. Within minutes Jack had been disarmed and persuaded to return to his home in Beverly Hills, though the gun was later given back to him because it was licensed, as it had been since the unfortunate incident with Mauritz Stiller, and the police had no official right to confiscate it, despite Jack's avowed intention to use it in the manner Adela had reported to the police.

Now, relatively sober and cleaned up for the evening, John Gilbert looked like the attractive man he could still be on occasion, and Marlene was smitten. As Dolores del Rio had suspected, she threw herself into the project of saving John Gilbert from his inner demons as if nothing in her life had mattered to her until this moment. It wasn't just the drinking that bothered her. She dragged him reluctantly back to the cardiologist, who reiterated that Jack had already had a small heart attack and he had to make changes in his life.

Marlene took the doctor's words seriously, even if Jack was still sceptical. She made him chicken soup and apple strudel, bought his Christmas presents, decorated his tree with German candles and took him dining and dancing, frequently against his wishes. It was, to Jack, a surreal replay of his attempts to bring Garbo out into Hollywood society nine years previously; only this time he was playing Garbo's part of the reluctant debutante.

'Where are we going now?' complained Jack, who had fallen asleep after they had made love and was objecting to being shaken awake by Marlene.

'Nowhere. I just got off the phone to the psychiatrist. He said he'll come over here to see you. You don't have to leave the house.'

'I don't want to see a trick cyclist.'

'You've done so well to stop drinking. Don't waste it.'

'What's the point? I'll never work in this town again.'

'I don't want to hear this self-pity. You are a thirty-six-year-old handsome, virile man.'

'Who is doomed to be permanently unemployed.' Marlene affected not to hear his protestations but bent down and kissed him tenderly on the lips. Jack folded his arms around her and pulled her powerfully down on top of him. Marlene made a token attempt to wriggle free, but Jack was too strong for her – and besides she didn't want to. She was thrilled to have 'cured' his temporary impotence and if he was interested in sex, it meant he was interested in life again.

Afterwards she lay contentedly in his arms, but her mind was buzzing with plans.

'On Sunday we are going to Basil and Ouida Rathbone's party.'

Jack groaned. 'He'll just want to talk about working with Garbo on *Anna Karenina*.'

'Then you walk the other side of the room and talk to someone else,' replied Marlene tartly. 'Then afterwards we go to the premiere of *A Night at the Opera*.'

'Opera? I don't want to go to some goddamn opera, Marlene. Ina was always trying to get me to go to the opera.'

'What's your problem with opera? Opera is wonderful.'

'It's like Schnozzle Durante said: "In opera, when some guy gets stabbed, instead of bleeding, he sings." '

'It's OK,' she smiled. 'It's a movie, a comedy – the Marx Brothers. You like them.' Jack acknowledged that he liked the Marx Brothers. They did things he'd always wanted to do but had never dared. Irving Thalberg was notorious for keeping everyone waiting, no matter how important they were. Even at the height of his power and influence, Jack had suffered along with everyone else – except the Marx Brothers. On time for an appointment, they were told by the apologetic secretary that Thalberg was detained in an important conference and they should take up a seat in the waiting room. The Marx Brothers declined and instead they lit two cigars each, knelt on the floor and blew the smoke under the crack of Thalberg's office door. Minutes later a coughing, spluttering Thalberg and his visitor staggered out and the Marx Brothers' meeting went ahead. The next time they were delayed the brothers piled furniture in front of the door and left Thalberg to heave his way out of the office at eight o'clock at night.

Thereafter the Marx Brothers got Thalberg's full attention, and he made sure never to keep them waiting again. Jack liked the Marx Brothers and he would go to their premiere with Marlene.

The phone call from England depressed Jack. Marlene had been anxious to re-make a film called *The Garden of Allah* for producers in England. This time Jack didn't put up much of a protest about filming in England, if Marlene was prepared to come with him. The story concerned a Trappist monk who leaves the monastery with the recipe for its house brandy in his pocket in order to marry a beautiful, unsuspecting girl in the desert. The novel had been a scandalous success when it had been published in 1904 but it had already seemed out of date when MGM filmed it in 1927. Thalberg had once talked to Garbo about it, but she rejected it firmly as antiquated nonsense. Nevertheless, having accepted the idea that he would never star in a movie again, Jack had been keenly anticipating the prospect of going back to work, and the news that the film was being shelved because the copyright was so difficult to disentangle came as yet another blow.

Jack was sunbathing by the pool when Marlene arrived from her home studio, Paramount, with thrilling news. He was sleeping quietly in the sunshine, dressed only in a pair of black swimming shorts and a pair of dark glasses, which had slipped down his nose as he lay nodding in the sun. She sat on the edge of his chair, ran her fingers down his chest and started to tickle him.

'No!' he shouted in agonised laughter, but Marlene was enjoying his violent contortions too much to stop. Desperately Jack struggled to his feet and holding Marlene in a tight clinch deliberately fell into the pool with the fully dressed German star shrieking in his arms.

They were both lying naked on the side of the pool when Carlos delivered the large jug of iced tea that Marlene had insisted was the only liquid he was to be allowed during cocktail hour. Carlos affected not to notice the state of undress. Frankly, after living with Mr Gilbert for ten years, few things could shock him any longer. Marlene poured out two glasses of the iced tea and handed one to Jack.

'I think I might have some news for you.'

'They repealed Prohibition?'

'About three years ago.'

'That's good. Skol!' He raised his glass.

'About a part.'

'A part of what?'

'A part in *Desire*.'

'The Lubitsch film?' Jack sat up instantly, spilling a little of the tea on his chest but brushing it away. 'Tell me everything.'

'Well, you know Gary Cooper is the male lead, and this would be the fourth lead?'

'Fourth?'

'Lubitsch first, then me, then Coop, then you.'

'Fourth lead is fine.'

'Your part is Carlos Margoli, he's my partner, a jewel thief and a fake nobleman.'

'I can do that.'

'That's what I told Lubitsch.'

'And?'

'He's going to give you a test. In colour!'

'He is?' Jack couldn't have been happier. He foxtrotted with Dietrich round the pool and back into the water again with an enormous splash. Carlos came out to clear away the glasses in case the exuberant couple did any serious damage.

The test was a triumph for all concerned. Jack was intrigued by the huge Technicolor camera and by its results. He sat in the screening room with Lubitsch and Dietrich and saw himself looking perhaps older than his thirty-six years but comfortingly serious, a sober, solid presence. After all the scandal and rumour that had surrounded him, Lubitsch confessed his relief and surprise that Marlene had not oversold her latest project. Near the end of the test Lubitsch's voice off camera asked him to smile.

'You want the full works?'

'Whatever you can give me.'

Jack looked into the camera and his mouth started to open, revealing the gleaming teeth that had lost none of their lustre. The smile seemed to wipe ten years off Jack, and Lubitsch and Dietrich saw glimpses of the Gilbert of the mid- to late-1920s who had been the mainstay of Metro-Goldwyn-Mayer for so many years.

When the lights went up, Marlene kissed him. Lubitsch sat puffing contentedly on his cigar, contemplating how best to phrase it. It was clear to him that this jewel thief was the sort of part that would re-invent Jack as a character actor, still suave and dashing but no longer burdened by the responsibility of having to carry the entire picture. Finally he stood up and looked down on the two lovers.

'Mr Gilbert?'

'Yes, Mr Lubitsch?'

'I should be very honoured if you would accept the part of Carlos Margoli in my new film, which is to start shooting in September.'

Marlene leaped to her feet and embraced Lubitsch. Jack rose more slowly and, with as much dignity as his controlled excitement would permit, replied solemnly.

'Mr Lubitsch, I would love to – but I'm afraid I must talk to my agent first.'

Lubitsch's eyebrows rose a fraction of an inch. Dietrich turned round and punched Jack on the arm.

'Jesus, that hurt! Couldn't you tell I was joking? I'd give anything to be in a Lubitsch movie. Jesus!' He rubbed his arm as Marlene smiled sheepishly at Lubitsch.

They were no sooner in the car on the way home than Marlene detected a clouding of the spirit in Jack.

'I'm sorry I punched you.'

'What? Oh, don't worry about that.'

'Then what are you worrying about? You have a new career opening up for you.'

'Did you know I'm only two years older than Gary Cooper?'

'So?'

'They think I'm too old to get the girl now.'

'You knew what the part was when you agreed to test for it.'

'I'm just saying, they think I'm too old to get the girl now. Coop's only two years younger than me but he seems to come from a different generation.'

'He was an out-of-work cowpoke when you were the world's greatest lover.'

'All those guys – Cooper, Gable, Tracy, Cagney, Robinson – they're all pretty much my age, but they seem like today's heroes, and I seem like yesterday's. We're from different generations.'

Jack was not drunk when he talked about the gap that had opened up between himself and his near contemporaries. He was right, and Marlene knew it. It made her question whether, for all her powers of restoration, she was better off consigning Jack to the attic of Hollywood where he seemed to want to go. God knew the attic was full of such characters already.

Dietrich had worked with Gary Cooper in her first American film,

Morocco, and to the consternation of her besotted director, Josef von Sternberg, she and Cooper had done their best to set the desert on fire. Working with him again rekindled some of that old passion, but Marlene wasn't prepared to give up on Jack. Not just yet. Not until she opened the door one day and saw, standing in front of a big old Packard, the unmistakable figure of Greta Garbo. Instantly she knew what this was about.

'Hello, Marlene. Is Yackie in?' Dietrich indicated as much with a glance of her head in Jack's direction. She stepped aside to permit Garbo to enter the house for the first time for seven years. 'Jack!' called Marlene. 'Friend to see you. I'm going out!' and she banged the door behind her to make her feelings clear. Jack rose to his feet, his heart hammering away. Oh, for God's sake, this was hardly the time to have another heart attack. How he had dreamed of this moment. Was it really happening? Was she really coming back to him after all these years?

'I heard Marlene had moved in. Is she staying in my old room?'

'No. She sleeps in my bed. She likes it.' He didn't know why he was attacking the woman he still adored.

'So you had another heart attack.'

'It wasn't so much a heart attack . . . more of a heart . . . warning.'

'I told you about the drinking, Yackie.'

'No more lectures, Flicka. Please.'

'I didn't come here to lecture you.'

'No? Then why did you come? Could it be that you were jealous of Marlene?'

'I came to tell you I am leaving for Sweden tomorrow.' Jack nodded. Maybe she was telling him the truth. 'Do you want to walk round the pool? For old times' sake?'

Garbo smiled. It was that smile that had always been able to pierce the strongest armour he could wear. He slid open the door, and they walked out onto the terrace. The view of the Los Angeles basin was as stunning as ever. It was only five o'clock, but already the sun had lost its power and there was a chill sufficient to remind them both of the approach of winter. They sat down by the pool and looked at each other. Even now, after all the years and all the pain, there was still something left of Yackie and his Flicka.

'How was *Anna Karenina*? As good as our version?'

'More accurate title.'

'Well, they couldn't say Garbo and March in *Love*.'

'They didn't try.'

'Did you do the garlic trick with Freddie March?'

'You heard? It wasn't what you think. I am on a new diet.'

'You were always on a new diet.'

'It is such a pain. I think I give up all this and just stay in Sweden.'

'Well, you've got the dough, Flicka. You can tell L.B. to go fuck himself and live happily for the rest of your life.'

Garbo stood and walked to the end of the pool, staring down at the house that used to belong to King Vidor and Eleanor Boardman. Jack came and stood next to her, resisting the overpowering temptation to put his arm around her shoulder. After a while he could feel the tension rising. What was it she was looking for? What was she doing here?

'Greta, I loved you so much. Why wouldn't you marry me?'

'I couldn't be the sort of woman you wanted, you needed.'

'I would have done anything for you.'

Garbo smiled ruefully. 'You wouldn't have stopped drinking or boasting or fighting. Or trying to make me marry you.' Jack acknowledged the truth of her observations.

'Nobody can make you do anything you don't want to do,' he protested softly.

'That marriage to Ina Claire hurt me.'

'It was supposed to. What other reason did you think I had for marrying her? She's a very nice woman, incidentally. I don't know what the hell she was thinking of when she agreed to marry me.'

'Yackie, there have been so many women in your life.' It was true. He had had a lot of women and he had enjoyed their bodies and given of himself entirely to each of them. They had nothing to complain about. He had held nothing back. He would make love to them off screen with as much passion as he made love to his co-stars on screen. In many cases his lovers off screen were also his lovers on screen. Somehow he knew where he was with actresses. They knew how to respond to his physical approaches.

But there was always a proviso at the bottom of his declarations of love, however sincerely they were felt. There was always Garbo.

'Many women maybe, but only one Garbo. But then there was always Stiller.'

'You know there was never anything between Moje and me.'

'How can you say that?' Even at a distance of seven years he could feel the old anger and jealousy start to boil within him as she mentioned his old rival.

'Because it was true. He was never my lover. You were my first. You were always special.'

'I was your first man, but there were women as well as men. There was Salka or Mercedes or . . .'

'Yackie, don't, please. If there was only one Garbo for you then there was only one Yackie for me.'

He was greatly moved by this declaration of love. Was it not still dormant in her breast as it was in his?

'I loved you so much. Did you love me? Ever?'

'Maybe. When I came to America I was very young and very frightened. You were so kind and generous. And I was grateful. Is that the same as love? How can one express love if one has never experienced it? As much as I can love any man, I loved you.'

They had been standing side by side, talking in soft, low voices. He was aware that he was as in love with Garbo now as he had been after the first five minutes of their first scene together on the set of *Flesh and the Devil*. He knew there was some kind of reciprocal feeling but he had no idea how deep it went and he couldn't know until he had kissed her. He turned her body slightly to face him. If there were going to be any resistance it would be apparent now.

There was no resistance. She turned towards him that familiar face he had seen so often in his dreams, like her millions of admirers. How could he explain to Ina and Virginia, to Marlene and all the others that when he made love to their bodies he was seeing Garbo's face, kissing Garbo's lips? He was drunk again but with remembered passion this time, not alcohol. What one saw in other women when drunk, he couldn't help thinking, one saw in Garbo when entirely sober. He leaned forward to kiss her and closed his eyes. She still had time to draw away. He would make no attempt to pursue her. He felt the softest touch of her lips on his and the familiar smell of her body that was so distinctively Garbo. Then he felt her pliant body in his arms as she also briefly sought to recapture that feeling that had once overwhelmed them both.

They kissed for the longest time, but it was different from any kiss he had ever known. It was a kiss that was full of romance and passion. It was a post-coital kiss, not a prelude to foreplay. It was a kiss that acknowledged what a deep bond of love had once stretched between them, but that it was now broken. It was a kiss that said there would never be anyone else who could mean to them what they had meant to each other. It was a kiss that marked the end of the greatest romance of both their lives. When the kiss ended, there were no more words. What words could possibly compare with the depth of soul that kiss had reawakened?

He let her go. She strode in that distinctively mannish style back through the open glass door, through the living room and into the courtyard where her driver was waiting patiently in the Packard. When he heard the engine start he felt as if his heart would stop. He didn't care if Marlene ever came back. He had said a final farewell to the greatest love of his life. Life itself now seemed entirely pointless and trivial. Without Garbo there was no life.

Chapter Eighteen

He lost the part in *Desire* a few days later. When Garbo walked out of his life forever and Marlene left him for Gary Cooper, there didn't seem to be much point in pursuing the healthy regime Marlene had forced on him. So he had a drink. It tasted good so he had another. He had a heart attack, then another drink and then another small series of heart attacks and then . . . he was finished. Again. The personal-appearance tour Marlene had scheduled for him before she left was cancelled, and the offer of the part of Carlos Margoli in *Desire* was withdrawn by Paramount on medical grounds.

Jack could hardly complain and he didn't. To her credit, Marlene came back to him when she heard of this latest illness, despite the fact that it now appeared that all her efforts at reforming him had been in vain. She took him to her house and looked after him. She knew his heart, as it were, wasn't in it but Marlene was a kind and honourable woman and she was determined to see things through to the end. One afternoon it seemed like it was the end when Jack had a terrifying seizure in Marlene's pool. It was a surprise as well as a relief to her that he seemed to recover so quickly from what she had been convinced was a fatal attack.

The one thing she encouraged which gave Jack some long-delayed pleasure was the new relationship that was blossoming with his eleven-year-old daughter, Leatrice, whom he nicknamed Tinker after Tinker Bell in *Peter Pan*. He had not been much of a father, he was the first to admit, but he thoroughly enjoyed the time he spent with young Leatrice, playing her his Gilbert and Sullivan records and taking her for walks in the hills above the house in Tower Road. They sang all his favourite songs from 'Three Little Maids From School' to 'Take a Pair of Sparkling Eyes' and he recited the poems that he wanted her to learn.

On Christmas Eve he invited Leatrice to share a private early celebration with him. When the little girl stepped through the open front door she saw a tall, glittering tree decorated with frosted-glass ornaments and ablaze with real candles in the German tradition, clearly the work of Marlene, who had tactfully slipped away just before Leatrice was due to arrive.

When the girl saw the pile of presents under the tree, all wrapped in heavy gold paper and tied with silk ribbons, she raced towards them.

'Are these all for me, Daddy?' she cried in unalloyed delight. Jack laughed and wondered again why he had deprived himself of this innocent pleasure for so long. He must contact Virginia and make sure that Susan Ann, his daughter by Virginia, was similarly treated.

'Yes, Tinker. Of course they're all for you.' It was the cue for an orgy of paper tearing and box opening. Jack thought he had never heard anything in his life to compare with the sound of a happy child.

'Hey there, slow down. You'll have more fun if you take your time.' There was only a shriek from Leatrice as she drew out a pink satin nightgown with a matching slip and panties to go with the doll with real hair, the charm bracelet with tiny animals picked out in gold, the books, the wristwatch and a hand-carved ivory chess set. When she tore open the package to reveal a sky-blue silk dress she was just about halfway through.

There was Christmas cake and lemonade and everything a child could wish for. It was the happiest day of the little girl's life, and to make it perfect she had just one more wish.

'Only one?' asked Jack, eyeing the devastation round the living room.

'Well . . .' considered Leatrice, since he was asking . . .

'What is it?' said Jack quickly before the child's wild imagination led her much further down the yellow brick road.

'Can you come home with me and see my Christmas tree? I so want you to.'

Jack shook his head.

'I can't do that, Tinker, much as I'd like to.'

'Oh why?' wailed the child. The afternoon had gone so well it seemed a shame to ruin it right at the end.

'It might embarrass your mother.'

'No, it won't. She'd love to see you.'

'I'm sorry, Tinker, but you're talking to a Gilbert, and Gilberts never change their minds.'

'Well, I'm a Gilbert too,' the little girl replied spiritedly and grabbed his hand, pulling him outside towards the car that her mother had sent for her.

All the way over to her house Leatrice kept up a constant babble of information about her room and her life at school and her friends and how she had placed his photograph over her bed. Jack couldn't get a word in edgeways. Nothing he could have said would have stemmed the torrent of words.

When the car pulled up outside her house, Leatrice ran to the door, which was opened by her mother. She pointed to the figure of her father in the car and dashed inside to prepare her room for the first official visit from her father.

It had been many years since Leatrice Joy, then the second Mrs John Gilbert, had opened a telegram addressed to Jack from the actress Laurette Taylor and discovered irrefutable proof of yet another affair. She had since remarried but had always carried in her heart a soft spot for her child-like errant ex-husband. Like Jack's, her career, had peaked before the introduction of sound. Jack knew well enough how badly he had hurt her and couldn't bear to end this wonderful day on a sour note. He leant forward and spoke quietly to the chauffeur.

'Back to Tower Road, please.'

Leatrice Joy watched with understanding and raised a hand in a gentle farewell as the car carrying Jack slipped quietly through the wrought-iron gates and onto the road.

On New Year's Day 1936 Jack sent a handwritten note to the young Leatrice rescinding the invitation for her to visit him again. He was feeling unwell and he thought it would be better if they waited a few days until he was feeling better. He was sure she would understand. She did but she was disappointed nonetheless.

It was just nine days later when Jack's old friend Cedric Gibbons, shaving in his bathroom with the radio on in the background, heard the newsflash from the wire services. It was buried in a bulletin of seemingly trivial news from the studios:

Star moppet Shirley Temple today inked a new contract with Twentieth Century Fox studio to make three pictures in 1936. The first, *Captain January*, starts shooting next week. Producer David O. Selznick announced that he has paid fifty thousand dollars to acquire the film rights to the Civil War novel *Gone With The Wind* by first-time author Margaret Mitchell, which is due to be published by Macmillan next month. And silent-movie star Jack Gilbert died today of heart failure at his home in Beverly Hills. He was thirty-six years old.

Poor Jack, thought Cedric Gibbons. Even in death he could only manage third billing behind a kid and an unknown author from Atlanta.

Nevertheless Cedric knew exactly what sort of ghoulish media feeding frenzy this news would provoke, and so did Marlene. Together they raced over to the house on Tower Road, but already the jostling reporters and photographers had overwhelmed the faithful Carlos. Together Cedric and Marlene barricaded themselves in the bathroom in an attempt to stop them taking pictures of Jack's distorted face, the result of Jack's swallowing his tongue at the end.

When the police eventually arrived and had restored order, Cedric and Marlene interrogated the nurse who had administered the last injection to Jack.

'I did everything I could,' she protested. 'I called the fire brigade.'

'Was he on fire?'

'No. It's the fire brigade that has a resuscitator that can pump air into his lungs.'

'And what happened last night?'

'He had trouble sleeping so I gave him a shot of sodium pentathol to get him back to sleep.'

'And how long did that take?'

'I don't know.'

'You don't know?'

'No. I left as soon as I gave it to him.'

'You left him alone in the house?' Cedric and Marlene were outraged, but it was too late. Jack was gone and, as soon as the telephone rang and the two friends turned to deal with it, so was the nurse.

'Who's going to make the funeral arrangements?' asked Marlene when she had put the phone down to another macabre enquiry.

'I'll call the studio. MGM killed him. The least they can do is bury him.'

There was a pause as they looked at each other, waiting for one of them to frame the question that hovered on both their lips.

'Who's going to tell Garbo?' asked Marlene eventually.

Cedric thought about it and sighed.

'She's in Sweden. It'll come better from me.'

Even if box-office figures suggested that America was transferring its affection to new gods, Europe still loved Garbo, and the trip she took to Sweden as soon as re-takes on *Anna Karenina* had been completed was to be one of her happiest returns to the land she still considered to be her home. After teasing Mercedes into making the 8,000-mile journey for the enticing prospect of dining with her in the elegant waterfront restaurant of the Grand Hotel, Garbo wallowed in the pleasures of the encroaching winter. Although her childhood had been poor and deprived, she had loved her family, which had been so cruelly deprived of first her father and then her sister, Alva. Being back in Stockholm at Christmas and New Year gave her the chance to indulge in all the activities that were not possible in southern California – ice-skating, skiing and sleigh riding. It was unfortunate that her health was not that strong and that she spent much of the time in bed.

On 10 January 1936 Garbo was well enough to attend a performance of Schiller's *Maria Stuart*. Intervals were always difficult for her. She could reach her two aisle seats just as the curtain was going up and she could depart rapidly as the audience was applauding, but if she were not invited into the management's private rooms, intervals meant she had to evade the crowds as best she could, and she didn't like informing the management that she was in the house because the news invariably escaped.

On this night it was as well she was not hiding because the telegram boy found her easily. She opened the telegram from Cedric Gibbons and read it, horror-struck. She remembered what had happened on the set of *Wild Orchids*, when Victor and Edith Seastrom's telegram had told her of the death of Moje Stiller. This was just as bad, possibly worse, for the world would now beat a path to her door demanding to learn of her response. And what could she say? What could she ever say to those who demanded she encapsulate in words her deepest feelings for her first lover? The news from Hollywood was not entirely unexpected, just like the telegram from the Seastroms telling her about Moje, but it was equally devastating. Yackie, her Yackie, was dead. In the incongruous surroundings of the crush bar of a Swedish theatre, she could see in front of her not the broken-down alcoholic wreck she had seen a few weeks before, but the dashing matinee idol, the movie star who loved her unconditionally. Still wearing her floor-length camel-hair coat in the blazing heat of the crush bar in the Dramatiska Teatern, Greta Garbo began to sob inwardly for the lost love of her youth.

Chapter Nineteen

~~~~~

Jack's predecessor as the Great Lover of the Silent Screen had been Rudolf Valentino, whose own untimely death had led to chaotic scenes inside and outside the funeral parlour in New York where the body awaited the funeral. This time there was to be no repetition, although just to make sure, twenty-five policemen were assigned to the task of controlling the crowds on the day of the funeral.

A stellar cast, Marlene noted with approval, had turned out for Jack's farewell performance. Gary Cooper was looking after her because she was very distressed, but present in the Beverly Hills mortuary chapel alongside Leatrice Joy and her daughter were long-time MGM associates of her former husband like Irving Thalberg, Cedric Gibbons, King Vidor, Monta Bell, Myrna Loy, Irene Mayer Selznick and her husband, David, but not of course her father, L.B Mayer. Marlene was so overcome with emotion that she collapsed in the aisle of the chapel, in what looked to the assembled spectators to be an unnecessary and atypically overdramatic star turn. The cameras were on hand to record the collapse for the waiting throngs who had hoped for something like this.

Marlene was horrified when she realised that she had deflected attention from her deceased ex-lover to herself. Marlene had been the one woman who had genuinely cared for Jack at the end, when he had been roundly rejected by the business he had loved to destruction. When Jack's estate was auctioned, she sent Harry Edington off to buy all the bedroom furniture, the rugs, the wall hangings and the sheets on which she and Jack had made love. The bed itself was sold to the Summit Hotel in Uniontown, Pennsylvania, where it took pride of place in the honeymoon suite.

At the end of the service David Selznick offered his condolences in his typical egocentric fashion.

'It's a tragedy, Leatrice, a real tragedy.'

'I know, David.'

'I just bought this book, you see.'

'A book?'

'Not just any book. I've bought the rights to the biggest bestseller ever written.'

'Oh?' Leatrice didn't want to offend the rising son-in-law. He was, they all said, going to be the most important producer in Hollywood.

'It's called *Gone With The Wind* and it's written by this southern belle, Margaret Mitchell. I'd have cast Jack like a shot as Rhett Butler. It's a tragedy.' And he wandered away bemoaning the fact that Jack's death had robbed him of a very exciting camera test. If he cast Clark Gable as Rhett Butler he would have to go on bended knees to his father-in-law, Louis B. Mayer, to ask for the loan of the MGM contracted star, a position he found entirely distasteful.

The previous most important producer in Hollywood, Irving Thalberg, who himself had only a few months to live, immediately buttonholed Leatrice. Thalberg had been made a pallbearer because of his former close relationship with Jack. The powerful executive looked in poor health as he tried to assuage his own guilt.

'You know, Leatrice, Jack was on the verge of a real comeback. I had drawn up a contract for him but I don't think he wanted it any more.'

Leatrice could not bring herself to make any comment. They were all guilty. Thalberg perhaps more than most because he had been a good friend of Jack's when he was successful but seemed to vanish when L.B. decided it was time for Jack to be destroyed. Almost everyone there except their daughter had hurt him as well as loved him. This nonsense from Thalberg was more than she could stand. She grabbed her daughter's arm and pulled her into the limousine.

Garbo, of course, was still in Sweden but even if she had been in town it was generally presumed that she would not have attended. That didn't lessen the world's eagerness for her reaction. When she returned to America, travelling on the SS *Gripsholm* under the assumed name Mary Holmquist, the ravenous press was waiting for her. To the traditional accompaniment of foghorns the liner pulled into New York harbour. Hubert Voight, the MGM press chief in New York, who had met Jack and Ina with the devastating reviews of *His Glorious Night*, was the man the studio always sent to shepherd Garbo through customs and the crowd of journalists clamouring for an interview.

'It's no good demanding. Miss Garbo will be giving no interviews. If you let me get through to her cabin, I'll try to get a statement from her. Just let me through here. C'mon, guys, OK, I'll see what I can do.'

Eventually he forced his way through the throng and knocked on the door of Garbo's cabin.

'Miss Garbo, it's me, Hubert Voight. You remember me, I'm the MGM press chief in New York.'

The door was unlocked, and Voight shoved his way gratefully inside. He did his best to calm her, to explain that if she just gave them a few words on her reaction to Jack's death, they would probably leave her alone, but if she tried to get through without saying a word, they would just tail her and make her life a misery until she did so.

'You can't blame them, Miss Garbo. You're the biggest movie star in the world. They just want to know what you're feeling.'

'I'm feeling tired.'

'I'm sure you are, but I need more than that.'

'It is none of their business. You know I do not give interviews.'

'I know that, but these guys have bosses too. They need something, anything. You don't have to meet with them. I can give it to them.'

'No.'

'You nearly married Jack Gilbert. Twice.'

Garbo smiled. 'Three times.'

'Really?' Voight tried to adopt a soft, companionable tone and not let the confrontation outside infect the atmosphere inside her cabin.

'He always said you were the biggest love of his life. He told me so himself one night.'

'He shouldn't have been talking like that.'

'Oh, but he loved you so much.'

'It was our business. Nobody else's.'

'I know he died with your name on his lips. Let me tell them that.' It made for a good story. It was what the public wanted to hear. Who cared whether or not it was true?

'You don't know that. You can tell them nothing. Except . . .'

Voight seized on her slight deviation from her blanket refusal. 'Yes? Except what?'

'What I always tell journalists. They seem to like it so much.'

'What's that, Miss Garbo?'

'Tell them . . . I want to be alone.'

Postscript

〜〜〜〜〜

After the death of John Gilbert in 1936 Greta Garbo made four more films for MGM. The last one, *Two-Faced Woman*, directed by George Cukor in 1941, was a disastrous attempt to remould Garbo into an all-American woman because there was no chance to export her films to a European continent torn apart by war. It marked the end of her career.

Irving Thalberg was not around to advise and guide her. He died of heart failure at the age of thirty-seven, just eight months after his friend, Jack Gilbert. Louis B. Mayer remained in sole charge of production at MGM until 1951, when he was finally deposed by the hated Nicholas Schenck, with whom he had been sworn enemies since the projected takeover by William Fox was aborted in 1929. He died, bitter and frustrated, in 1957. Metro-Goldwyn-Mayer kept its name, but its status as Hollywood's biggest and best studio declined soon after the departure of L.B. Mayer and the termination of the contracts of the stars which had given it its unique lustre.

At the age of thirty-six, the age at which Jack Gilbert died, Greta Garbo retired from the screen. For twenty years there were rumours of a comeback but, whatever the announcements of optimistic producers, Garbo was not to be tempted. Despite her retirement, the world's obsession with Greta Garbo scarcely diminished and she remained an object of fascination, even as she lived out her final years as a recluse in a seven-room apartment on East 52nd Street in New York.

She had a short-lived but very public affair with the flamboyant conductor Leopold Stokowski, and a very odd liaison with the aesthetic English photographer and designer Cecil Beaton. Her final puzzling relationship was with George Schlee, who lived with his wife, the Russian designer Valentina, on the ninth floor of Garbo's New York apartment building.

Greta Garbo died in 1990 at the age of eighty-four, leaving an estate estimated at $55 million. The auction of her art collection, antique treasures and assorted bric-a-brac raised $19 million. She never married and the final resting place of her ashes was never made public. Even in death she wanted to be alone. It was, it must be said, one way of stopping Jack Gilbert from proposing to her again.